BRIGHTER CHILD® BOOK OF

MATH TIMED TESTS

GRADES 3-5

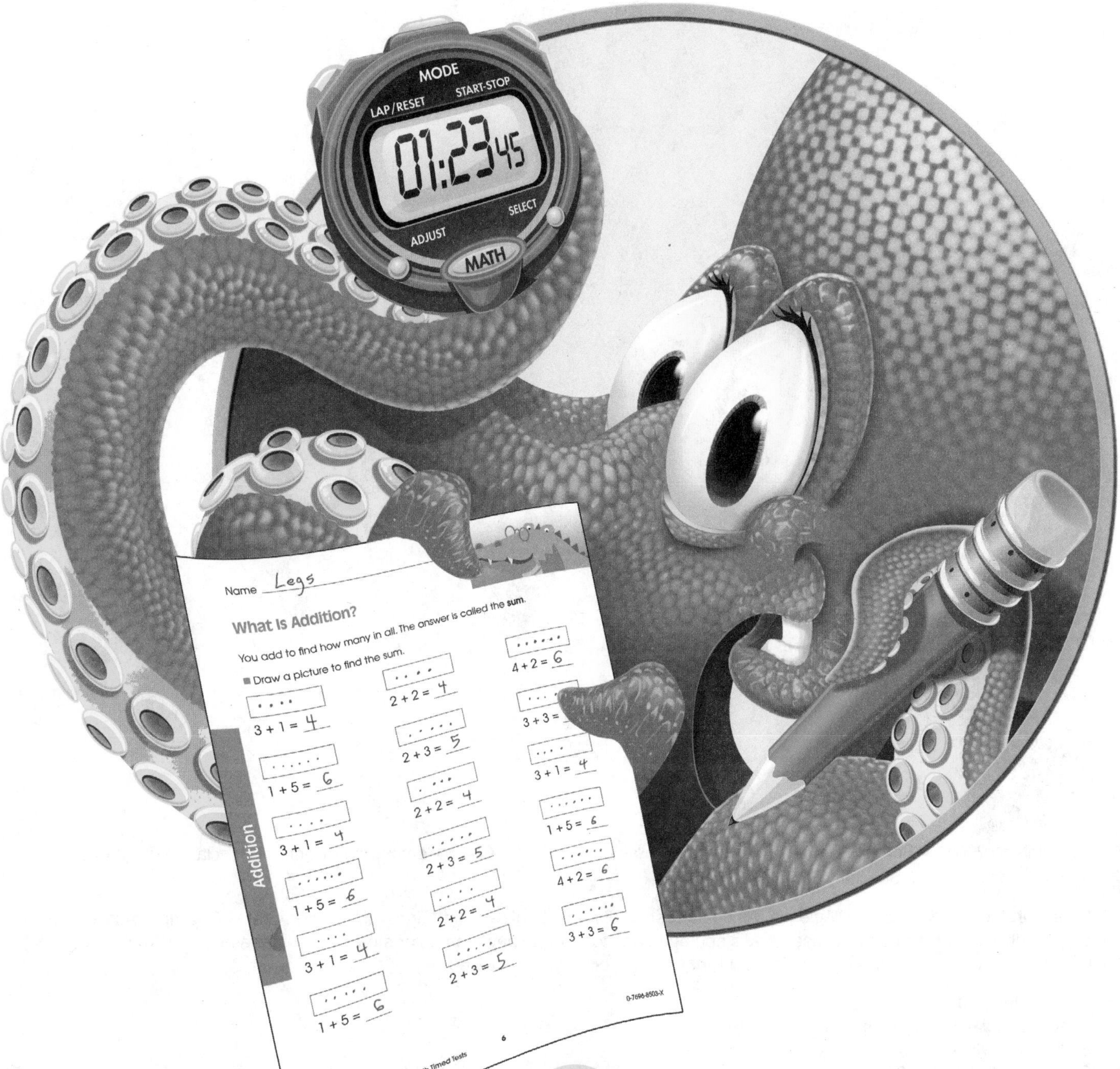

BRIGHTER CHILD®
Columbus, Ohio

Send all inquiries to:
School Specialty Publishing
8720 Orion Place
Columbus, OH 43240-2111

ISBN 0-7696-8503-X

1 2 3 4 5 6 QPD 12 11 10 09

Table of Contents

Table of Contents

ADDITION

Name ______________________

What Is Addition?

You add to find how many in all. The answer is called the **sum**.

3 birds plus 2 more birds equals 5 birds in all.

There are two ways to show the addition.

$3 + 2 = 5$

$$\begin{array}{r} 3 \\ +\,2 \\ \hline 5 \end{array}$$

You can draw a picture to find a sum.

Example: Find the sum. 2 + 4 = ____

Step 1: Draw 2 dots. ⟶ ● ●

Step 2: Draw 4 more dots. ⟶ ● ● ● ●

Step 3: Count all the dots.

Answer: 2 + 4 = 6

■ Draw a picture to find the sum.

3 + 1 = ____	2 + 2 = ____	4 + 2 = ____
1 + 5 = ____	2 + 3 = ____	3 + 3 = ____

Name ______________________________

What Is Addition?

You can use counters to find a sum. You will need some pennies.

Example: Find the sum. 3 + 2 = _____

Step 1: Put 3 pennies in the box. →

Step 2: Put 2 more pennies in the box. →

Step 3: Count all the pennies. →

Answer: 3 + 2 = <u>5</u>

■ Use counters to find the sum.

4 + 3 = _____ 2 + 4 = _____ 3 + 4 = _____

4	5	2	2	3
+ 4	+ 1	+ 5	+ 1	+ 2
___	___	___	___	___

You can use a number line to find a sum.

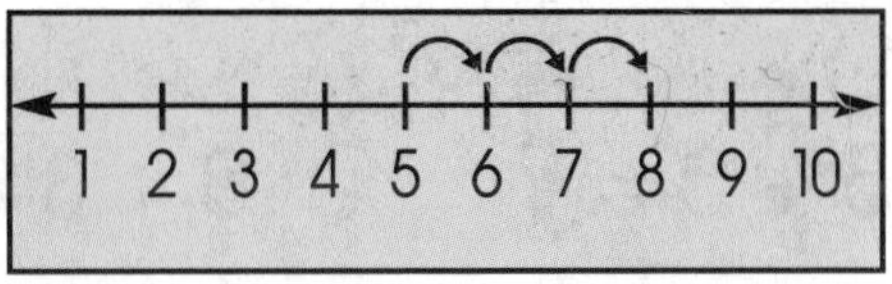

Example: Find the sum. 5 + 3 = _____

Step 1: Put your finger on 5.

Step 2: Move your finger 3 spaces to the right.

Step 3: Read the number your finger is on.

Answer: 5 + 3 = <u>8</u>

■ Use the number line to find the sum.

4 + 1 = _____ 5 + 3 = _____ 3 + 5 = _____

5	4	1	5	5
+ 2	+ 5	+ 2	+ 4	+ 5
___	___	___	___	___

Name ______________________________

Adding Zero

Zero is called the **identity element of addition**. This means that, when zero is added to a number, that number does not change.

Example: 3 + 0 = 3

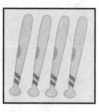

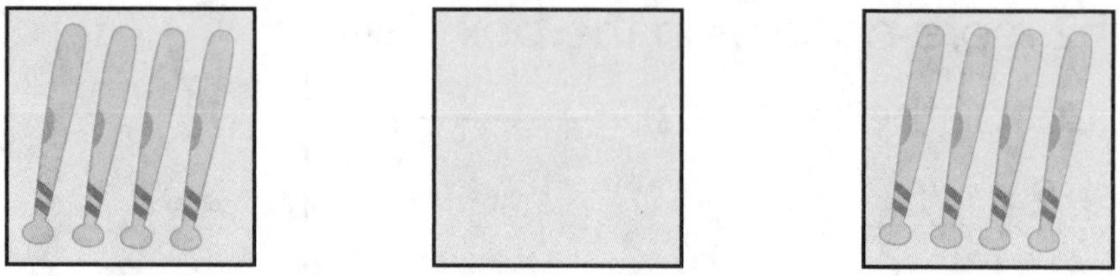

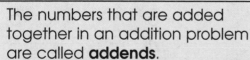

4 + 0 = 4

■ Add.

2 + 0 = ____	3 + 0 = ____	1 + 0	0 + 4	0 + 0	3 + 0
0 + 6 = ____	0 + 4 = ____				
0 + 1 = ____	4 + 0 = ____	0 + 5	6 + 0	0 + 6	4 + 0
5 + 0 = ____	0 + 3 = ____				
1 + 0 = ____	0 + 2 = ____	0 + 2	0 + 3	5 + 0	2 + 0
0 + 5 = ____	6 + 0 = ____				

The numbers that are added together in an addition problem are called **addends**.
The answer in an addition problem is called the **sum**.

5 + **0** = **5**
addend **addend** **sum**

5 addend
+0 addend
5 sum

Name ____________________________________

Counting On

If one of the addends in an addition fact is a lesser number like 1, 2, or 3, you can find the sum by "counting on" from the other addend.

Example: 3 + 2 Start at 3. Count on by moving 2 jumps on the number line. The sum is 5.

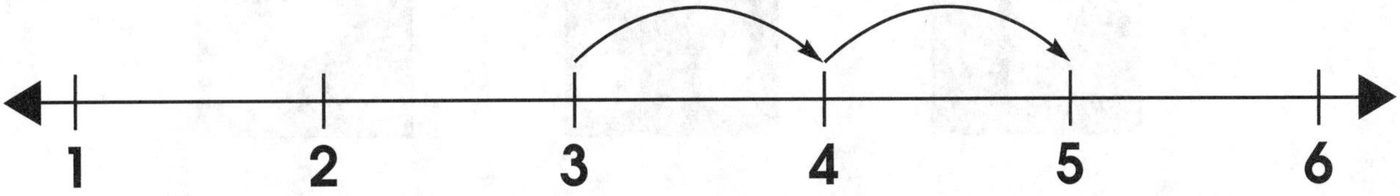

■ Complete each **T** by counting on by the number at the top. Use the number line to help you.

+ 1	
5	____
3	____
4	____
2	____
0	____

+ 2	
4	____
0	____
3	____
1	____

+ 3	
2	____
1	____
0	____

Counting numbers are all the whole numbers beginning with 1 and going as far as you want. 1, 2, 3, 4, . . .

Hint: Always add the smaller addend to the larger one, no matter which comes first.

Name ______________________________

Changing the Order of the Addends

The **commutative property of addition** says that the sum is always the same no matter how the addends are arranged.

Example: 3 + 2 = 5 is the same as 2 + 3 = 5.

3 + 2 = 5

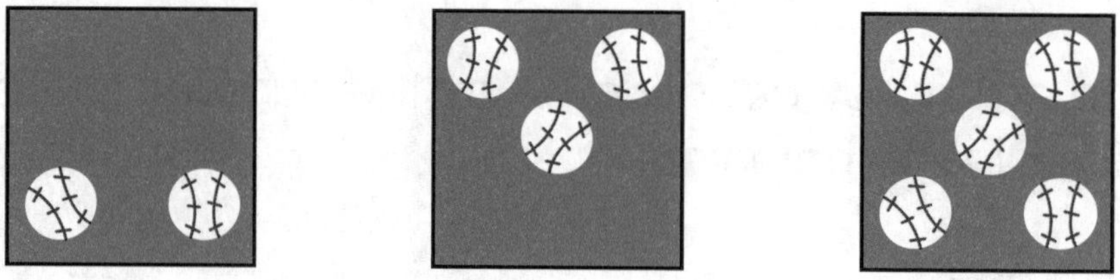

2 + 3 = 5

■ Use the commutative property to solve the problems below.

1 + 3 = ____	4 + 2 = ____	2 + 3 = ____
3 + 1 = ____	2 + 4 = ____	3 + 2 = ____
1 + 2 = ____	1 + 4 = ____	5 + 1 = ____
2 + 1 = ____	4 + 1 = ____	1 + 5 = ____

Name ______________________________

Adding Doubles

Doubles are basic facts in which the addends are the same number.

Examples: 1 + 1 = 2

2 + 2 = 4

3 + 3 = 6

■ Add.

0 + 0 = ____   2 + 2 = ____

3 + 3 = ____   1 + 1 = ____

$$\begin{array}{r} 2 \\ +\ 2 \\ \hline \end{array} \qquad \begin{array}{r} 1 \\ +\ 1 \\ \hline \end{array} \qquad \begin{array}{r} 0 \\ +\ 0 \\ \hline \end{array} \qquad \begin{array}{r} 3 \\ +\ 3 \\ \hline \end{array}$$

The sums of doubles are always even numbers, like 0, 2, 4, and 6. This is true even if the addends are odd numbers like 1 and 3.

Name ______________________

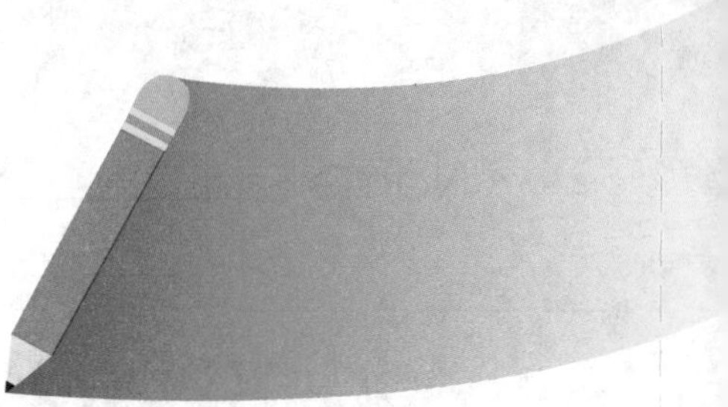

Practice

■ Add.

1	0	2	2	0	1	3	0	0
+ 4	+ 6	+ 1	+ 4	+ 5	+ 2	+ 3	+ 4	+ 1
0	2	0	3	1	0	1	5	3
+ 0	+ 2	+ 2	+ 2	+ 0	+ 3	+ 4	+ 0	+ 2
2	4	3	1	1	4	0	4	2
+ 3	+ 0	+ 3	+ 3	+ 4	+ 2	+ 3	+ 1	+ 0
3	1	1	2	6	1	2	3	5
+ 0	+ 5	+ 1	+ 2	+ 0	+ 3	+ 3	+ 1	+ 1

Score: ______________

Name ____________________

Practice

■ Add.

3 + 3 = ___	2 + 4 = ___	2 + 1 = ___	4 + 2 = ___
0 + 1 = ___	1 + 2 = ___	5 + 0 = ___	0 + 3 = ___
1 + 0 = ___	3 + 2 = ___	1 + 3 = ___	2 + 2 = ___
0 + 2 = ___	0 + 4 = ___	5 + 1 = ___	3 + 1 = ___
2 + 1 = ___	3 + 3 = ___	0 + 5 = ___	1 + 4 = ___

0 + 0 = ___ 1 + 1 = ___

2 + 3 = ___ 2 + 0 = ___

1 + 5 = ___ 5 + 1 = ___

4 + 0 = ___ 0 + 6 = ___

0 + 5 = ___ 3 + 1 = ___

3 + 0 = ___ 1 + 4 = ___

4 + 1 = ___ 6 + 0 = ___

3 + 2 = ___ 2 + 2 = ___

Sums Through Six

Score: ___________

Circle any problems that you still find difficult to remember. Make your own flash cards to help you master these problems.

Name ______________________________

Timed Test

■ Improve your speed on these basic facts. Ask someone to time you. Record your time and score on each Timed Test page.

0 + 5 = ____	1 + 1 = ____	0 + 2 = ____	2 + 1 = ____
1 + 4 = ____	5 + 0 = ____	3 + 2 = ____	6 + 0 = ____
2 + 0 = ____	2 + 3 = ____	1 + 0 = ____	1 + 5 = ____
3 + 3 = ____	4 + 2 = ____	2 + 4 = ____	5 + 1 = ____
0 + 1 = ____	0 + 3 = ____	1 + 2 = ____	2 + 2 = ____
4 + 1 = ____	1 + 3 = ____	4 + 0 = ____	3 + 1 = ____
3 + 0 = ____	0 + 6 = ____	0 + 4 = ____	0 + 0 = ____
2 + 4 = ____	3 + 3 = ____	1 + 5 = ____	3 + 2 = ____
1 + 4 = ____	5 + 0 = ____	4 + 2 = ____	2 + 2 = ____
3 + 1 = ____	1 + 1 = ____	2 + 0 = ____	1 + 2 = ____

Score: __________ Time: __________ minutes __________ seconds

Name ______________________________

Timed Test

1 + 4 = ____ 2 + 3 = ____

0	3	3	1
+ 5	+ 1	+ 0	+ 2

5 + 1 = ____ 1 + 3 = ____

0 + 6 = ____ 4 + 0 = ____

4	0	3	3
+ 2	+ 0	+ 3	+ 2

2 + 4 = ____ 0 + 3 = ____

2 + 0 = ____ 2 + 1 = ____

1	4	2	0
+ 0	+ 1	+ 0	+ 1

6 + 0 = ____ 1 + 5 = ____

0 + 4 = ____ 5 + 0 = ____

0	1	2	5
+ 2	+ 1	+ 2	+ 1

3 + 3 = ____ 4 + 1 = ____

2 + 1 = ____ 3 + 2 = ____

1	1	0	2
+ 2	+ 0	+ 4	+ 4

1 + 1 = ____ 6 + 0 = ____

Score: ________ Time: ________ minutes ________ seconds

Name ______________________________

Timed Test

Sums Through Six

1 + 4 = ____ 2 + 2 = ____

0 + 3 = ____ 3 + 0 = ____

3	4	5	2
+ 3	+ 0	+ 0	+ 1

2 + 3 = ____ 0 + 6 = ____

1 + 2 = ____ 4 + 1 = ____

1	0	1	6
+ 1	+ 2	+ 0	+ 0

2 + 4 = ____ 1 + 3 = ____

0 + 4 = ____ 0 + 3 = ____

3	5	3	0
+ 2	+ 1	+ 1	+ 0

4 + 2 = ____ 0 + 1 = ____

3 + 1 = ____ 3 + 2 = ____

1	2	1	0
+ 5	+ 0	+ 2	+ 5

2 + 0 = ____ 1 + 2 = ____

2 + 2 = ____ 4 + 1 = ____

4	0	2	1
+ 2	+ 6	+ 2	+ 4

Score: ____________ Time: ____________ minutes ____________ seconds

Name ______________________________

Adding Zero

Remember: Zero is the identity element of addition. When zero is added to a number, that number does not change.

Example: $7 + 0 = 7$

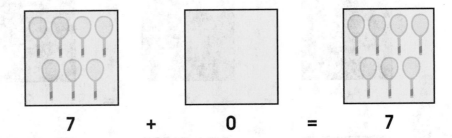

7 **+** **0** **=** **7**

■ Complete the **T** by adding zero to each number on the left. Then, write a number sentence for each problem.

	+0					
7	____	____	+	____	=	____
5	____	____	+	____	=	____
9	____	____	+	____	=	____
4	____	____	+	____	=	____
8	____	____	+	____	=	____
3	____	____	+	____	=	____
0	____	____	+	____	=	____
6	____	____	+	____	=	____

Name ________________________

Changing the Order of the Addends

Remember: The commutative property of addition says that the sum is always the same no matter how the addends are arranged.

Example: 6 + 3 = 9 is the same as 3 + 6 = 9.

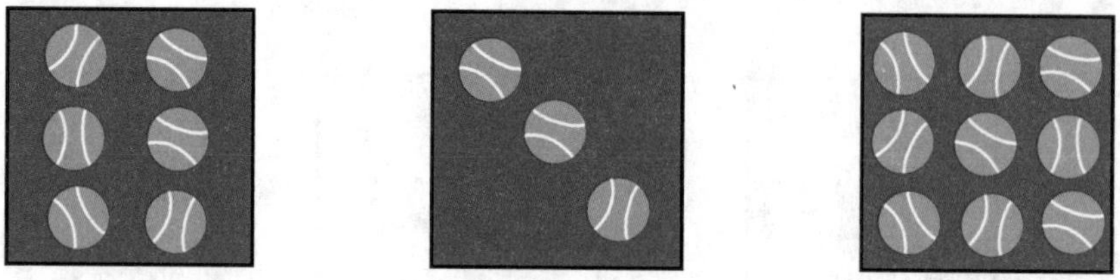

6 + 3 = 9

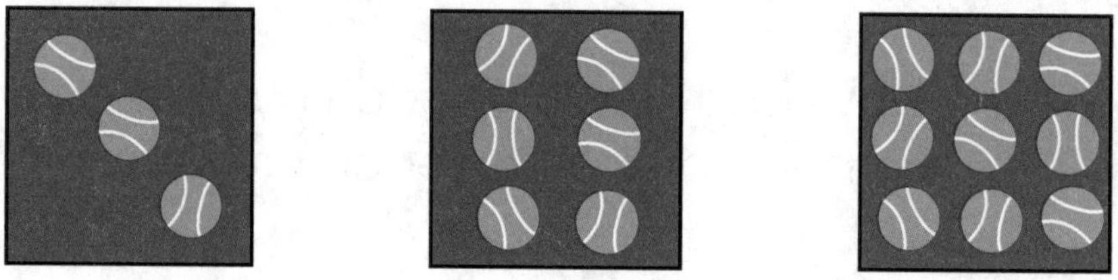

3 + 6 = 9

■ Write another addition fact using the numbers in each fact below.

7 + 1 = 8	6 + 4 = 10	9 + 0 = 9
____ + ____ = ____	____ + ____ = ____	____ + ____ = ____
6 + 1 = 7	6 + 2 = 8	9 + 1 = 10
____ + ____ = ____	____ + ____ = ____	____ + ____ = ____
7 + 2 = 9	8 + 1 = 9	8 + 2 = 10
____ + ____ = ____	____ + ____ = ____	____ + ____ = ____

Name ______________________________

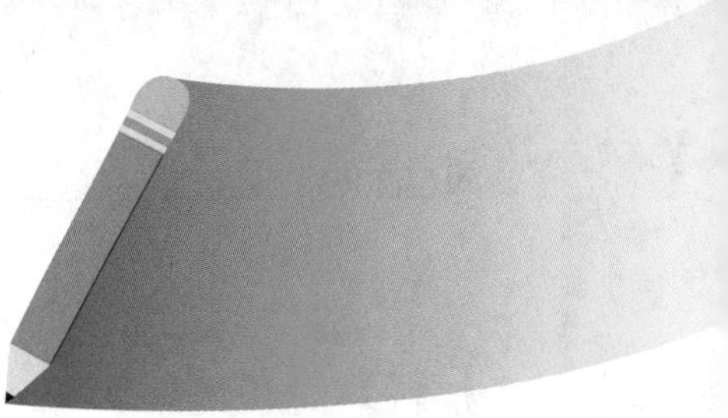

Practice

■ Add.

6	3	9	0	2	6	4	3	5
+ 3	+ 6	+ 0	+ 9	+ 6	+ 2	+ 4	+ 5	+ 3
9	1	4	5	8	0	8	2	1
+ 1	+ 9	+ 5	+ 4	+ 0	+ 8	+ 2	+ 8	+ 6
6	3	4	3	7	8	1	5	2
+ 1	+ 4	+ 3	+ 7	+ 3	+ 1	+ 8	+ 2	+ 5
5	7	2	6	4	0	7	7	1
+ 5	+ 2	+ 7	+ 4	+ 6	+ 7	+ 0	+ 1	+ 7

Score: ______________

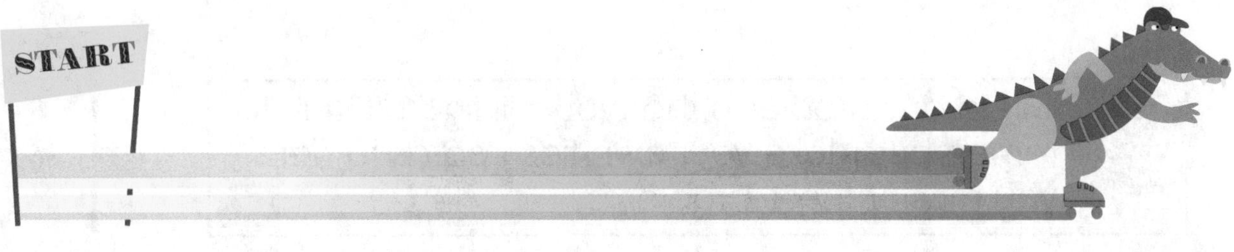

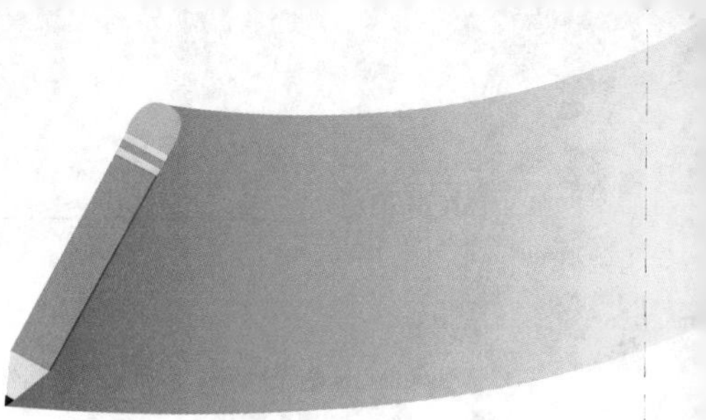

Name _____

Practice

■ Add.

6	4	6	1
+ 4	+ 5	+ 2	+ 8

9 + 1 = ____   4 + 6 = ____

2 + 5 = ____   7 + 0 = ____

4	2	3	8
+ 4	+ 6	+ 7	+ 1

6 + 3 = ____   0 + 8 = ____

0 + 9 = ____   5 + 5 = ____

0	7	3	8
+ 7	+ 3	+ 6	+ 2

8 + 0 = ____   1 + 9 = ____

4 + 3 = ____   1 + 6 = ____

2	5	1	5
+ 8	+ 2	+ 7	+ 3

6 + 1 = ____   9 + 0 = ____

2 + 7 = ____   3 + 4 = ____

5	7	7	6
+ 4	+ 2	+ 3	+ 4

Score: _____

 Circle any problems that you still find difficult to remember. Make your own flash cards to help you master these problems.

Name ______________________________

Timed Test

■ Improve your speed on these basic facts. Ask someone to time you. Record your time and score on each Timed Test page.

0 + 8 = ____	5 + 3 = ____	5 + 4 = ____	2 + 6 = ____
2 + 5 = ____	2 + 8 = ____	0 + 7 = ____	7 + 0 = ____
7 + 3 = ____	8 + 0 = ____	5 + 2 = ____	3 + 7 = ____
1 + 6 = ____	3 + 6 = ____	3 + 5 = ____	8 + 1 = ____
7 + 1 = ____	6 + 4 = ____	4 + 6 = ____	0 + 9 = ____
3 + 4 = ____	1 + 8 = ____	2 + 7 = ____	6 + 2 = ____
6 + 1 = ____	4 + 5 = ____	1 + 7 = ____	4 + 3 = ____
6 + 3 = ____	8 + 2 = ____	4 + 4 = ____	5 + 5 = ____
1 + 9 = ____	7 + 2 = ____	9 + 1 = ____	9 + 0 = ____
3 + 7 = ____	2 + 8 = ____	5 + 4 = ____	4 + 6 = ____

Score: __________ Time: __________ minutes __________ seconds

Name ____________________

Timed Test

3 + 5 = ____ 6 + 1 = ____

$\begin{array}{r} 9 \\ +0 \\ \hline \end{array}$ $\begin{array}{r} 3 \\ +6 \\ \hline \end{array}$ $\begin{array}{r} 6 \\ +2 \\ \hline \end{array}$ $\begin{array}{r} 1 \\ +6 \\ \hline \end{array}$

9 + 1 = ____ 3 + 7 = ____

6 + 3 = ____ 7 + 1 = ____

$\begin{array}{r} 7 \\ +3 \\ \hline \end{array}$ $\begin{array}{r} 4 \\ +6 \\ \hline \end{array}$ $\begin{array}{r} 3 \\ +4 \\ \hline \end{array}$ $\begin{array}{r} 4 \\ +4 \\ \hline \end{array}$

1 + 9 = ____ 0 + 8 = ____

7 + 2 = ____ 5 + 3 = ____

$\begin{array}{r} 0 \\ +9 \\ \hline \end{array}$ $\begin{array}{r} 8 \\ +0 \\ \hline \end{array}$ $\begin{array}{r} 5 \\ +2 \\ \hline \end{array}$ $\begin{array}{r} 2 \\ +7 \\ \hline \end{array}$

2 + 8 = ____ 1 + 7 = ____

4 + 5 = ____ 6 + 4 = ____

$\begin{array}{r} 5 \\ +4 \\ \hline \end{array}$ $\begin{array}{r} 1 \\ +8 \\ \hline \end{array}$ $\begin{array}{r} 7 \\ +0 \\ \hline \end{array}$ $\begin{array}{r} 4 \\ +3 \\ \hline \end{array}$

8 + 2 = ____ 0 + 7 = ____

5 + 5 = ____ 7 + 3 = ____

$\begin{array}{r} 5 \\ +5 \\ \hline \end{array}$ $\begin{array}{r} 8 \\ +1 \\ \hline \end{array}$ $\begin{array}{r} 2 \\ +6 \\ \hline \end{array}$ $\begin{array}{r} 2 \\ +5 \\ \hline \end{array}$

2 + 5 = ____ 1 + 8 = ____

Score: ________ Time: ________ minutes ________ seconds

 0-7696-8503-X

Name ____________________

Timed Test

Sums Through Ten

0 + 8 = ____ 7 + 0 = ____

8	1	6	4
+ 0	+ 9	+ 3	+ 3

8 + 1 = ____ 0 + 9 = ____

4 + 4 = ____ 4 + 6 = ____

6	0	3	8
+ 1	+ 7	+ 7	+ 2

2 + 5 = ____ 3 + 4 = ____

6 + 2 = ____ 5 + 2 = ____

2	5	1	9
+ 7	+ 5	+ 6	+ 1

1 + 8 = ____ 1 + 7 = ____

3 + 6 = ____ 5 + 3 = ____

5	7	2	6
+ 4	+ 2	+ 8	+ 4

9 + 0 = ____ 7 + 1 = ____

6 + 4 = ____ 7 + 3 = ____

3	7	2	4
+ 5	+ 3	+ 6	+ 5

2 + 6 = ____ 5 + 4 = ____

Score: ________ Time: ________ minutes ________ seconds

Name ______________________________

Thinking of Tens

Another way to remember certain sums is to think about tens.

Example: 8 + 6 = 14

Think: How much of 6 would be added to 8 to equal 10?
The answer is 8 + 2 = 10, with 4 left over. Therefore, 8 + 6 = 14.

■ Complete each of these number sentences.

9 + 4 is 9 + _____ (or 10), with _____ left over. Therefore, 9 + 4 = _____.

5 + 8 is _____ + 8 (or 10), with _____ left over. Therefore, 5 + 8 = _____.

9 + 7 is 9 + _____ (or 10), with _____ left over. Therefore, 9 + 7 = _____.

5 + 9 is _____ + 9 (or 10), with _____ left over. Therefore, 5 + 9 = _____.

4 + 7 is _____ + 7 (or 10), with _____ left over. Therefore, 4 + 7 = _____.

■ Think about tens as you complete these facts.

6 + 7 = _____	8 + 5 = _____	9 + 6 = _____	6 + 8 = _____
9 + 8 = _____	4 + 9 = _____	4 + 7 = _____	9 + 5 = _____
8 + 7 = _____	5 + 8 = _____	5 + 7 = _____	7 + 9 = _____
5 + 6 = _____	8 + 4 = _____	5 + 9 = _____	6 + 9 = _____

Name ______________________________

Adding Doubles

Remember: Two addends that are the same number are called doubles.

Example: 6 + 6 = 12

■ Add.

9 + 9 = ____ 7 + 7 = ____ 8 + 8 = ____ 6 + 6 = ____

8	6	7	9
+ 8	+ 6	+ 7	+ 9
____	____	____	____

■ Add these doubles down and across.

3	3	
3	3	

4	4	
4	4	

Remember: The sums of doubles are always even numbers, like 10, 12, and 14. This is true even if the addends are odd numbers like 7 and 9.

Name ______________________________

Practice

■ Add.

8	7	4	6
+ 9	+ 6	+ 7	+ 5
8	8	9	6
+ 7	+ 5	+ 8	+ 7
3	5	9	8
+ 8	+ 8	+ 7	+ 3
6	7	9	5
+ 9	+ 8	+ 4	+ 6
7	9	4	9
+ 7	+ 6	+ 9	+ 3

7 + 4 = ____ 9 + 2 = ____

8 + 8 = ____ 6 + 8 = ____

6 + 6 = ____ 5 + 9 = ____

3 + 9 = ____ 4 + 8 = ____

8 + 4 = ____ 7 + 9 = ____

7 + 5 = ____ 9 + 5 = ____

9 + 9 = ____ 5 + 7 = ____

8 + 6 = ____ 2 + 9 = ____

Score: ______________

Name ______________________

Practice

■ Add.

9 + 8	6 + 7	5 + 6	8 + 3
3 + 8	7 + 8	6 + 5	9 + 6
7 + 6	9 + 9	3 + 9	8 + 5
8 + 6	5 + 8	9 + 4	6 + 9
8 + 8	9 + 2	8 + 7	9 + 3

9 + 7 = ____	5 + 7 = ____
4 + 8 = ____	8 + 9 = ____
9 + 5 = ____	7 + 5 = ____
6 + 8 = ____	8 + 7 = ____
7 + 9 = ____	4 + 9 = ____
4 + 7 = ____	8 + 4 = ____
7 + 7 = ____	7 + 4 = ____
6 + 6 = ____	5 + 9 = ____

Score: ____________

Circle any problems that you still find difficult to remember. Make your own flash cards to help you master these problems.

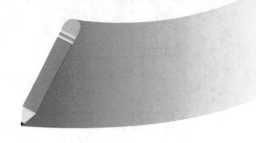

Name ____________________

Timed Test

■ Improve your speed on these basic facts. Ask someone to time you. Record your time and score on each Timed Test page.

9 + 6 = ____	9 + 8 = ____	8 + 6 = ____	5 + 7 = ____
5 + 8 = ____	5 + 9 = ____	4 + 7 = ____	9 + 2 = ____
2 + 9 = ____	7 + 6 = ____	9 + 4 = ____	7 + 8 = ____
9 + 5 = ____	3 + 9 = ____	6 + 8 = ____	8 + 8 = ____
7 + 4 = ____	8 + 3 = ____	8 + 5 = ____	6 + 5 = ____
9 + 3 = ____	6 + 7 = ____	3 + 8 = ____	4 + 6 = ____
5 + 6 = ____	8 + 7 = ____	9 + 7 = ____	7 + 9 = ____
8 + 9 = ____	4 + 8 = ____	7 + 5 = ____	4 + 9 = ____
8 + 4 = ____	6 + 9 = ____	9 + 9 = ____	6 + 6 = ____
7 + 8 = ____	8 + 6 = ____	7 + 7 = ____	3 + 9 = ____

Score: ________ Time: ________ minutes ________ seconds

Name ____________________

Timed Test

Sums Through Eighteen

3 + 8 = ____ 8 + 8 = ____

8 + 4 = ____ 6 + 5 = ____

9 + 7 = ____ 7 + 6 = ____

5 + 6 = ____ 8 + 9 = ____

7 + 9 = ____ 5 + 7 = ____

9 + 6 = ____ 8 + 6 = ____

4 + 8 = ____ 6 + 7 = ____

9 + 3 = ____ 9 + 9 = ____

6 + 9 = ____ 5 + 9 = ____

8 + 7 = ____ 2 + 9 = ____

4 + 7 ____	9 + 4 ____	2 + 9 ____	9 + 5 ____
7 + 4 ____	8 + 7 ____	6 + 6 ____	8 + 3 ____
7 + 5 ____	9 + 2 ____	4 + 9 ____	7 + 8 ____
9 + 8 ____	5 + 8 ____	3 + 9 ____	8 + 5 ____
6 + 8 ____	7 + 7 ____	7 + 9 ____	8 + 4 ____

Score: __________ Time: __________ minutes __________ seconds

Name ____________________

Timed Test

Sums Through Eighteen

4 + 7 = ____ 7 + 4 = ____

8 + 7 = ____ 8 + 4 = ____

7 + 6 = ____ 9 + 6 = ____

7 + 8 = ____ 6 + 8 = ____

3 + 9 = ____ 9 + 4 = ____

5 + 9 = ____ 8 + 5 = ____

5 + 6 = ____ 9 + 2 = ____

4 + 9 = ____ 9 + 8 = ____

6 + 6 = ____ 2 + 9 = ____

6 + 7 = ____ 6 + 9 = ____

9 + 9	3 + 8	7 + 9	9 + 3
8 + 8	4 + 8	5 + 8	7 + 7
8 + 3	5 + 7	9 + 5	7 + 5
6 + 9	6 + 7	9 + 7	8 + 9
6 + 5	8 + 6	8 + 4	9 + 9

SUBTRACTION

What Is Subtraction?

You subtract to find how many are left. The answer is called the **difference**.

5 birds take away 2 birds equals 3 birds.

There are two ways to show the subtraction.

$$5 - 2 = 3 \qquad \begin{array}{r} 5 \\ -2 \\ \hline 3 \end{array}$$

You can draw a picture to find how many are left.

Example: Find the difference.   6 – 2 = _____

Step 1: Draw 6 dots. ⟶ ● ● ● ● ● ●

Step 2: Cross out 2 dots. ⟶ ✗ ✗ ● ● ● ●

Step 3: Count the remaining dots.

Answer: 6 – 2 = __4__

■ Draw a picture to find the difference.

4 – 1 = ___   4 – 2 = ___   6 – 2 = ___

6 – 5 = ___   5 – 3 = ___   6 – 3 = ___

Name ______________________

What Is Subtraction?

You can use counters to find the difference. You will need some pennies.

Example: Find the difference. 5 – 2 = ____

Step 1: Put 5 pennies in the box. ⟶

Step 2: Take out 2 pennies. ⟶

Step 3: Count the pennies that are left. ⟶

Answer: 5 – 2 = 3

■ Use counters to find the difference.

6 – 3 = ____ 6 – 4 = ____ 7 – 4 = ____

5	4	7	3	5
– 4	– 1	– 5	– 1	– 2

You can use a number line to find the difference.

Example: Find the answer. 8 – 3 = ____

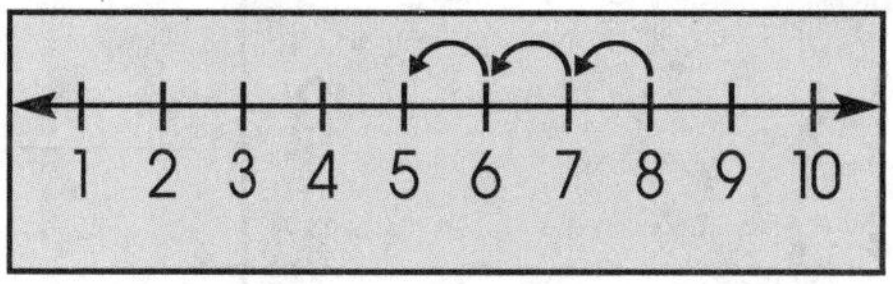

Step 1: Put your finger on 8.

Step 2: Move your finger 3 spaces to the left.

Step 3: Read the number your finger is on.

Answer: 8 – 3 = 5

■ Use the number line to find the difference.

4 – 1 = ____ 5 – 3 = ____ 8 – 5 = ____

4	7	3	6	6
– 2	– 5	– 2	– 4	– 5

Subtraction

Name ______________________________

Subtracting Zero

Just as it is in addition, zero is the **identity element of subtraction.** This means that, when zero is subtracted from a number, the difference is that number.

Example: 3 – 0 = 3

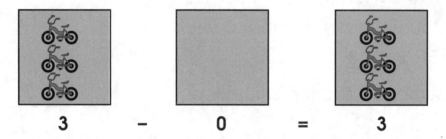

3 – 0 = 3

■ Complete this **T** by subtracting zero from each number.

	– 0
1	____
3	____
2	____
0	____

■ Write the difference for each fact.

2 – 0 = ____ 0 – 0 = ____

1 – 0 = ____ 3 – 0 = ____

1	3	2	0
– 0	– 0	– 0	– 0
____	____	____	____

The answer in a subtraction problem is called the **difference**. The number from which the other is subtracted is called the **minuend**. The number being taken away is called the **subtrahend**.

Name ______________________________

Subtracting Doubles

When the subtrahend is the same as the minuend, the difference is always zero.

Example: 2 – 2 = 0

2 - 2 = 0

Remember: If the difference is zero, the minuend and the subtrahend are the same number.

Example: If 6 – ? = 0, then 6 – 6 = 0.

■ Complete these facts by writing the missing numbers.

5 – 5 = ____

6 – ____ = 0

____ – 4 = 0

1 – 1 = ____

8 – 8 = ____

7 – ____ = 0

____ – 9 = 0

____ – 3 = 0

6 – 6 =	1 – □ = 0	□ – 9 = 0	2 – □ = 0
□ – 4 = 0	8 – 8 =	5 – □ = 0	□ – 3 = 0

Differences Through Three

Name ______________________________

Counting Back

When the subtrahend is a lesser number like 1, 2, or 3, you can "count back" to find the difference.

Example: 3 – 1 = 2

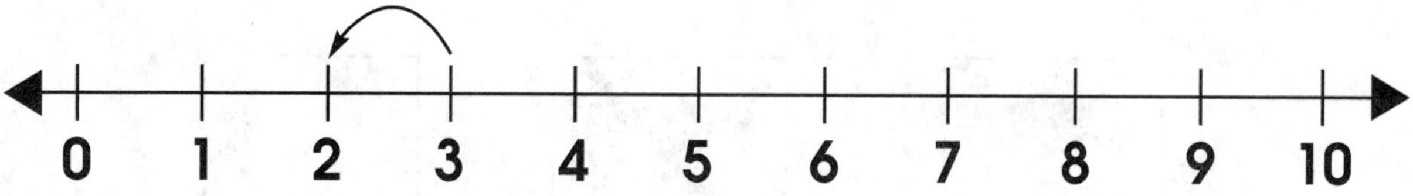

■ Complete each **T** by counting back by the number at the top. Use the number line to help you.

– 1	
3	___
2	___
1	___
4	___

– 2	
2	___
5	___
4	___
3	___

– 3	
4	___
6	___
5	___
3	___

■ Subtract.

6 – 3 = ____ 3 – 2 = ____

4 – 1 = ____ 4 – 3 = ____

5 – 2 = ____ 4 – 2 = ____

$\begin{array}{r} 5 \\ -\,3 \\ \hline \end{array}$ $\begin{array}{r} 4 \\ -\,1 \\ \hline \end{array}$ $\begin{array}{r} 5 \\ -\,2 \\ \hline \end{array}$

$\begin{array}{r} 2 \\ -\,1 \\ \hline \end{array}$ $\begin{array}{r} 6 \\ -\,3 \\ \hline \end{array}$ $\begin{array}{r} 3 \\ -\,2 \\ \hline \end{array}$

Name ______________________________

Using Addition

You can use addition facts to help you learn subtraction facts. This is because addition and subtraction are inverse operations.

Example: You already know that $3 + 2 = 5$.

Then, $5 - 2 = 3$.

And, $5 - 3 = 2$.

■ Write two different subtraction facts using the numbers in each addition sentence.

$3 + 1 = 4$	$2 + 0 = 2$	$1 + 0 = 1$
___ − ___ = ___	___ − ___ = ___	___ − ___ = ___
___ − ___ = ___	___ − ___ = ___	___ − ___ = ___
$1 + 2 = 3$	$3 + 0 = 3$	$2 + 3 = 5$
___ − ___ = ___	___ − ___ = ___	___ − ___ = ___
___ − ___ = ___	___ − ___ = ___	___ − ___ = ___

■ Write an addition fact using the numbers in each subtraction sentence.

$3 - 2 = 1$	$4 - 1 = 3$	$5 - 3 = 2$
___ + ___ = ___	___ + ___ = ___	___ + ___ = ___
$2 - 0 = 2$	$3 - 3 = 0$	$4 - 2 = 2$
___ + ___ = ___	___ + ___ = ___	___ + ___ = ___

Name ____________________

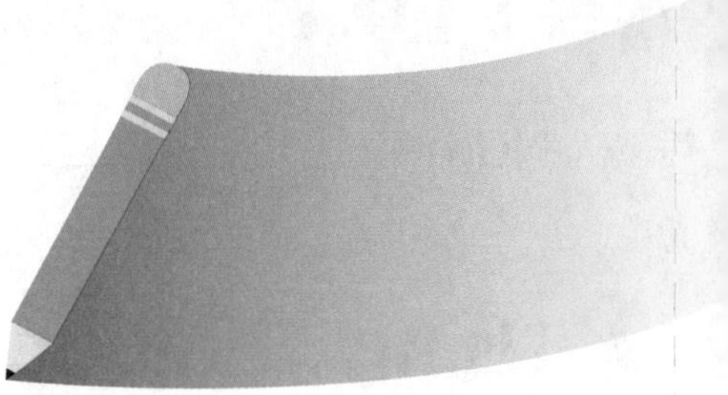

Practice

■ Subtract.

0 − 0	8 − 7	9 − 8	7 − 6	8 − 8	5 − 4	3 − 2	1 − 1	4 − 3
10 − 9	7 − 7	7 − 5	3 − 3	9 − 6	2 − 2	8 − 5	1 − 0	5 − 2
9 − 7	5 − 3	4 − 2	11 − 8	12 − 9	9 − 9	11 − 9	8 − 6	2 − 1
3 − 0	6 − 3	3 − 1	2 − 0	10 − 8	7 − 4	6 − 5	6 − 4	10 − 7

Score: ____________

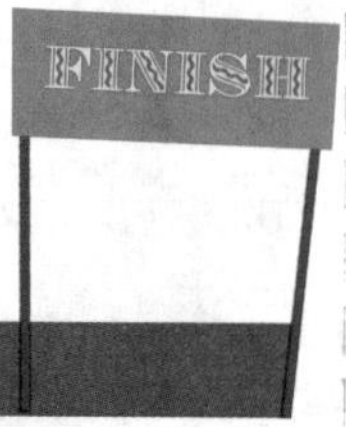

Name ______________________________

Practice

■ Subtract.

8	11	4	6
− 6	− 9	− 3	− 6
10	5	2	3
− 9	− 3	− 2	− 2
7	9	11	6
− 6	− 9	− 8	− 4
8	0	5	7
− 5	− 0	− 4	− 5
3	8	6	5
− 1	− 8	− 5	− 2

9 − 8 = ____	4 − 1 = ____
1 − 0 = ____	2 − 0 = ____
4 − 2 = ____	6 − 3 = ____
5 − 5 = ____	7 − 7 = ____
8 − 7 = ____	10 − 7 = ____
2 − 1 = ____	7 − 4 = ____
3 − 0 = ____	12 − 9 = ____
1 − 1 = ____	9 − 7 = ____

Differences Through Three

Score: ____________

FINISH

Circle any problems that you still find difficult to remember. Make your own flash cards to help you master these problems.

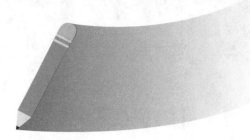

Name ______________________________

Timed Test

3	6	11	2	11	4	3	6
− 1	− 6	− 8	− 0	− 9	− 3	− 0	− 5
6	2	5	6	10	1	5	9
− 3	− 2	− 3	− 4	− 8	− 0	− 2	− 8
9	0	4	9	12	5	4	10
− 6	− 0	− 4	− 9	− 9	− 5	− 2	− 9
7	3	8	8	4	7	7	2
− 5	− 2	− 6	− 7	− 1	− 7	− 4	− 1
5	8	3	9	8	10	1	7
− 4	− 5	− 3	− 7	− 8	− 7	− 1	− 6

Score: __________ Time: __________ minutes __________ seconds

Name ______________________________

Timed Test

8 − 7 = ____	2 − 0 = ____
1 − 0 = ____	3 − 3 = ____
7 − 4 = ____	6 − 4 = ____
5 − 4 = ____	10 − 9 = ____
1 − 1 = ____	4 − 2 = ____
7 − 5 = ____	5 − 5 = ____
3 − 0 = ____	9 − 7 = ____
11 − 9 = ____	8 − 5 = ____
3 − 2 = ____	10 − 7 = ____
12 − 9 = ____	7 − 7 = ____

11 − 8 ____	7 − 6 ____	4 − 4 ____	6 − 3 ____
6 − 5 ____	4 − 1 ____	8 − 8 ____	5 − 2 ____
2 − 1 ____	8 − 6 ____	0 − 0 ____	9 − 6 ____
3 − 1 ____	9 − 9 ____	10 − 8 ____	2 − 2 ____
5 − 3 ____	4 − 3 ____	9 − 8 ____	6 − 6 ____

Differences Through Three

Score: __________ Time: __________ minutes __________ seconds

Name ______________________________

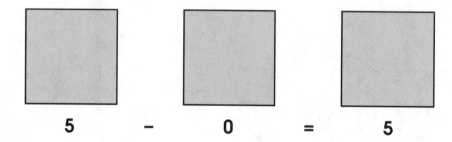

Subtracting Zero

Knowing that zero is the identity element of subtraction helps you to know three of the facts in this new group. Just remember that zero subtracted from any number is that number.

Example: 5 – 0 = 5

■ Draw X's in these boxes to show this is true.

☐		☐		☐
5	**–**	**0**	**=**	**5**

■ Complete this **T** by subtracting zero from each number.

	– 0
4	____
5	____
6	____

■ Now, write the answers for these facts.

6 – 0 = ____ 4 – 0 = ____

5 – 0 = ____

5	4	6
– 0	– 0	– 0
____	____	____

Name ____________________________________

Using Addition

You already have learned that addition and subtraction are opposite operations.

Example: If 1 + 4 = 5, then, 5 − 4 = 1. And, 5 − 1 = 4.

Notice that the sum in an addition fact becomes the minuend in a related subtraction fact.

Example: 1 + 4 = 5 → 5 − 4 = 1

■ Write two different subtraction facts using the numbers in each addition sentence.

6 + 2 = 8	5 + 3 = 8	5 + 1 = 6
___ − ___ = ___	___ − ___ = ___	___ − ___ = ___
___ − ___ = ___	___ − ___ = ___	___ − ___ = ___
5 + 2 = 7	**3 + 6 = 9**	**5 + 4 = 9**
___ − ___ = ___	___ − ___ = ___	___ − ___ = ___
___ − ___ = ___	___ − ___ = ___	___ − ___ = ___
3 + 4 = 7	**4 + 2 = 6**	**6 + 1 = 7**
___ − ___ = ___	___ − ___ = ___	___ − ___ = ___
___ − ___ = ___	___ − ___ = ___	___ − ___ = ___

Name ____________________

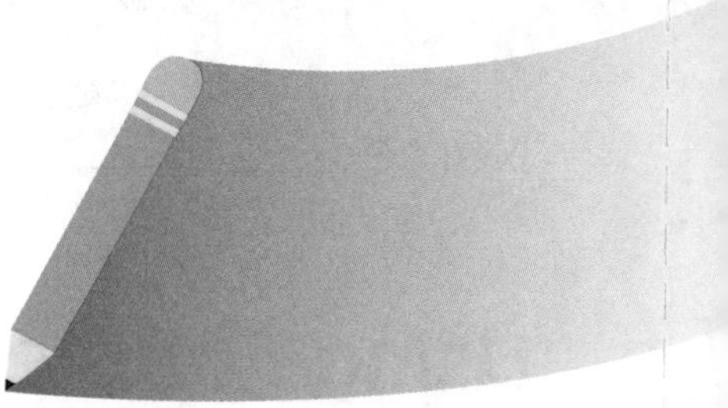

Practice

■ Subtract.

5 − 0	13 − 9	7 − 3	15 − 9	12 − 7	12 − 6	6 − 2	11 − 6	9 − 3
10 − 6	7 − 2	6 − 0	13 − 7	4 − 0	9 − 4	8 − 2	13 − 8	5 − 1
12 − 8	6 − 1	10 − 5	14 − 9	11 − 7	14 − 8	10 − 4	11 − 5	8 − 4
7 − 1	9 − 5	8 − 3	9 − 4	7 − 0	15 − 9	8 − 4	13 − 9	11 − 6

Score: ____________

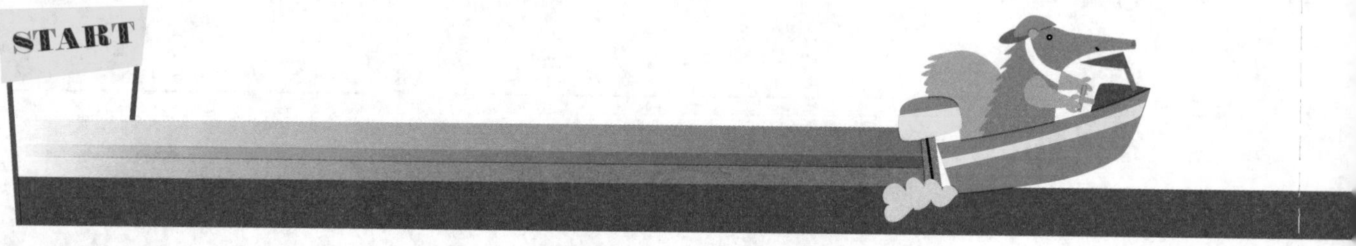

Name ______________________________

Practice

■ Subtract.

12 − 7	10 − 6	7 − 2	9 − 3
6 − 2	5 − 0	7 − 3	7 − 1
11 − 6	8 − 2	11 − 7	12 − 6
8 − 3	14 − 8	4 − 0	9 − 4
13 − 7	8 − 2	9 − 5	11 − 5

5 − 1 = ____ 6 − 1 = ____

13 − 8 = ____ 15 − 9 = ____

8 − 4 = ____ 10 − 5 = ____

6 − 0 = ____ 14 − 9 = ____

10 − 4 = ____ 12 − 8 = ____

13 − 9 = ____ 14 − 8 = ____

11 − 5 = ____ 7 − 1 = ____

9 − 4 = ____ 13 − 6 = ____

Differences Through Six

Score: ____________

FINISH

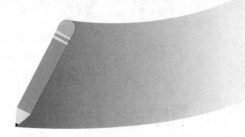

Name ______________________________

Timed Test

■ Complete these facts as accurately and as quickly as you can.

5	6	14	9	7	13	6	15
− 1	− 1	− 9	− 5	− 2	− 9	− 0	− 9
11	9	10	8	12	10	4	13
− 7	− 3	− 5	− 2	− 7	− 6	− 0	− 7
9	7	8	12	11	5	12	6
− 4	− 3	− 3	− 8	− 5	− 0	− 6	− 2
8	7	10	11	14	13	6	9
− 4	− 1	− 4	− 6	− 8	− 8	− 1	− 3
12	14	11	8	6	5	12	10
− 8	− 9	− 7	− 2	− 2	− 0	− 7	− 5

Score: ________ Time: ________ minutes ________ seconds

Name ______________________

Timed Test

Differences Through Six

9 – 5 = ____	11 – 7 = ____
11 – 5 = ____	14 – 9 = ____
6 – 2 = ____	10 – 5 = ____
13 – 8 = ____	14 – 8 = ____
8 – 3 = ____	5 – 1 = ____
6 – 0 = ____	15 – 9 = ____
12 – 8 = ____	4 – 0 = ____
8 – 2 = ____	7 – 2 = ____
5 – 0 = ____	12 – 7 = ____
9 – 3 = ____	8 – 4 = ____

15 – 9	4 – 0	7 – 2	12 – 7
8 – 4	6 – 1	13 – 9	11 – 6
7 – 3	7 – 1	9 – 4	10 – 6
13 – 7	10 – 4	12 – 6	9 – 5
6 – 2	8 – 3	10 – 5	11 – 7

Score: ________ Time: ________ minutes ________ seconds

Name ______________________

Timed Test

The rest of the Timed Tests in this section will include some of the differences through 3 to help you remember what you have already learned.

7 − 3 = ____ 6 − 1 = ____

12	6	11	8
− 6	− 0	− 6	− 8

11 − 7 = ____ 7 − 6 = ____

8 − 2 = ____ 9 − 4 = ____

10	14	5	12
− 5	− 8	− 1	− 8

12 − 9 = ____ 6 − 4 = ____

10 − 6 = ____ 13 − 8 = ____

6	11	9	14
− 3	− 5	− 5	− 9

13 − 7 = ____ 1 − 0 = ____

3 − 3 = ____ 6 − 2 = ____

8	9	13	7
− 4	− 3	− 9	− 2

5 − 0 = ____ 12 − 7 = ____

8 − 7 = ____ 7 − 1 = ____

2	8	10	15
− 0	− 3	− 4	− 9

4 − 0 = ____ 11 − 9 = ____

Score: ________ Time: ________ minutes ________ seconds

Name ______________________________

Counting Back

Remember: You can count back to find the difference when the subtrahend is a lesser number like 1, 2, or 3.

Example: 10 – 1 = 9

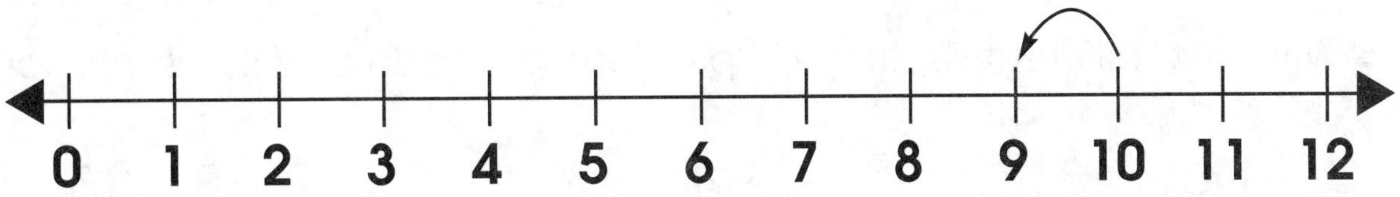

■ Complete these **T**'s by subtracting the numbers at the top from those along the side. You may use the number line to help you count.

	– 1
10	____
9	____
8	____

	– 2
11	____
9	____
10	____

	– 3
10	____
12	____
11	____

■ Subtract.

9 – 2 = ____   11 – 3 = ____

10 – 3 = ____   8 – 1 = ____

11 – 2 = ____   12 – 3 = ____

8	10	11
– 1	– 2	– 3
____	____	____
10	12	9
– 1	– 3	– 1
____	____	____

Differences Through Nine

Name ____________________

Using Addition

Use the higher addition facts and what you know about opposite operations to help you discover the higher subtraction facts.

Example: If 9 + 6 = 15, then, 15 – 9 = 6. And, 15 – 6 = 9.

■ Write two different subtraction problems for each addition sentence.

7 + 6 = 13	9 + 4 = 13	7 + 8 = 15
___ – ___ = ___	___ – ___ = ___	___ – ___ = ___
___ – ___ = ___	___ – ___ = ___	___ – ___ = ___
9 + 6 = 15	7 + 4 = 11	9 + 4 = 13
___ – ___ = ___	___ – ___ = ___	___ – ___ = ___
___ – ___ = ___	___ – ___ = ___	___ – ___ = ___
5 + 7 = 12	9 + 8 = 17	9 + 7 = 16
___ – ___ = ___	___ – ___ = ___	___ – ___ = ___
___ – ___ = ___	___ – ___ = ___	___ – ___ = ___

■ Write one subtraction fact related to each addition sentence.

7 + 7 = 14	8 + 8 = 16	9 + 9 = 18
___ – ___ = ___	___ – ___ = ___	___ – ___ = ___

Name ______________________________

Practice

■ Subtract.

12	15	12	8
− 5	− 7	− 4	− 1

13	11	16	13
− 4	− 3	− 7	− 6

16	18	10	9
− 8	− 9	− 1	− 2

8	12	16	14
− 0	− 3	− 9	− 6

14	9	15	11
− 5	− 0	− 8	− 2

14 − 6 = ____ 17 − 9 = ____

11 − 4 = ____ 10 − 2 = ____

13 − 5 = ____ 15 − 8 = ____

15 − 6 = ____ 11 − 2 = ____

14 − 7 = ____ 17 − 8 = ____

9 − 1 = ____ 12 − 5 = ____

7 − 0 = ____ 15 − 7 = ____

10 − 3 = ____ 8 − 1 = ____

Score: ____________

FINISH

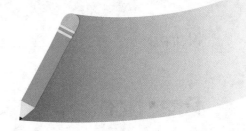

Differences Through Nine

Name ______________________________

Practice

■ Subtract.

7 − 0	13 − 4	12 − 4	16 − 8
11 − 4	9 − 0	16 − 9	15 − 7
18 − 9	9 − 2	12 − 3	13 − 6
15 − 6	10 − 2	14 − 6	12 − 5
10 − 3	14 − 7	11 − 2	13 − 5

8 − 1 = ____ 11 − 2 = ____

14 − 5 = ____ 13 − 5 = ____

11 − 3 = ____ 10 − 1 = ____

17 − 8 = ____ 15 − 8 = ____

12 − 5 = ____ 16 − 7 = ____

8 − 0 = ____ 9 − 2 = ____

17 − 9 = ____ 11 − 4 = ____

9 − 1 = ____ 13 − 6 = ____

Score: ____________

Circle any problems that you still find difficult to remember. Make your own flash cards to help you master these problems.

FINISH

Name ______________________________

Timed Test

12 − 4	13 − 6	13 − 5	16 − 9	14 − 5	9 − 2	16 − 7	18 − 9
9 − 1	10 − 3	17 − 8	15 − 6	8 − 1	11 − 4	17 − 9	15 − 8
13 − 4	11 − 3	16 − 8	12 − 5	15 − 7	14 − 6	9 − 0	14 − 7
10 − 2	12 − 3	10 − 1	8 − 0	7 − 0	11 − 2	13 − 5	15 − 7
16 − 8	11 − 4	16 − 9	8 − 1	12 − 4	14 − 6	9 − 2	17 − 8

Differences Through Nine

Name ____________________

Timed Test

Differences Through Nine

$17 - 8 =$ ____ $10 - 2 =$ ____

$15 - 8 =$ ____ $18 - 9 =$ ____

$7 - 0 =$ ____ $12 - 3 =$ ____

$9 - 1 =$ ____ $11 - 3 =$ ____

$16 - 8 =$ ____ $13 - 4 =$ ____

$10 - 3 =$ ____ $16 - 7 =$ ____

$11 - 2 =$ ____ $9 - 0 =$ ____

$13 - 5 =$ ____ $14 - 7 =$ ____

$10 - 1 =$ ____ $15 - 6 =$ ____

$12 - 5 =$ ____ $9 - 2 =$ ____

$\begin{array}{r} 16 \\ -7 \\ \hline \end{array}$	$\begin{array}{r} 17 \\ -9 \\ \hline \end{array}$	$\begin{array}{r} 11 \\ -4 \\ \hline \end{array}$	$\begin{array}{r} 8 \\ -0 \\ \hline \end{array}$
$\begin{array}{r} 9 \\ -0 \\ \hline \end{array}$	$\begin{array}{r} 16 \\ -9 \\ \hline \end{array}$	$\begin{array}{r} 14 \\ -6 \\ \hline \end{array}$	$\begin{array}{r} 8 \\ -1 \\ \hline \end{array}$
$\begin{array}{r} 15 \\ -7 \\ \hline \end{array}$	$\begin{array}{r} 14 \\ -7 \\ \hline \end{array}$	$\begin{array}{r} 13 \\ -6 \\ \hline \end{array}$	$\begin{array}{r} 14 \\ -5 \\ \hline \end{array}$
$\begin{array}{r} 12 \\ -4 \\ \hline \end{array}$	$\begin{array}{r} 15 \\ -6 \\ \hline \end{array}$	$\begin{array}{r} 9 \\ -2 \\ \hline \end{array}$	$\begin{array}{r} 17 \\ -8 \\ \hline \end{array}$
$\begin{array}{r} 7 \\ -0 \\ \hline \end{array}$	$\begin{array}{r} 18 \\ -9 \\ \hline \end{array}$	$\begin{array}{r} 11 \\ -2 \\ \hline \end{array}$	$\begin{array}{r} 10 \\ -3 \\ \hline \end{array}$

Score: ________ Time: ________ minutes ________ seconds

Name ______________________________

Timed Test

12 – 5 = ____ 14 – 6 = ____

16 – 7 = ____ 10 – 1 = ____

9 – 2 = ____ 8 – 1 = ____

11 – 2 = ____ 7 – 0 = ____

13 – 5 = ____ 15 – 8 = ____

9 – 1 = ____ 12 – 4 = ____

14 – 5 = ____ 11 – 3 = ____

13 – 6 = ____ 18 – 9 = ____

9 – 0 = ____ 15 – 7 = ____

10 – 2 = ____ 16 – 8 = ____

17	12	15	14
– 8	– 4	– 6	– 7
13	11	18	10
– 4	– 3	– 9	– 3
15	8	12	16
– 7	– 0	– 3	– 8
16	11	17	12
– 9	– 4	– 9	– 5
14	8	10	13
– 5	– 1	– 2	– 6

Score: __________ Time: __________ minutes __________ seconds

Name ______________________________

All-Addition Review

■ Here are 60 addition facts. Prove to yourself that you are an expert in addition. Concentrate on accuracy.

8 + 2 = ____	1 + 8 = ____	4 + 1 = ____	7 + 8 = ____
6 + 8 = ____	5 + 9 = ____	8 + 0 = ____	3 + 9 = ____
0 + 7 = ____	7 + 4 = ____	2 + 5 = ____	4 + 9 = ____
4 + 5 = ____	9 + 6 = ____	5 + 7 = ____	7 + 1 = ____
7 + 2 = ____	9 + 5 = ____	6 + 3 = ____	4 + 4 = ____
3 + 6 = ____	1 + 7 = ____	8 + 7 = ____	3 + 5 = ____
6 + 7 = ____	5 + 2 = ____	6 + 9 = ____	5 + 0 = ____
2 + 4 = ____	9 + 8 = ____	4 + 7 = ____	1 + 2 = ____
4 + 0 = ____	5 + 8 = ____	6 + 2 = ____	4 + 8 = ____
1 + 5 = ____	5 + 6 = ____	2 + 8 = ____	2 + 7 = ____
9 + 0 = ____	2 + 6 = ____	7 + 5 = ____	5 + 3 = ____
3 + 2 = ____	2 + 3 = ____	8 + 9 = ____	7 + 6 = ____
8 + 8 = ____	7 + 7 = ____	9 + 7 = ____	8 + 1 = ____
7 + 3 = ____	3 + 4 = ____	9 + 9 = ____	4 + 2 = ____
4 + 6 = ____	1 + 6 = ____	8 + 3 = ____	9 + 1 = ____

Name ______________________________

All-Subtraction Review

■ Here are 60 subtraction facts. Prove to yourself that you are also an expert in subtraction. Concentrate on accuracy.

4 – 0 = ___	16 – 9 = ___	13 – 6 = ___	7 – 3 = ___
11 – 4 = ___	17 – 9 = ___	15 – 9 = ___	2 – 1 = ___
9 – 3 = ___	2 – 2 = ___	16 – 7 = ___	13 – 4 = ___
4 – 3 = ___	14 – 5 = ___	9 – 5 = ___	6 – 2 = ___
8 – 2 = ___	10 – 7 = ___	5 – 3 = ___	9 – 6 = ___
10 – 5 = ___	5 – 5 = ___	9 – 4 = ___	11 – 3 = ___
14 – 9 = ___	9 – 2 = ___	6 – 5 = ___	12 – 7 = ___
5 – 4 = ___	13 – 5 = ___	8 – 3 = ___	9 – 7 = ___
11 – 5 = ___	12 – 6 = ___	14 – 6 = ___	12 – 3 = ___
12 – 9 = ___	15 – 6 = ___	18 – 9 = ___	12 – 8 = ___
4 – 2 = ___	12 – 4 = ___	5 – 2 = ___	11 – 2 = ___
6 – 6 = ___	16 – 8 = ___	13 – 8 = ___	5 – 1 = ___
8 – 4 = ___	14 – 7 = ___	15 – 7 = ___	14 – 8 = ___
11 – 7 = ___	13 – 9 = ___	10 – 8 = ___	12 – 5 = ___
9 – 8 = ___	11 – 6 = ___	11 – 9 = ___	13 – 7 = ___

MULTIPLICATION

Name ________________________________

What Is Multiplication?

You multiply to find how many there are in all in groups that are equal. The answer is called the **product**.

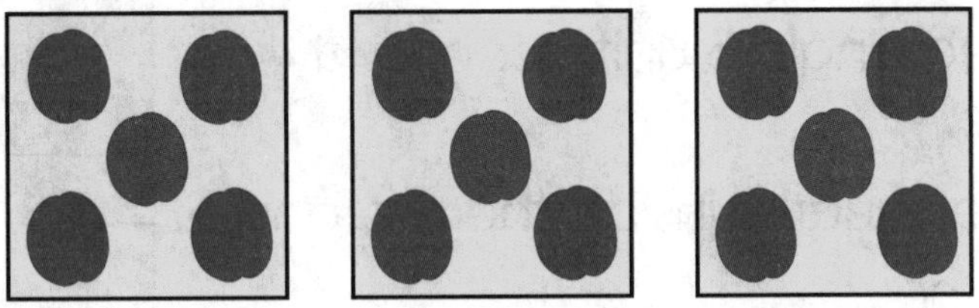

5 plums + 5 plums + 5 plums

Here are two ways to show the multiplication. You read the problem this way: **3 times 5 equals 15**.

$3 \times 5 = 15$

$$\begin{array}{r} 3 \\ \times 5 \\ \hline 15 \end{array}$$

You can draw a picture to find a product.

Example: Find the answer. 4 x 2 = _____

Step 1: Draw 4 sets of 2 dots. ● ●   ● ●   ● ●   ● ●

Step 2: Count all the dots.

Answer: 4 x 2 = __8__

■ Draw a picture to find the product.

3 x 2 = _____

2 x 4 = _____

5 x 2 = _____

2 x 3 = _____

4 x 3 = _____

3 x 4 = _____

Name ______________________________

What Is Multiplication?

Multiplication

You can use grid paper to find the product.

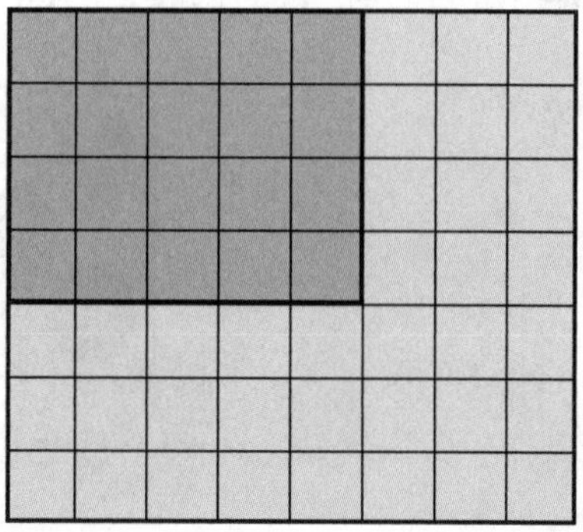

Example: Find the product. 4 x 5 = ____

Step 1: Draw a rectangle 5 units long and 4 units wide.

Step 2: Count the squares inside the rectangle.

Answer: 4 x 5 = 20

■ Use grid paper to find the product.

3 x 3 = ____ 2 x 5 = ____ 4 x 4 = ____

3 x 5	2 x 2	6 x 2	3 x 4	6 x 3

You can use a number line to find the product.

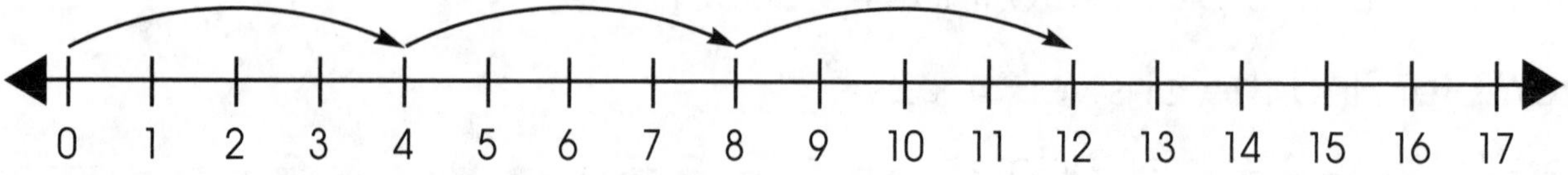

Example: Find the product. 3 x 4 = ____

Step 1: Put your finger on 0.

Step 2: Make 3 moves to the right of 4 spaces each.

Step 3: Read the number your finger is on.

Answer: 3 x 4 = 12

■ Use the number line to find the product.

3 x 3 = ____ 2 x 5 = ____ 4 x 4 = ____

4 x 2	3 x 4	3 x 2	2 x 6	3 x 5

Name ______________________________

Products Through Nine

The answer in multiplication is called the **product**. The numbers multiplied together are called **factors**.

Example: 0 x 4 = 0.

0	x	4	=	0
factor		factor		product

$$\begin{array}{rl} 0 & \textbf{factor} \\ \times 4 & \textbf{factor} \\ \hline 0 & \textbf{product} \end{array}$$

There are three important things to remember about the multiplication facts on this page.

- When one of the factors is 0, the product is always 0.
  Example: 6 x 0 = 0
- When one of the factors is 1, the product is the same as the other factor. One is the **identity element of multiplication**.
  Example: 5 x 1 = 5
- The order of the factors does not change the product.
  Example: 3 x 1 = 3 and 1 x 3 = 3

■ Find the products for these basic facts.

0 x 3 = ____	0 x 5 = ____	7 x 0 = ____	1 x 7 = ____
6 x 0 = ____	9 x 1 = ____	4 x 1 = ____	0 x 9 = ____
0 x 7 = ____	1 x 0 = ____	0 x 4 = ____	0 x 8 = ____
4 x 1 = ____	3 x 0 = ____	1 x 3 = ____	1 x 2 = ____
7 x 1 = ____	5 x 1 = ____	9 x 0 = ____	2 x 0 = ____

Zero and One as Factors

Name ____________________

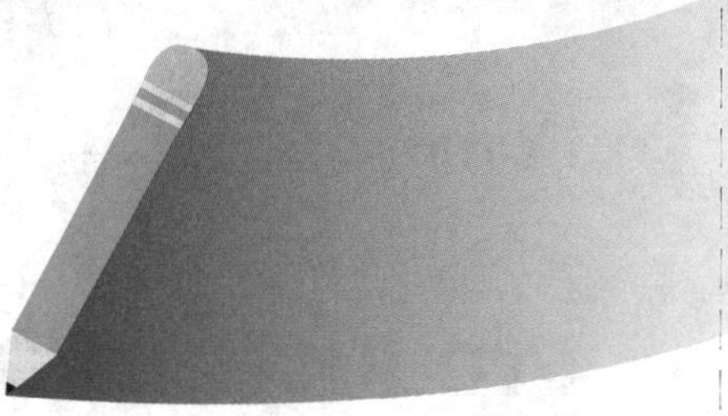

Practice

■ Multiply.

0 x 0	1 x 2	2 x 0	4 x 1	9 x 0	5 x 1	0 x 3	1 x 9	0 x 5
1 x 1	5 x 0	1 x 8	0 x 7	9 x 1	7 x 1	1 x 7	0 x 9	0 x 8
4 x 0	8 x 0	1 x 4	1 x 0	3 x 1	1 x 3	3 x 0	0 x 1	0 x 4
2 x 1	6 x 0	8 x 1	1 x 5	0 x 6	6 x 1	7 x 0	0 x 2	1 x 6

Score: ____________

Circle any problems that you still find difficult to remember. Make your own flash cards to help you master these problems.

Name ____________________

Timed Test

■ Improve your speed on these basic multiplication facts. Ask someone to time you. Record your time and score below.

1 x 0 = ____	2 x 1 = ____
1 x 4 = ____	0 x 4 = ____
0 x 2 = ____	7 x 1 = ____
6 x 0 = ____	9 x 0 = ____
1 x 9 = ____	0 x 5 = ____
2 x 0 = ____	7 x 0 = ____
0 x 9 = ____	1 x 7 = ____
1 x 3 = ____	4 x 0 = ____
5 x 0 = ____	1 x 5 = ____
0 x 7 = ____	9 x 1 = ____

0 x 3	1 x 5	4 x 1	8 x 1
6 x 1	1 x 6	9 x 1	3 x 0
1 x 1	0 x 6	0 x 0	5 x 1
1 x 8	3 x 1	0 x 8	1 x 2
0 x 1	8 x 0	1 x 3	7 x 1

Zero and One as Factors

Score: ________ Time: ________ minutes ________ seconds

Name ____________________

Products Through Eighteen

Remember: The answer in multiplication is called the **product**. The numbers that are multiplied together are called **factors**.

Multiplication is like addition in some ways. Like a sum, a product represents how many in all. What makes multiplication different is that one of the factors represents the number of things in a group and the other factor represents the number of groups.

Example: 2 x 4 = ?

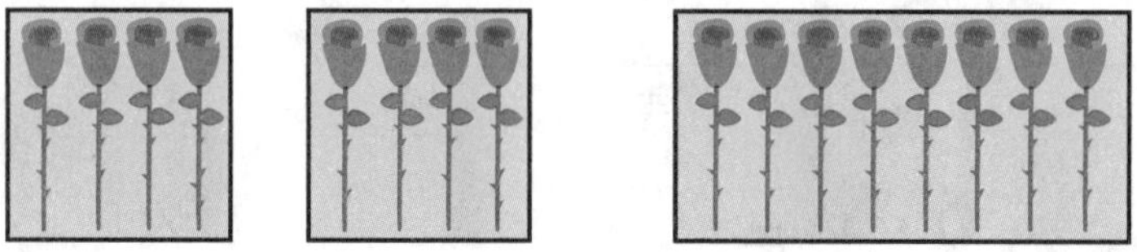

There are 2 groups of 4 roses each. Therefore, there are 8 roses in all.

2 x 4 = 8

Notice that the product is the same if you think of the problem as 4 groups of 2 roses each.

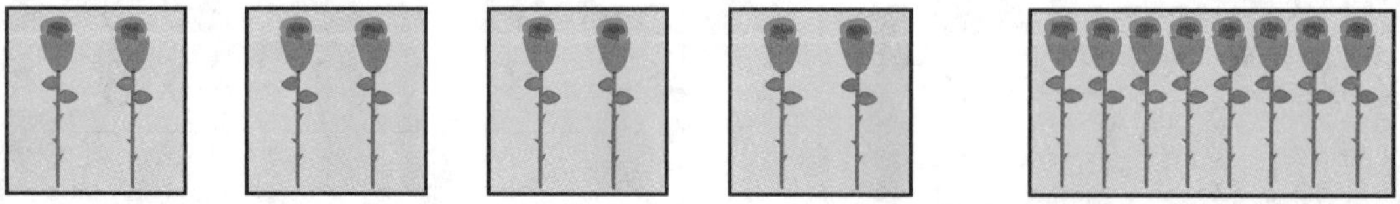

Notice that the product of 2 and another factor is always an even number, such as 0, 2, 4, 6, 8, 10, 12, 14, 16, or 18. These numbers are the first ten multiples of 2. They are the same as the products of 2 times any number from 0 through 9.

■ Complete these **T**'s by multiplying the numbers by 2.

x 2	
4	____
1	____

x 2	
5	____
3	____

x 2	
9	____
7	____

x 2	
0	____
6	____

x 2	
2	____
8	____

Name ______________________________

Practice

■ Multiply.

2 x 3	4 x 2	2 x 0	6 x 2
2 x 1	2 x 6	2 x 4	7 x 2
2 x 7	0 x 2	9 x 2	1 x 2
5 x 2	2 x 9	2 x 8	2 x 3
1 x 2	2 x 6	3 x 2	2 x 9

2 x 5 = ____ 4 x 2 = ____

9 x 2 = ____ 2 x 0 = ____

3 x 2 = ____ 6 x 2 = ____

0 x 2 = ____ 2 x 7 = ____

2 x 1 = ____ 5 x 2 = ____

2 x 9 = ____ 2 x 4 = ____

8 x 2 = ____ 7 x 2 = ____

2 x 3 = ____ 2 x 8 = ____

Score: ____________

Circle any problems that you still find difficult to remember. Make your own flash cards to help you master these problems.

Name ______________________________

Timed Test

■ Complete these facts as accurately and as quickly as you can.

Two as a Factor

2 x 7 = ____   3 x 2 = ____

2 x 5 = ____   9 x 2 = ____

0 x 2 = ____   2 x 0 = ____

2 x 1 = ____   5 x 2 = ____

6 x 2 = ____   2 x 3 = ____

2 x 6 = ____   2 x 8 = ____

3 x 2 = ____   9 x 2 = ____

7 x 2 = ____   4 x 2 = ____

1 x 2 = ____   2 x 2 = ____

2 x 4 = ____   2 x 9 = ____

2 x 0	0 x 2	7 x 2	2 x 3
6 x 2	1 x 2	2 x 9	2 x 5
2 x 4	2 x 8	3 x 2	2 x 1
9 x 2	5 x 2	2 x 6	4 x 2
2 x 7	2 x 5	7 x 2	2 x 2

Score: ________   Time: ________ minutes ________ seconds

Name ________________________________

Products Through Twenty-Seven

When you multiply a number by 3, you triple that number. It is the same as adding that number three times.

Example: 3 x 4 = ?

Therefore, 3 x 4 = 12.

Notice that the product is the same if you multiply 4 by 3. In this case, it would be 4 groups of 3 each. Therefore, 4 x 3 = 12.

The first ten multiples of 3 are 0, 3, 6, 9, 12, 15, 18, 21, 24, 27. They are the same as the products of 3 times any number from 0 through 9.

- Complete this circle by multiplying each of the numbers by 3.

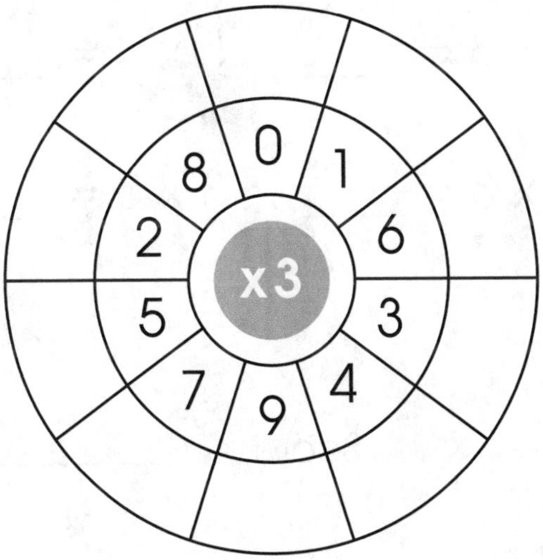

- Now, complete these facts.

5 x 3	9 x 3	3 x 1	3 x 8
6 x 3	3 x 2	0 x 3	3 x 5
2 x 3	3 x 4	8 x 3	3 x 9

Name ______________________

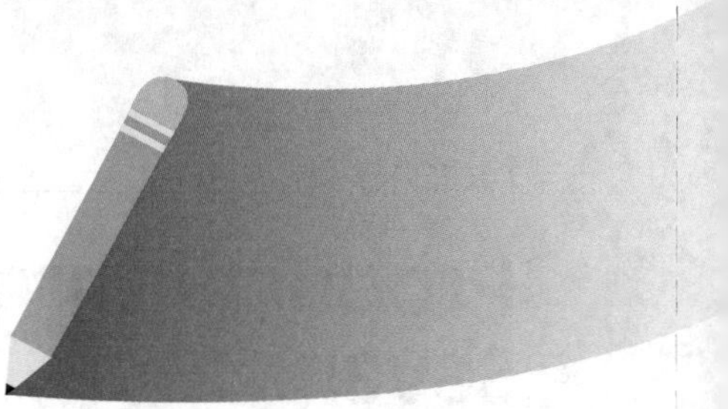

Practice

■ Multiply.

3 x 3	3 x 0	5 x 3	3 x 2
9 x 3	3 x 6	2 x 3	3 x 7
3 x 4	8 x 3	1 x 3	3 x 9
6 x 3	4 x 3	3 x 5	7 x 3
0 x 3	2 x 3	3 x 1	3 x 8

3 x 0 = ____ 6 x 3 = ____

0 x 3 = ____ 3 x 1 = ____

3 x 8 = ____ 3 x 5 = ____

3 x 7 = ____ 4 x 3 = ____

8 x 3 = ____ 9 x 3 = ____

3 x 4 = ____ 3 x 2 = ____

1 x 3 = ____ 5 x 3 = ____

7 x 3 = ____ 3 x 3 = ____

Score: ____________

Circle any problems that you still find difficult to remember. Make your own flash cards to help you master these problems.

Name ______________________________

Timed Test

■ Complete these facts as accurately and as quickly as you can.

3 x 6 = ____	3 x 3 = ____
3 x 5 = ____	3 x 1 = ____
0 x 3 = ____	3 x 4 = ____
3 x 2 = ____	1 x 3 = ____
3 x 0 = ____	3 x 9 = ____
6 x 3 = ____	2 x 3 = ____
3 x 8 = ____	3 x 3 = ____
9 x 3 = ____	8 x 3 = ____
3 x 7 = ____	4 x 3 = ____
5 x 3 = ____	3 x 1 = ____

3	5	4	0
x 8	x 3	x 3	x 3
3	1	3	6
x 1	x 3	x 4	x 3
3	7	3	9
x 6	x 3	x 0	x 3
2	3	8	3
x 3	x 3	x 3	x 7
3	3	3	3
x 5	x 2	x 9	x 6

Three as a Factor

Score: ____________ Time: ____________ minutes ____________ seconds

 0-7696-8503-X

Name ____________________

Products Through Thirty-Six

The first ten multiples of 4 are 0, 4, 8, 12, 16, 20, 24, 28, 32, and 36. They are the same as the products of 4 times any number from 0 through 9.

Example: 4 x 5 = ?

Remember to think of one of the factors as the number of groups in all and the other as the number of objects in one group.

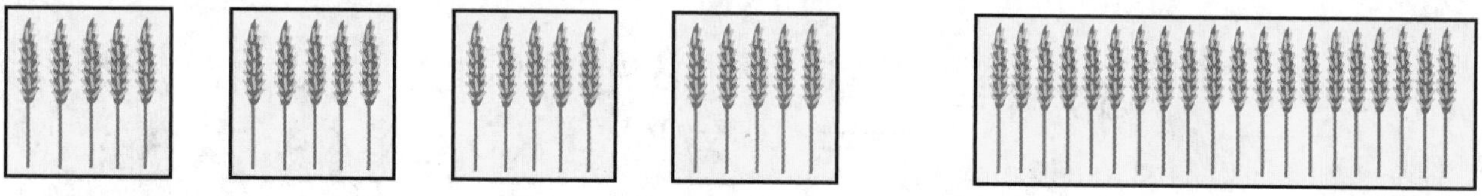

Therefore, 4 x 5 = 20.

- Complete these **T**'s by multiplying each of the numbers by 4.

x 4	
6	____
9	____
0	____
8	____
4	____

x 4	
2	____
7	____
1	____
3	____
5	____

- Now, complete these facts.

4 x 9 = ____ 4 x 7 = ____

3 x 4 = ____ 2 x 4 = ____

4 x 2 = ____ 4 x 3 = ____

8 x 4 = ____ 4 x 0 = ____

1 x 4 = ____ 5 x 4 = ____

6 x 4 = ____ 0 x 4 = ____

4 x 1 = ____ 4 x 6 = ____

Name ______________________________

Practice

■ Multiply.

4 x 2	4 x 6	4 x 0	9 x 4
3 x 4	4 x 5	8 x 4	4 x 3
0 x 4	5 x 4	7 x 4	1 x 4
4 x 8	4 x 1	6 x 4	2 x 4
9 x 4	4 x 6	4 x 7	4 x 4

4 x 1 = ____	0 x 4 = ____
5 x 4 = ____	4 x 3 = ____
4 x 6 = ____	7 x 4 = ____
3 x 4 = ____	1 x 4 = ____
4 x 4 = ____	4 x 5 = ____
6 x 4 = ____	4 x 8 = ____
9 x 4 = ____	8 x 4 = ____
2 x 4 = ____	4 x 0 = ____

Four as a Factor

Score: ____________

Circle any problems that you still find difficult to remember. Make your own flash cards to help you master these problems.

Name ____________________

Timed Test

■ Complete these facts as accurately and as quickly as you can.

Four as a factor

4 x 4 = ____ 4 x 5 = ____

2 x 4 = ____ 5 x 4 = ____

4 x 8 = ____ 8 x 4 = ____

0 x 4 = ____ 4 x 0 = ____

4 x 3 = ____ 4 x 2 = ____

3 x 4 = ____ 4 x 6 = ____

6 x 4 = ____ 7 x 4 = ____

1 x 4 = ____ 9 x 4 = ____

4 x 7 = ____ 4 x 5 = ____

4 x 9 = ____ 4 x 1 = ____

4	8	9	4
x 5	x 4	x 4	x 3
4	7	0	4
x 4	x 4	x 4	x 1
4	4	4	5
x 6	x 0	x 9	x 4
4	4	1	6
x 2	x 8	x 4	x 4
9	3	4	2
x 4	x 4	x 7	x 4

Score: ________ Time: ________ minutes ________ seconds

Name ______________________________

Products Through Forty-Five

The first ten multiples of 5 are 0, 5, 10, 15, 20, 25, 30, 35, 40, and 45. They are the same as the products of 5 times any number from 0 through 9.

Example: 5 x 3 = ?

Therefore, 5 x 3 = 15.

Remember, 3 x 5 is also 15.

Notice that when one of the factors is 5, the product always ends in a 5 or 0.

- Complete this circle by multiplying each of the numbers by 5.

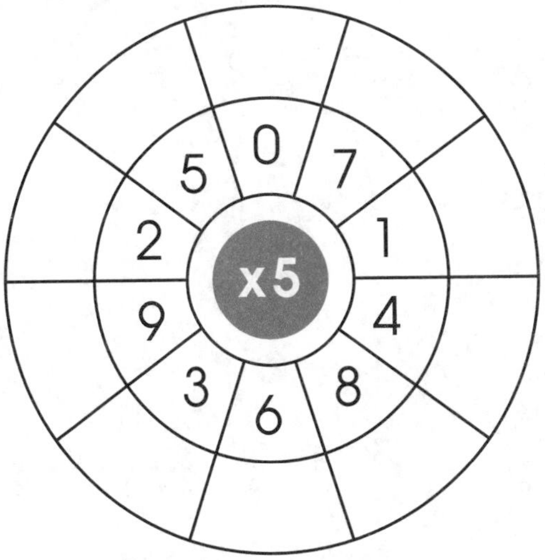

- Now, complete these facts.

5 x 8	5 x 4	5 x 2	7 x 5
5 x 7	1 x 5	5 x 0	6 x 5
5 x 9	3 x 5	8 x 5	5 x 5

Five as a Factor

0-7696-8503-X

Name ______________________________

Practice

Five as a Factor

■ Multiply.

5	8	6	5
x 5	x 5	x 5	x 4
3	5	1	5
x 5	x 8	x 5	x 3
5	9	7	5
x 2	x 5	x 5	x 6
0	5	4	5
x 5	x 1	x 5	x 9
5	2	5	5
x 7	x 5	x 3	x 0

5 x 0 = ____	5 x 6 = ____
5 x 9 = ____	2 x 5 = ____
0 x 5 = ____	7 x 5 = ____
5 x 3 = ____	9 x 5 = ____
8 x 5 = ____	4 x 5 = ____
5 x 5 = ____	5 x 7 = ____
6 x 5 = ____	5 x 2 = ____
5 x 8 = ____	3 x 5 = ____

Score: ______________

Circle any problems that you still find difficult to remember. Make your own flash cards to help you master these problems.

Name ______________________________

Timed Test

■ Complete these facts as accurately and as quickly as you can.

5 x 8 = ____   5 x 5 = ____

7 x 5 = ____   1 x 5 = ____

2 x 5 = ____   3 x 5 = ____

5 x 7 = ____   6 x 5 = ____

4 x 5 = ____   5 x 1 = ____

5 x 0 = ____   9 x 5 = ____

8 x 5 = ____   5 x 3 = ____

5 x 6 = ____   5 x 4 = ____

0 x 5 = ____   5 x 9 = ____

5 x 2 = ____   4 x 5 = ____

5 x 3	7 x 5	5 x 1	6 x 5
4 x 5	5 x 2	5 x 0	9 x 5
3 x 5	8 x 5	5 x 5	5 x 4
2 x 5	9 x 5	1 x 5	5 x 7
5 x 8	5 x 6	5 x 9	0 x 5

Five as a Factor

Score: ________   Time: ________ minutes ________ seconds

Name ____________________

Products Through Fifty-Four

The first ten multiples of 6 are 0, 6, 12, 18, 24, 30, 36, 42, 48, and 54. They are the same as the products of 6 times any number from 0 through 9.

Example: 6 x 4 = ?

6 groups of 4 each

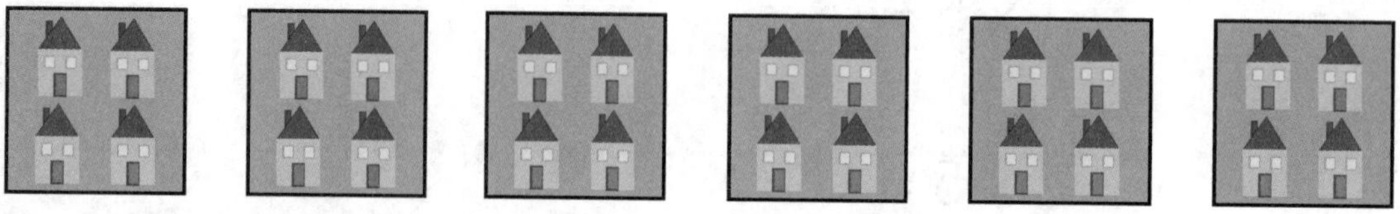

Therefore, 6 x 4 = 24.

Remember, 4 x 6 is also 24.

Notice that when you learn each set of facts, you are actually learning facts from other sets. For example, when you learned that 3 x 6 = 18, you also learned 6 x 3 = 18. This cuts down on the number of new facts you actually have to learn.

■ Complete these facts that you have already learned in which 6 is a factor.

6 x 4 ___	6 x 0 ___	6 x 5 ___
6 x 2 ___	6 x 3 ___	6 x 1 ___

■ Complete these **T**'s by multiplying each of the numbers by 6.

x 6	
3	___
0	___
5	___
2	___
7	___

x 6	
9	___
4	___
6	___
1	___
8	___

Name ________________________________

Practice

■ Multiply.

0 x 6	9 x 6	6 x 6	6 x 3
6 x 0	4 x 6	2 x 6	6 x 7
6 x 1	3 x 6	6 x 8	1 x 6
7 x 6	6 x 9	6 x 5	6 x 2
8 x 6	4 x 6	6 x 3	5 x 6

6 x 6 = ____ 6 x 8 = ____

3 x 6 = ____ 0 x 6 = ____

6 x 3 = ____ 6 x 2 = ____

2 x 6 = ____ 4 x 6 = ____

6 x 9 = ____ 6 x 4 = ____

8 x 6 = ____ 5 x 6 = ____

1 x 6 = ____ 6 x 7 = ____

6 x 5 = ____ 6 x 0 = ____

Six as a Factor

Score: ____________

Circle any problems that you still find difficult to remember. Make your own flash cards to help you master these problems.

Name _____

Timed Test

■ Complete these facts as accurately and as quickly as you can.

6 x 3 = ____   7 x 6 = ____

$$\begin{array}{cccc} 6 & 6 & 4 & 6 \\ \underline{\times 1} & \underline{\times 3} & \underline{\times 6} & \underline{\times 5} \end{array}$$

1 x 6 = ____   2 x 6 = ____

0 x 6 = ____   8 x 6 = ____

$$\begin{array}{cccc} 6 & 3 & 9 & 6 \\ \underline{\times 8} & \underline{\times 6} & \underline{\times 6} & \underline{\times 6} \end{array}$$

6 x 9 = ____   6 x 6 = ____

6 x 2 = ____   4 x 6 = ____

$$\begin{array}{cccc} 2 & 6 & 6 & 1 \\ \underline{\times 6} & \underline{\times 0} & \underline{\times 7} & \underline{\times 6} \end{array}$$

6 x 5 = ____   6 x 0 = ____

6 x 7 = ____   6 x 3 = ____

$$\begin{array}{cccc} 6 & 6 & 0 & 6 \\ \underline{\times 4} & \underline{\times 9} & \underline{\times 6} & \underline{\times 2} \end{array}$$

9 x 6 = ____   5 x 6 = ____

6 x 4 = ____   7 x 6 = ____

$$\begin{array}{cccc} 5 & 8 & 3 & 7 \\ \underline{\times 6} & \underline{\times 6} & \underline{\times 6} & \underline{\times 6} \end{array}$$

6 x 8 = ____   6 x 1 = ____

Score: _____   Time: _____ minutes _____ seconds

Six as a Factor

Name ______________________________

Products Through Sixty-Three

The first ten multiples of 7 are 0, 7, 14, 21, 28, 35, 42, 49, 56, and 63. They are the same as the products of 7 times any number from 0 through 9.

Example: 7 x 5 = ?

7 groups of 5 each

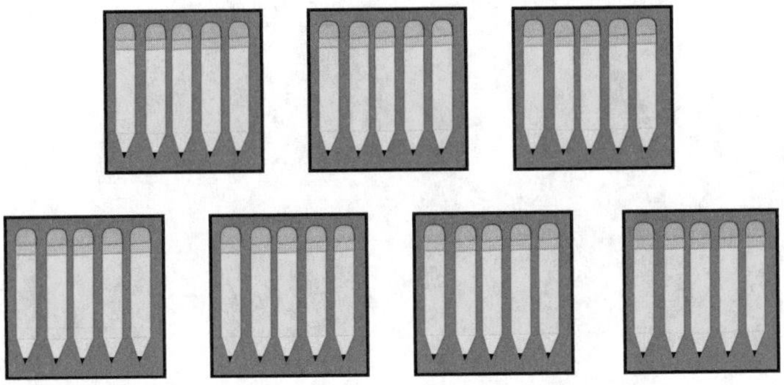

Therefore, 7 x 5 = 35.

Remember, 5 x 7 is also 35.

■ Complete these facts that you have already learned in which 7 is a factor.

3 x 7	1 x 7	5 x 7	2 x 7
0 x 7	4 x 7	6 x 7	

■ Complete this circle by multiplying each of the numbers by 7.

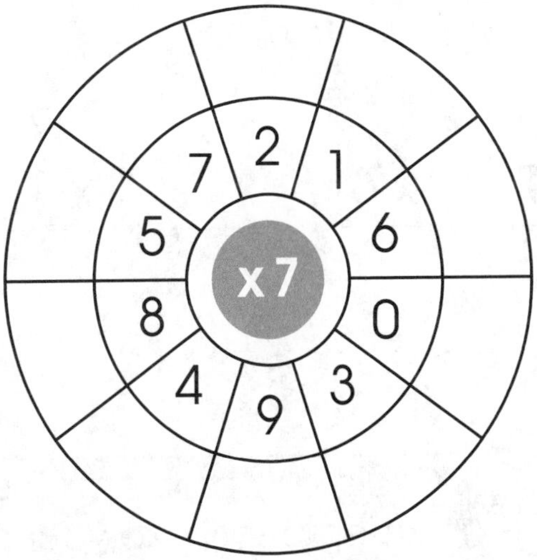

Name ______________________________

Practice

■ Multiply.

7	5	7	9
x 7	x 7	x 4	x 7
7	3	7	4
x 0	x 7	x 8	x 7
7	6	1	7
x 3	x 7	x 7	x 9
7	8	7	0
x 5	x 7	x 2	x 7
2	7	7	7
x 7	x 6	x 8	x 1

7 x 4 = ____	7 x 5 = ____
2 x 7 = ____	3 x 7 = ____
7 x 1 = ____	9 x 7 = ____
7 x 7 = ____	7 x 2 = ____
7 x 8 = ____	5 x 7 = ____
1 x 7 = ____	0 x 7 = ____
7 x 3 = ____	7 x 6 = ____
8 x 7 = ____	4 x 7 = ____

Score: ______________

Circle any problems that you still find difficult to remember. Make your own flash cards to help you master these problems.

Name ________________________

Timed Test

■ Complete these facts as accurately and as quickly as you can.

7 x 6 = ____   1 x 7 = ____

0 x 7	7 x 3	7 x 8	7 x 6

8 x 7 = ____   7 x 9 = ____

2 x 7 = ____   3 x 7 = ____

7 x 2	6 x 7	7 x 5	7 x 4

5 x 7 = ____   7 x 1 = ____

0 x 7 = ____   6 x 7 = ____

7 x 9	5 x 7	1 x 7	4 x 7

7 x 2 = ____   7 x 8 = ____

7 x 0 = ____   9 x 7 = ____

7 x 1	9 x 7	2 x 7	3 x 7

4 x 7 = ____   7 x 4 = ____

7 x 7 = ____   2 x 7 = ____

8 x 7	7 x 5	7 x 7	7 x 0

7 x 5 = ____   7 x 3 = ____

Seven as a Factor

Score: ________   Time: ________ minutes ________ seconds

Name ______________________________

Timed Test

Seven as a Factor

7 x 8 = ____ 7 x 4 = ____

7 x 2 = ____ 7 x 1 = ____

5 x 7 = ____ 7 x 9 = ____

1 x 7 = ____ 7 x 2 = ____

3 x 7 = ____ 7 x 3 = ____

7 x 0 = ____ 7 x 5 = ____

6 x 7 = ____ 0 x 7 = ____

7 x 7 = ____ 4 x 7 = ____

2 x 7 = ____ 9 x 7 = ____

8 x 7 = ____ 7 x 6 = ____

7 x 6	0 x 7	7 x 1	4 x 7
7 x 8	9 x 7	7 x 3	2 x 7
6 x 7	7 x 7	3 x 7	5 x 7
7 x 2	4 x 7	1 x 7	7 x 5
7 x 9	8 x 7	7 x 4	7 x 0

Score: ________ Time: ________ minutes ________ seconds

0-7696-8503-X

Name ______________________________

Products Through Seventy-Two

The first ten multiples of 8 are 0, 8, 16, 24, 32, 40, 48, 56, 64, and 72. They are the same as the products of 8 times any number from 0 through 9.

Example: 8 x 6 = ?

8 groups of 6 each

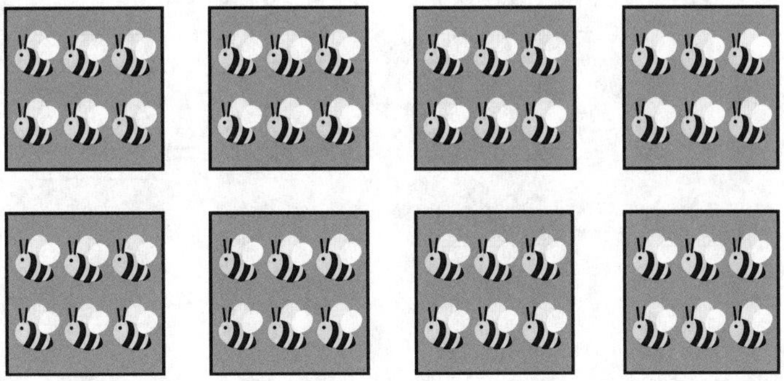

Therefore, 8 x 6 = 48.

Remember, 6 x 8 is also 48.

■ Complete these facts that you have already learned in which 8 is a factor.

6 x 8 ___	1 x 8 ___	4 x 8 ___	0 x 8 ___
2 x 8 ___	5 x 8 ___	7 x 8 ___	3 x 8 ___

■ Complete these **T**'s by multiplying each of the numbers by 8.

x 8	
5	___
1	___
4	___
9	___
0	___

x 8	
6	___
3	___
7	___
2	___
8	___

Name ______________________________

Practice

Eight as a Factor

■ Multiply.

8 x 0	8 x 6	0 x 8	9 x 8
8 x 4	5 x 8	8 x 9	1 x 8
8 x 5	8 x 3	6 x 8	8 x 8
3 x 8	8 x 2	7 x 8	4 x 8
8 x 1	8 x 7	2 x 8	5 x 8

8 x 9 = ____	2 x 8 = ____
8 x 3 = ____	8 x 8 = ____
9 x 8 = ____	0 x 8 = ____
4 x 8 = ____	8 x 2 = ____
8 x 1 = ____	8 x 7 = ____
8 x 4 = ____	1 x 8 = ____
8 x 6 = ____	6 x 8 = ____
7 x 8 = ____	5 x 8 = ____

Score: ______________

FINISH

Circle any problems that you still find difficult to remember. Make your own flash cards to help you master these problems.

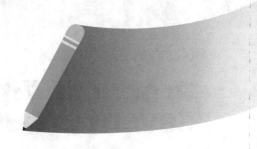

Name ______________________________

Timed Test

■ Complete these facts as accurately and as quickly as you can.

8 x 4 = ____ 6 x 8 = ____

8 x 0 = ____ 0 x 8 = ____

7 x 8 = ____ 3 x 8 = ____

5 x 8 = ____ 8 x 3 = ____

8 x 6 = ____ 8 x 9 = ____

9 x 8 = ____ 2 x 8 = ____

4 x 8 = ____ 8 x 7 = ____

1 x 8 = ____ 8 x 2 = ____

8 x 8 = ____ 8 x 1 = ____

8 x 5 = ____ 3 x 8 = ____

8	2	0	5
x 3	x 8	x 8	x 8

3	8	8	6
x 8	x 8	x 0	x 8

8	1	8	9
x 7	x 8	x 2	x 8

8	8	8	8
x 4	x 6	x 1	x 9

8	2	4	7
x 5	x 8	x 8	x 8

Score: __________ Time: __________ minutes __________ seconds

Name ____________________

Timed Test

Eight as a Factor

8 x 9 = ____ 8 x 6 = ____

6 x 8 = ____ 1 x 8 = ____

8 x 2 = ____ 4 x 8 = ____

0 x 8 = ____ 8 x 3 = ____

7 x 8 = ____ 9 x 8 = ____

8 x 5 = ____ 8 x 8 = ____

5 x 8 = ____ 2 x 8 = ____

8 x 7 = ____ 8 x 1 = ____

8 x 0 = ____ 8 x 4 = ____

9 x 8 = ____ 3 x 8 = ____

8 x 4	3 x 8	8 x 0	1 x 8
9 x 8	4 x 8	8 x 3	8 x 6
2 x 8	8 x 9	5 x 8	7 x 8
8 x 5	0 x 8	8 x 4	8 x 7
8 x 1	6 x 8	2 x 8	8 x 8

Score: ________ Time: ________ minutes ________ seconds

Name ______________________________________

Products Through Eighty-One

The first ten multiples of 9 are 0, 9, 18, 27, 36, 45, 54, 63, 72, and 81. They are the same as the products of 9 times any number from 0 through 9.

Example: 9 x 4 = ?

9 groups of 4 each

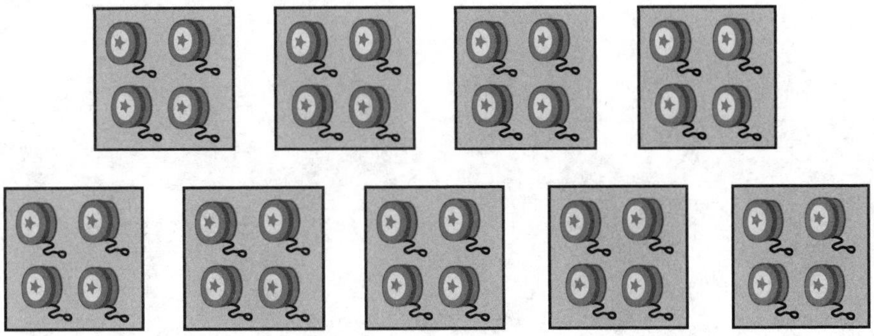

Therefore, 9 x 4 = 36. Remember, 4 x 9 is also 36.

- Complete these facts that you have already learned in which 9 is a factor.

2	0	5	6
x 9	x 9	x 9	x 9
___	___	___	___

4	7	1	8	3
x 9	x 9	x 9	x 9	x 9
___	___	___	___	___

Here is the only new fact in this set in which 9 is a factor:

9 x 9 = ____

- Complete these **T**'s by multiplying all the numbers by 9.

x 9	
4	____
3	____
6	____
7	____
2	____

x 9	
1	____
5	____
9	____
0	____
8	____

Nine as a Factor

Name ______________________________

Practice

■ Complete these facts as accurately and as quickly as you can.

8 x 9	9 x 5	9 x 9	1 x 9
9 x 4	9 x 8	3 x 9	0 x 9
9 x 6	9 x 7	7 x 9	2 x 9
9 x 1	9 x 3	5 x 9	9 x 0
4 x 9	9 x 2	9 x 8	6 x 9

9 x 4 = ____	9 x 9 = ____
5 x 9 = ____	1 x 9 = ____
0 x 9 = ____	7 x 9 = ____
9 x 6 = ____	3 x 9 = ____
9 x 7 = ____	9 x 2 = ____
4 x 9 = ____	9 x 8 = ____
9 x 0 = ____	2 x 9 = ____
6 x 9 = ____	9 x 3 = ____

Score: ____________

Circle any problems that you still find difficult to remember. Make your own flash cards to help you master these problems.

Name ______________________________

Timed Test

■ Complete these facts as accurately and as quickly as you can.

0 x 9 = ____ 5 x 9 = ____

7 x 9 = ____ 8 x 9 = ____

9 x 0 = ____ 4 x 9 = ____

6 x 9 = ____ 9 x 3 = ____

1 x 9 = ____ 9 x 6 = ____

9 x 5 = ____ 9 x 2 = ____

9 x 9 = ____ 9 x 1 = ____

9 x 8 = ____ 2 x 9 = ____

8 x 9 = ____ 9 x 7 = ____

9 x 4 = ____ 3 x 9 = ____

9 x 1	4 x 9	0 x 9	1 x 9
8 x 9	9 x 7	3 x 9	9 x 2
7 x 9	9 x 5	4 x 9	9 x 0
5 x 9	9 x 3	2 x 9	9 x 8
6 x 9	9 x 6	9 x 9	9 x 4

Score: ________ Time: ________ minutes ________ seconds

 0-7696-8503-X

Name ______________________________

Timed Test

Nine as a Factor

9 x 1 = ____ 4 x 9 = ____

5 x 9 = ____ 0 x 9 = ____

3 x 9 = ____ 9 x 7 = ____

9 x 5 = ____ 7 x 9 = ____

8 x 9 = ____ 9 x 9 = ____

1 x 9 = ____ 9 x 3 = ____

9 x 6 = ____ 9 x 2 = ____

9 x 7 = ____ 9 x 8 = ____

9 x 0 = ____ 2 x 9 = ____

6 x 9 = ____ 9 x 4 = ____

9 x 4	9 x 9	9 x 2	7 x 9
9 x 1	9 x 6	1 x 9	6 x 9
9 x 3	5 x 9	9 x 8	9 x 7
3 x 9	9 x 5	0 x 9	4 x 9
8 x 9	9 x 0	5 x 9	2 x 9

Score: __________ Time: __________ minutes __________ seconds

Name ______________________________

Practice

■ Multiply.

5 x 6	2 x 5	3 x 3	4 x 4	8 x 8	1 x 0	7 x 2	6 x 7
2 x 4	9 x 6	5 x 5	9 x 4	0 x 0	6 x 3	3 x 2	7 x 9
1 x 7	8 x 0	4 x 3	6 x 8	0 x 4	4 x 9	8 x 7	1 x 8
9 x 5	8 x 1	7 x 3	2 x 2	5 x 7	4 x 5	8 x 9	1 x 6
3 x 4	3 x 9	6 x 6	5 x 4	0 x 1	7 x 8	3 x 1	9 x 7

Continue this Review on the next page.

Name ______________________

Practice

9 x 1	3 x 8	2 x 3	4 x 6	0 x 6	5 x 8	1 x 5	6 x 5
3 x 0	7 x 4	0 x 9	5 x 2	8 x 5	3 x 5	4 x 1	0 x 2
2 x 0	6 x 1	2 x 7	7 x 0	1 x 2	9 x 8	5 x 0	7 x 7
8 x 2	9 x 0	7 x 5	1 x 4	0 x 7	6 x 4	4 x 7	2 x 9
5 x 9	9 x 2	5 x 3	0 x 3	9 x 9	3 x 7	8 x 4	1 x 3

Circle any problems that you still find difficult to remember. Make your own flash cards to help you master these problems.

Score: ______________

Name ______________________________

Timed Test

All-Multiplication Review

■ Complete these facts as accurately and as quickly as you can.

5 x 4 = ____	2 x 1 = ____	0 x 1 = ____	5 x 5 = ____
1 x 0 = ____	0 x 4 = ____	7 x 3 = ____	4 x 1 = ____
9 x 6 = ____	6 x 3 = ____	8 x 0 = ____	9 x 2 = ____
4 x 4 = ____	9 x 8 = ____	9 x 1 = ____	5 x 3 = ____
9 x 3 = ____	4 x 2 = ____	9 x 7 = ____	4 x 5 = ____
3 x 4 = ____	8 x 3 = ____	2 x 8 = ____	6 x 4 = ____
0 x 9 = ____	2 x 7 = ____	8 x 1 = ____	2 x 0 = ____
3 x 3 = ____	7 x 4 = ____	3 x 5 = ____	3 x 2 = ____
9 x 9 = ____	8 x 4 = ____	1 x 1 = ____	6 x 0 = ____
1 x 3 = ____	6 x 2 = ____	7 x 9 = ____	0 x 2 = ____

Continue this Timed Test on the next page.

Name ____________________

Timed Test

6 x 9 = ____	6 x 6 = ____	2 x 4 = ____	8 x 6 = ____
4 x 0 = ____	4 x 6 = ____	7 x 1 = ____	5 x 7 = ____
5 x 6 = ____	0 x 3 = ____	1 x 9 = ____	2 x 9 = ____
4 x 9 = ____	5 x 9 = ____	8 x 9 = ____	7 x 7 = ____
1 x 4 = ____	2 x 6 = ____	9 x 5 = ____	4 x 8 = ____
3 x 1 = ____	8 x 5 = ____	8 x 7 = ____	1 x 7 = ____
2 x 2 = ____	5 x 2 = ____	1 x 5 = ____	6 x 8 = ____
7 x 6 = ____	1 x 8 = ____	7 x 8 = ____	3 x 9 = ____
0 x 7 = ____	3 x 7 = ____	3 x 0 = ____	2 x 3 = ____
3 x 6 = ____	5 x 0 = ____	0 x 8 = ____	9 x 0 = ____

Score: ________ Time: ________ minutes ________ seconds

Name ____________________

Timed Test

0 x 0 = ____	5 x 7 = ____	8 x 8 = ____	0 x 5 = ____
1 x 7 = ____	0 x 9 = ____	0 x 4 = ____	5 x 8 = ____
4 x 5 = ____	6 x 1 = ____	3 x 3 = ____	2 x 6 = ____
2 x 9 = ____	8 x 0 = ____	4 x 9 = ____	8 x 5 = ____
3 x 7 = ____	2 x 5 = ____	0 x 7 = ____	1 x 8 = ____
8 x 4 = ____	7 x 6 = ____	2 x 2 = ____	7 x 9 = ____
2 x 1 = ____	9 x 2 = ____	1 x 0 = ____	9 x 8 = ____
7 x 0 = ____	1 x 3 = ____	4 x 6 = ____	5 x 4 = ____
5 x 3 = ____	6 x 5 = ____	8 x 1 = ____	6 x 9 = ____
9 x 9 = ____	4 x 1 = ____	6 x 2 = ____	0 x 1 = ____

Continue this Timed Test on the next page.

Name ________________________________

Products Through One Hundred Twenty

Now you will learn about some higher facts.

The first thirteen multiples of 10 are 0, 10, 20, 30, 40, 50, 60, 70, 80, 90, 100, 110, and 120. They are the same as the products of 10 times any number from 0 through 12.

Here are some things to remember about the basic facts in which 10 is one of the factors:

- The product of 10 and another counting number always ends in 0. Here's a shortcut to find a product of 10 and another number: Simply annex (attach) a zero at the end of the other factor.

Examples: 10 x 6 = 60, 10 x 3 = 30, and 10 x 10 = 100

- Changing the order of the factors does not change the product. So, 10 x 7 is the same as 7 x 10.
- As you have learned with other facts, 10 x 0 is 0 and 10 x 1 is 10.

■ Complete these **T**'s by multiplying each of the numbers by 10.

x 10	
6	____
2	____
12	____
4	____
7	____
9	____
1	____

x 10	
5	____
3	____
11	____
0	____
8	____
10	____

■ Now, complete these facts.

10 x 5 = ____	10 x 9 = ____
4 x 10 = ____	10 x 3 = ____
10 x 12 = ____	10 x 7 = ____
10 x 11 = ____	2 x 10 = ____
10 x 10 = ____	10 x 8 = ____
6 x 10 = ____	7 x 10 = ____
10 x 0 = ____	10 x 2 = ____
11 x 10 = ____	1 x 10 = ____

Name ______________________________

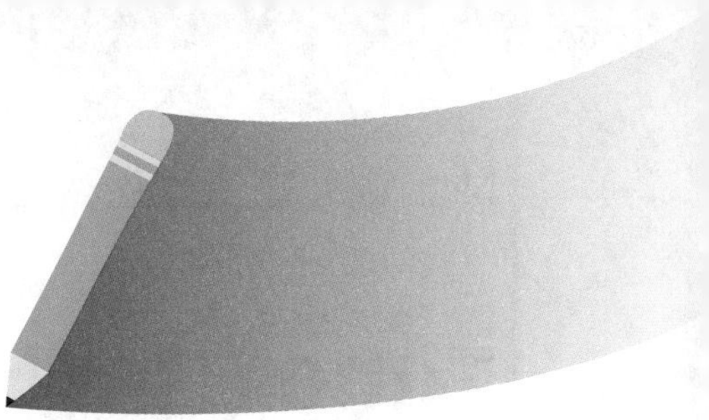

Practice

■ Complete these facts as accurately and as quickly as you can.

10 x 8	10 x 5	10 x 3	10 x 12
11 x 10	10 x 8	12 x 10	10 x 4
10 x 9	10 x 2	10 x 4	10 x 0
10 x 7	10 x 6	10 x 2	10 x 9
10 x 5	10 x 1	10 x 12	10 x 7

10 x 6 = ____ 7 x 10 = ____

0 x 10 = ____ 10 x 12 = ____

10 x 2 = ____ 10 x 4 = ____

6 x 10 = ____ 1 x 10 = ____

3 x 10 = ____ 12 x 10 = ____

10 x 7 = ____ 10 x 10 = ____

10 x 11 = ____ 11 x 10 = ____

10 x 0 = ____ 10 x 1 = ____

Score: ____________

Circle any problems that you still find difficult to remember. Make your own flash cards to help you master these problems.

Name ____________________

Timed Test

■ Complete these facts as accurately and as quickly as you can.

10 x 4 = ____ 2 x 10 = ____

12 x 10 = ____ 10 x 8 = ____

10 x 1 = ____ 10 x 11 = ____

10 x 3 = ____ 8 x 10 = ____

5 x 10 = ____ 10 x 5 = ____

10 x 9 = ____ 6 x 10 = ____

3 x 10 = ____ 10 x 10 = ____

10 x 2 = ____ 1 x 10 = ____

10 x 12 = ____ 10 x 7 = ____

4 x 10 = ____ 10 x 6 = ____

10 x 1	11 x 10	10 x 5	10 x 9
10 x 7	12 x 10	10 x 9	10 x 8
10 x 0	10 x 4	10 x 11	10 x 5
10 x 6	10 x 3	10 x 10	10 x 7
10 x 2	10 x 4	10 x 12	10 x 1

Ten as a Factor

Score: ________ Time: ________ minutes ________ seconds

Name ____________________

Products Through One Hundred Thirty-Two

The first thirteen multiples of 11 are 0, 11, 22, 33, 44, 55, 66, 77, 88, 99, 110, 121, and 132. They are the same as the products of 11 times any number from 0 through 12.

Here are some things to remember about the basic facts in which 11 is one of the factors:

- All of the products from 11 x 2 through 11 x 9 are easy to remember because both digits in each product are the same as the second factor. Thus, 11 x 2 is 22, 11 x 5 is 55, and 11 x 9 is 99.
- That leaves only three other facts to learn. The first of these you already know: 11 x 10 is 110. The other two are new: 11 x 11 is 121 and 11 x 12 is 132.
- Changing the order of the factors does not change the product. So, 11 x 7 is the same as 7 x 11.
- As you have learned with other facts, 11 x 0 is 0 and 11 x 1 is 11.

■ Complete this circle by multiplying each of the numbers by 11.

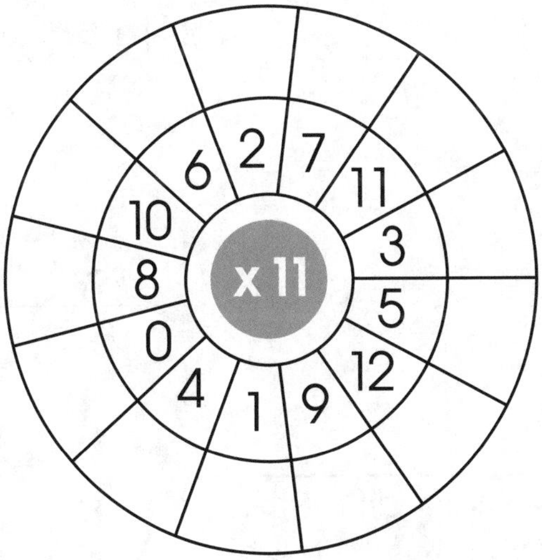

■ Now, complete these facts.

11 x 3 = ____	2 x 11 = ____
8 x 11 = ____	11 x 7 = ____
11 x 6 = ____	4 x 11 = ____
0 x 11 = ____	10 x 11 = ____
11 x 2 = ____	6 x 11 = ____
7 x 11 = ____	11 x 12 = ____
11 x 5 = ____	9 x 11 = ____

Name ______________________

Practice

Eleven as a Factor

■ Multiply.

12 x 11	11 x 10	11 x 0	11 x 4
11 x 6	10 x 11	11 x 9	11 x 5
11 x 5	11 x 8	11 x 3	11 x 7
11 x 1	11 x 8	11 x 3	11 x 12
11 x 4	11 x 2	11 x 11	11 x 5

11 x 1 = ____	11 x 5 = ____
12 x 11 = ____	1 x 11 = ____
3 x 11 = ____	4 x 11 = ____
11 x 8 = ____	11 x 10 = ____
2 x 11 = ____	11 x 2 = ____
9 x 11 = ____	11 x 11 = ____
11 x 0 = ____	11 x 7 = ____
8 x 11 = ____	5 x 11 = ____

Score: ______________

Circle any problems that you still find difficult to remember. Make your own flash cards to help you master these problems.

Name ____________________

Timed Test

■ Complete these facts as accurately and as quickly as you can.

1 x 11 = ____	11 x 5 = ____
5 x 11 = ____	12 x 11 = ____
11 x 6 = ____	11 x 0 = ____
11 x 4 = ____	11 x 8 = ____
6 x 11 = ____	7 x 11 = ____
11 x 1 = ____	11 x 11 = ____
11 x 7 = ____	10 x 11 = ____
11 x 12 = ____	9 x 11 = ____
2 x 11 = ____	11 x 10 = ____
11 x 3 = ____	0 x 11 = ____

11 x 4 ____	11 x 1 ____	10 x 11 ____	11 x 6 ____
11 x 0 ____	11 x 10 ____	12 x 11 ____	11 x 5 ____
11 x 9 ____	11 x 2 ____	11 x 11 ____	11 x 9 ____
11 x 0 ____	11 x 3 ____	11 x 6 ____	11 x 3 ____
11 x 7 ____	11 x 12 ____	11 x 5 ____	11 x 1 ____

Eleven as a Factor

Score: ________ Time: ________ minutes ________ seconds

Name ________________________________

Products Through One Hundred Forty-Four

The first thirteen multiples of 12 are 0, 12, 24, 36, 48, 60, 72, 84, 96, 108, 120, 132, and 144. They are the same as the products of 12 times any number from 0 through 12.

Here are some things to remember about the basic facts in which 12 is one of the factors:

- Changing the order of the factors does not change the product. Therefore, you already know that 12 x 10 is 120 and 10 x 12 is 120.
- As you have learned with other facts, 12 x 0 is 0 and 12 x 1 is 12.

■ Complete these **T**'s by multiplying each of the numbers by 12.

x 12	
6	____
10	____
8	____
1	____
5	____
3	____
2	____

x 12	
12	____
0	____
4	____
7	____
9	____
11	____

■ Now, complete these facts.

12 x 2 = ____   12 x 0 = ____

12 x 5 = ____   12 x 9 = ____

12 x 4 = ____   12 x 3 = ____

12 x 12 = ____   12 x 8 = ____

12 x 6 = ____   12 x 7 = ____

12 x 1 = ____   12 x 10 = ____

12 x 11 = ____

Name ______________________________

Practice

■ Multiply.

12 x 1	12 x 12	12 x 9	12 x 6
12 x 1	12 x 3	12 x 8	12 x 1
12 x 4	12 x 9	12 x 8	12 x 0
12 x 10	12 x 5	12 x 7	10 x 12
12 x 11	12 x 2	12 x 6	12 x 3

12 x 9 = ____ 12 x 4 = ____

4 x 12 = ____ 2 x 12 = ____

12 x 0 = ____ 12 x 10 = ____

10 x 12 = ____ 6 x 12 = ____

3 x 12 = ____ 11 x 12 = ____

9 x 12 = ____ 1 x 12 = ____

12 x 3 = ____ 12 x 12 = ____

5 x 12 = ____ 12 x 6 = ____

Score: ____________

Circle any problems that you still find difficult to remember. Make your own flash cards to help you master these problems.

Name ______________________________

Timed Test

■ Complete these facts as accurately and as quickly as you can.

1 x 12 = ____	12 x 2 = ____
6 x 12 = ____	7 x 12 = ____
12 x 1 = ____	12 x 9 = ____
12 x 12 = ____	5 x 12 = ____
12 x 8 = ____	12 x 4 = ____
12 x 5 = ____	0 x 12 = ____
9 x 12 = ____	11 x 12 = ____
12 x 0 = ____	12 x 3 = ____
12 x 6 = ____	8 x 12 = ____
3 x 12 = ____	12 x 7 = ____

12 x 8 ____	12 x 7 ____	12 x 0 ____	12 x 4 ____
12 x 6 ____	12 x 5 ____	12 x 12 ____	12 x 3 ____
12 x 5 ____	12 x 6 ____	12 x 9 ____	10 x 12 ____
12 x 1 ____	12 x 1 ____	12 x 8 ____	12 x 11 ____
12 x 7 ____	12 x 0 ____	12 x 2 ____	12 x 10 ____

Score: __________ Time: __________ minutes __________ seconds

Name ______________________

Timed Test

11 x 11 = ____	12 x 8 = ____	1 x 11 = ____	9 x 10 = ____
3 x 11 = ____	2 x 11 = ____	2 x 10 = ____	11 x 5 = ____
10 x 3 = ____	10 x 7 = ____	7 x 10 = ____	9 x 11 = ____
8 x 10 = ____	0 x 12 = ____	11 x 10 = ____	12 x 0 = ____
12 x 12 = ____	11 x 12 = ____	6 x 12 = ____	10 x 10 = ____
5 x 12 = ____	12 x 4 = ____	10 x 6 = ____	11 x 8 = ____
11 x 3 = ____	1 x 10 = ____	0 x 10 = ____	12 x 3 = ____
11 x 4 = ____	12 x 9 = ____	12 x 7 = ____	11 x 5 = ____
5 x 10 = ____	4 x 12 = ____	9 x 12 = ____	10 x 4 = ____
10 x 11 = ____	11 x 2 = ____	10 x 2 = ____	11 x 6 = ____

Score: ____________ Time: ____________ minutes ____________ seconds

DIVISION

Name ______________________________

What Is Division?

You divide to answer questions such as how many groups of 3's are there in 12. The answer is called the **quotient**.

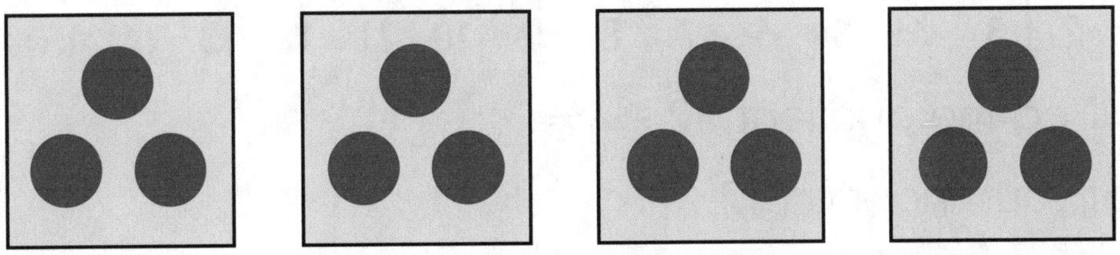

12 grapes divided into groups of 3 equals 4 equal groups.

Here are two ways to show the division.

$12 \div 3 = 4$ $\qquad$ $\begin{array}{r} 4 \\ 3\overline{)12} \end{array}$

You read the problem this way: **12 divided by 3 equals 4.**

You can draw a picture to find a quotient.

Example: Find the quotient. $8 \div 2 =$ _____

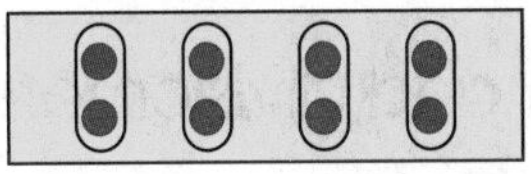

Step 1: Draw 8 dots. Group them into 2's.

Step 2: Count all the groups.

Answer: $8 \div 2 =$ __4__

■ Draw a picture to find the quotient.

$6 \div 2 =$ _____ $\qquad$ $8 \div 4 =$ _____ $\qquad$ $10 \div 2 =$ _____

$6 \div 3 =$ _____ $\qquad$ $12 \div 3 =$ _____ $\qquad$ $12 \div 4 =$ _____

Name ______________________________

What Is Division?

You can use a number line to find a quotient.

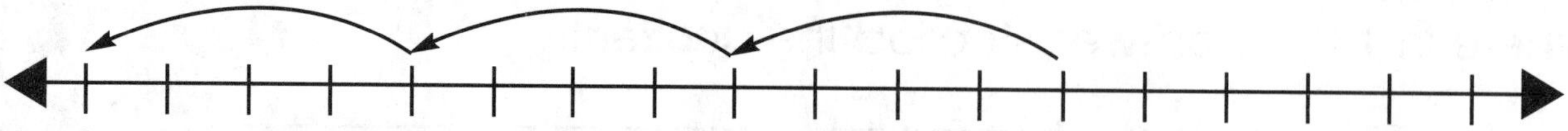

Example: Find the quotient. $12 \div 4 =$ ____

Step 1: Put your finger on 12.

Step 2: Make moves to the left of 4 spaces each, ending on zero.

Step 3: Count the number of moves you made.

Answer: $12 \div 4 =$ __3__

■ Use the number line to find the quotient.

$8 \div 2 =$ ____ $15 \div 5 =$ ____ $16 \div 4 =$ ____

$2\overline{)8}$ $4\overline{)12}$ $2\overline{)6}$ $6\overline{)12}$ $5\overline{)15}$

Multiplication and division are **inverse operations**. $10 \div 2 = 5$ $5 \times 2 = 10$

You can use multiplication facts to find the quotient.

Example: Find the quotient. $20 \div 5 =$ ____

Think: Some number times 5 equals 20. ____ $\times 5 = 20$

Since $4 \times 5 = 20$, then $20 \div 5 =$ __4__

Answer: $20 \div 5 =$ __4__

■ Use a multiplication fact to find the quotient.

$9 \div 3 =$ ____ $10 \div 5 =$ ____ $16 \div 2 =$ ____

$5\overline{)15}$ $2\overline{)4}$ $2\overline{)12}$ $6\overline{)18}$ $3\overline{)18}$

Name ______________________________

Dividends Through Eighteen

Division is the operation in which a number is divided into equal parts. The **dividend** is the number being divided. The **divisor** is the number of equal parts, and the **quotient** is the number in each part.

Example: 15 ÷ 3 = 5
dividend **divisor** **quotient**

5 **quotient**
divisor $3\overline{)15}$ **dividend**

When you divide a number by 1, the quotient will always be the same as the dividend.

Example: 6 ÷ 1 = 6

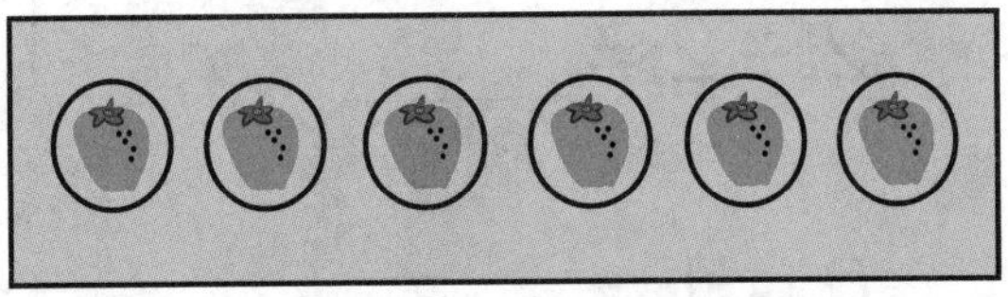

When you divide a number by 2, the quotient is half of the dividend.

Example: 6 ÷ 2 = 3

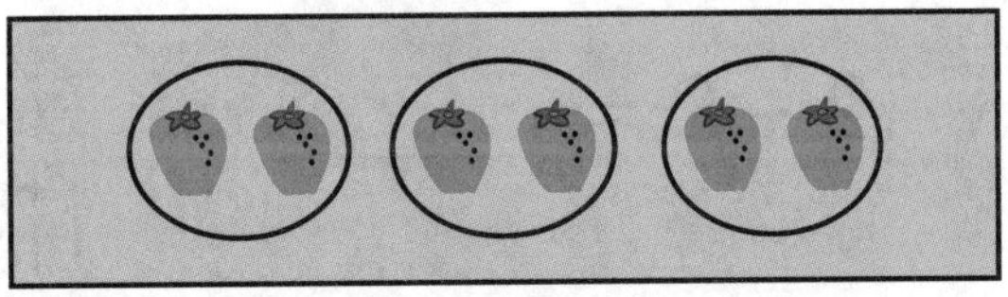

■ Find the quotient for these facts.

6 ÷ 1 = ____	18 ÷ 2 = ____	10 ÷ 2 = ____	0 ÷ 1 = ____
7 ÷ 1 = ____	6 ÷ 2 = ____	8 ÷ 1 = ____	5 ÷ 1 = ____
16 ÷ 2 = ____	14 ÷ 2 = ____	8 ÷ 2 = ____	1 ÷ 1 = ____
2 ÷ 1 = ____	9 ÷ 1 = ____	12 ÷ 2 = ____	4 ÷ 2 = ____

Name ______________________________

Practice

■ Divide.

$2 \div 1 =$ ____ $8 \div 2 =$ ____

$6 \div 2 =$ ____ $4 \div 1 =$ ____

$7 \div 1 =$ ____ $14 \div 2 =$ ____

$10 \div 2 =$ ____ $2 \div 2 =$ ____

$9 \div 1 =$ ____ $0 \div 1 =$ ____

$8 \div 1 =$ ____ $18 \div 2 =$ ____

$3 \div 1 =$ ____ $12 \div 2 =$ ____

$0 \div 2 =$ ____ $4 \div 2 =$ ____

$16 \div 2 =$ ____ $5 \div 1 =$ ____

$6 \div 1 =$ ____ $1 \div 1 =$ ____

$2\overline{)0}$ $1\overline{)4}$

$2\overline{)8}$ $2\overline{)12}$

$2\overline{)18}$ $1\overline{)0}$

$1\overline{)5}$ $1\overline{)9}$

$2\overline{)14}$ $2\overline{)6}$

$1\overline{)3}$ $2\overline{)16}$

$1\overline{)6}$ $2\overline{)2}$

$1\overline{)8}$ $1\overline{)1}$

FINISH

Circle any problems that you still find difficult to remember. Make your own flash cards to help you master these problems.

Score: ____________

Name ______________________________

Timed Test

■ Complete these facts as accurately and as quickly as you can.

$0 \div 1 =$ ____ $1 \div 1 =$ ____

$9 \div 1 =$ ____ $6 \div 1 =$ ____

$6 \div 2 =$ ____ $8 \div 2 =$ ____

$16 \div 2 =$ ____ $4 \div 2 =$ ____

$2 \div 1 =$ ____ $12 \div 2 =$ ____

$8 \div 2 =$ ____ $4 \div 1 =$ ____

$18 \div 2 =$ ____ $2 \div 2 =$ ____

$7 \div 1 =$ ____ $3 \div 1 =$ ____

$14 \div 2 =$ ____ $5 \div 1 =$ ____

$10 \div 2 =$ ____ $0 \div 2 =$ ____

$2\overline{)4}$ $2\overline{)8}$ $2\overline{)2}$

$1\overline{)2}$ $2\overline{)6}$ $1\overline{)9}$

$1\overline{)1}$ $1\overline{)3}$ $2\overline{)10}$

$2\overline{)16}$ $2\overline{)14}$ $1\overline{)5}$

$1\overline{)4}$ $2\overline{)0}$ $1\overline{)7}$

$1\overline{)8}$ $1\overline{)0}$ $2\overline{)12}$

$1\overline{)6}$ $2\overline{)18}$

One and Two as Divisors

Score: ________   Time: ________ minutes ________ seconds

Name ______________________________

Dividends Through Twenty-Seven

Now, think about what happens when a number is divided by 3.

Example: 18 ÷ 3 = 6

The dividend is 18. If you put 3 objects in each group, you have 6 equal groups.

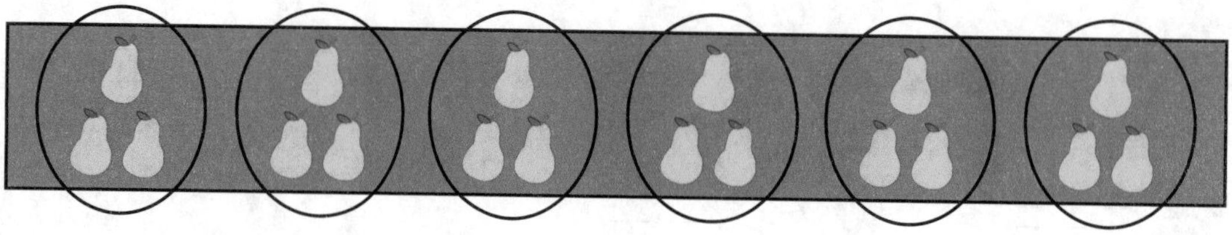

Division and multiplication are **inverse operations**.

Example: 6 x 3 = 18
18 ÷ 3 = 6

When you divide, you cannot have 0 as a divisor. It doesn't make sense to divide a number into zero groups. However, you could have a 0 as a dividend. But, no matter how many groups you divide 0 into, the quotient will always be 0.

Examples: 0 ÷ 2 = 0   0 ÷ 5 = 0

Apply what you have learned to the division facts of 3.

Examples: 0 ÷ 3 = 0   3 ÷ 1 = 3   3 ÷ 3 = 1

■ Complete this circle by dividing each of the numbers by 3.

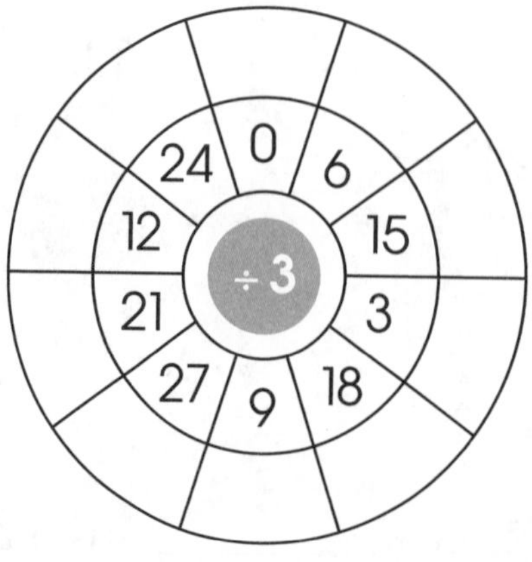

Name ______________________

Practice

■ Divide.

24 ÷ 3 = ____	12 ÷ 3 = ____	$3\overline{)21}$	$3\overline{)12}$
3 ÷ 3 = ____	9 ÷ 3 = ____	$3\overline{)3}$	$3\overline{)18}$
18 ÷ 3 = ____	0 ÷ 3 = ____	$3\overline{)27}$	$3\overline{)0}$
6 ÷ 3 = ____	27 ÷ 3 = ____	$3\overline{)6}$	$3\overline{)24}$
15 ÷ 3 = ____	24 ÷ 3 = ____	$3\overline{)15}$	$3\overline{)9}$
21 ÷ 3 = ____	18 ÷ 3 = ____	$3\overline{)27}$	$3\overline{)15}$
9 ÷ 3 = ____	6 ÷ 3 = ____	$3\overline{)18}$	$3\overline{)21}$
0 ÷ 3 = ____	3 ÷ 3 = ____	$3\overline{)24}$	$3\overline{)12}$
12 ÷ 3 = ____	15 ÷ 3 = ____		
27 ÷ 3 = ____	21 ÷ 3 = ____		

FINISH

Circle any problems that you still find difficult to remember. Make your own flash cards to help you master these problems.

Score: ____________

Name ____________________________________

Timed Test

■ Complete these facts as accurately and as quickly as you can.

15 ÷ 3 = ____ 24 ÷ 3 = ____

21 ÷ 3 = ____ 9 ÷ 3 = ____

3 ÷ 3 = ____ 12 ÷ 3 = ____

24 ÷ 3 = ____ 27 ÷ 3 = ____

18 ÷ 3 = ____ 0 ÷ 3 = ____

6 ÷ 3 = ____ 15 ÷ 3 = ____

12 ÷ 3 = ____ 18 ÷ 3 = ____

0 ÷ 3 = ____ 3 ÷ 3 = ____

9 ÷ 3 = ____ 6 ÷ 3 = ____

27 ÷ 3 = ____ 21 ÷ 3 = ____

$3\overline{)27}$ $3\overline{)21}$ $3\overline{)12}$

$3\overline{)0}$ $3\overline{)15}$ $3\overline{)6}$

$3\overline{)18}$ $3\overline{)9}$ $3\overline{)3}$

$3\overline{)12}$ $3\overline{)21}$ $3\overline{)6}$

$3\overline{)24}$ $3\overline{)9}$ $3\overline{)18}$

$3\overline{)3}$ $3\overline{)27}$ $3\overline{)15}$

$3\overline{)21}$ $3\overline{)0}$

Score: __________ Time: __________ minutes __________ seconds

Name ______________________________

Dividends Through Thirty-Six

Now, think about what happens when a number is divided by 4.

Example: $12 \div 4 = 3$

The dividend is 12. If you put 4 objects in each group, you have 3 equal groups.

Remember: Division and multiplication are inverse operations.

Example: $4 \times 3 = 12$
$12 \div 4 = 3$

Apply what you have learned to the division facts of 4.

Examples: $0 \div 4 = 0$ $4 \div 1 = 4$ $4 \div 4 = 1$

■ Complete these **T**'s by dividing each of the numbers by 4. Then, divide the problems on the right.

$\div 4$	
36	____
32	____
24	____
20	____
8	____

$\div 4$	
16	____
12	____
4	____
28	____
0	____

$4\overline{)24}$ $4\overline{)32}$ $4\overline{)28}$

$4\overline{)36}$ $4\overline{)4}$ $4\overline{)20}$

$4\overline{)12}$ $4\overline{)0}$ $4\overline{)16}$

$4\overline{)8}$

Four as a Divisor

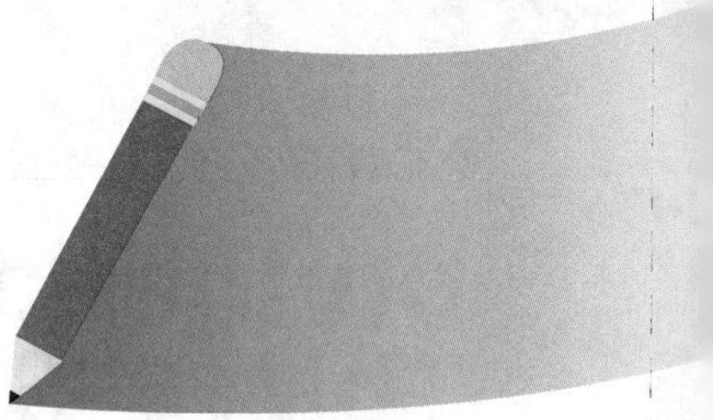

Name ______________________

Practice

■ Divide.

16 ÷ 4 = ____	12 ÷ 4 = ____
0 ÷ 4 = ____	4 ÷ 4 = ____
12 ÷ 4 = ____	28 ÷ 4 = ____
8 ÷ 4 = ____	20 ÷ 4 = ____
28 ÷ 4 = ____	36 ÷ 4 = ____
24 ÷ 4 = ____	4 ÷ 4 = ____
32 ÷ 4 = ____	16 ÷ 4 = ____
20 ÷ 4 = ____	0 ÷ 4 = ____
4 ÷ 4 = ____	24 ÷ 4 = ____
36 ÷ 4 = ____	16 ÷ 4 = ____

$4\overline{)20}$	$4\overline{)24}$
$4\overline{)4}$	$4\overline{)36}$
$4\overline{)28}$	$4\overline{)0}$
$4\overline{)8}$	$4\overline{)16}$
$4\overline{)32}$	$4\overline{)12}$
$4\overline{)16}$	$4\overline{)36}$
$4\overline{)32}$	$4\overline{)20}$
$4\overline{)24}$	$4\overline{)28}$

Circle any problems that you still find difficult to remember. Make your own flash cards to help you master these problems.

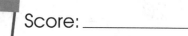

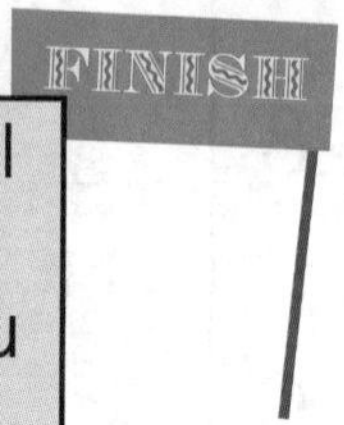

Score: ____________

Four as a Divisor

Name ____________________

Timed Test

■ Complete these facts as accurately and as quickly as you can.

$28 \div 4 =$ ____ $4 \div 4 =$ ____

$16 \div 4 =$ ____ $0 \div 4 =$ ____

$24 \div 4 =$ ____ $36 \div 4 =$ ____

$20 \div 4 =$ ____ $32 \div 4 =$ ____

$4 \div 4 =$ ____ $12 \div 4 =$ ____

$8 \div 4 =$ ____ $28 \div 4 =$ ____

$32 \div 4 =$ ____ $0 \div 4 =$ ____

$12 \div 4 =$ ____ $20 \div 4 =$ ____

$36 \div 4 =$ ____ $8 \div 4 =$ ____

$16 \div 4 =$ ____ $24 \div 4 =$ ____

$4\overline{)36}$	$4\overline{)0}$	$4\overline{)12}$
$4\overline{)4}$	$4\overline{)8}$	$4\overline{)32}$
$4\overline{)16}$	$4\overline{)36}$	$4\overline{)28}$
$4\overline{)20}$	$4\overline{)12}$	$4\overline{)8}$
$4\overline{)24}$	$4\overline{)0}$	$4\overline{)4}$
$4\overline{)8}$	$4\overline{)16}$	$4\overline{)20}$
$4\overline{)32}$	$4\overline{)28}$	

Four as a Divisor

Score: ________ Time: ________ minutes ________ seconds

Name ____________________

Dividends Through Forty-Five

Now, think about what happens when a number is divided by 5.

Example: 15 ÷ 5 = 3

The dividend is 15. If you put 5 objects in each group, you have 3 equal groups.

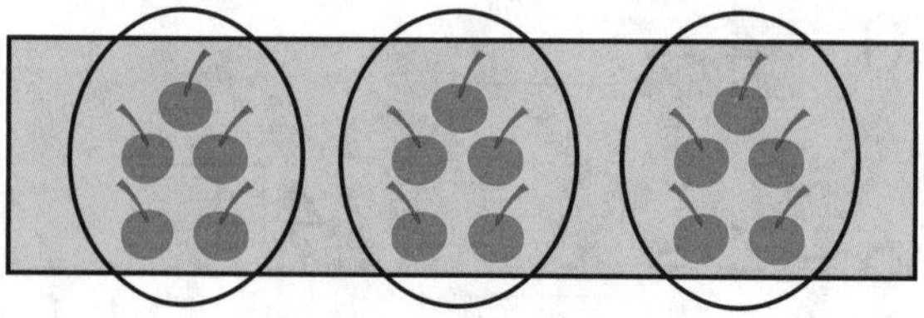

Remember: Division and multiplication are inverse operations.

Example: 5 x 3 = 15
15 ÷ 5 = 3

Apply what you have learned to the division facts of 5.

Examples: 0 ÷ 5 = 0 5 ÷ 1 = 5 5 ÷ 5 = 1

■ Complete this circle by dividing each of the numbers by 5. Then, divide the problems on the right.

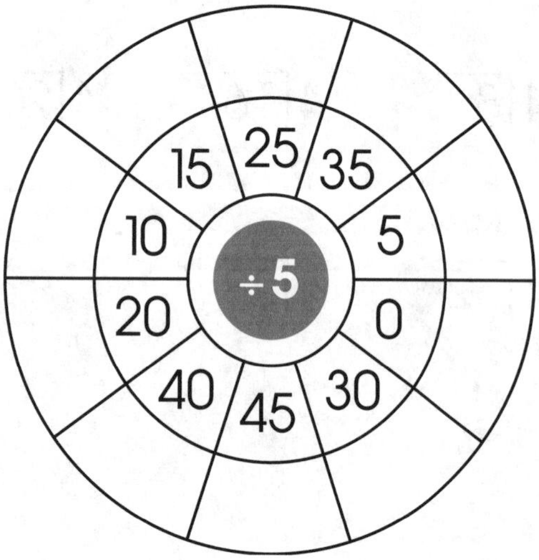

$5\overline{)15}$ $5\overline{)25}$ $5\overline{)0}$

$5\overline{)20}$ $5\overline{)40}$ $5\overline{)10}$

$5\overline{)35}$ $5\overline{)5}$ $5\overline{)30}$

$5\overline{)45}$

Name ____________________

Practice

■ Divide.

10 ÷ 5 = ____	5 ÷ 5 = ____	$5\overline{)15}$	$5\overline{)30}$
35 ÷ 5 = ____	45 ÷ 5 = ____	$5\overline{)5}$	$5\overline{)10}$
15 ÷ 5 = ____	20 ÷ 5 = ____	$5\overline{)45}$	$5\overline{)25}$
30 ÷ 5 = ____	40 ÷ 5 = ____	$5\overline{)35}$	$5\overline{)0}$
5 ÷ 5 = ____	0 ÷ 5 = ____	$5\overline{)40}$	$5\overline{)20}$
25 ÷ 5 = ____	15 ÷ 5 = ____	$5\overline{)15}$	$5\overline{)10}$
45 ÷ 5 = ____	35 ÷ 5 = ____	$5\overline{)20}$	$5\overline{)30}$
20 ÷ 5 = ____	10 ÷ 5 = ____	$5\overline{)45}$	$5\overline{)40}$
40 ÷ 5 = ____	30 ÷ 5 = ____		
0 ÷ 5 = ____	25 ÷ 5 = ____		

Circle any problems that you still find difficult to remember. Make your own flash cards to help you master these problems.

Score: ____________

Name ______________________________

Timed Test

■ Complete these facts as accurately and as quickly as you can.

$5 \div 5 =$ ____	$20 \div 5 =$ ____
$45 \div 5 =$ ____	$35 \div 5 =$ ____
$30 \div 5 =$ ____	$15 \div 5 =$ ____
$40 \div 5 =$ ____	$10 \div 5 =$ ____
$0 \div 5 =$ ____	$5 \div 5 =$ ____
$15 \div 5 =$ ____	$45 \div 5 =$ ____
$25 \div 5 =$ ____	$40 \div 5 =$ ____
$20 \div 5 =$ ____	$30 \div 5 =$ ____
$10 \div 5 =$ ____	$0 \div 5 =$ ____
$35 \div 5 =$ ____	$25 \div 5 =$ ____

$5\overline{)10}$	$5\overline{)40}$	$5\overline{)45}$
$5\overline{)20}$	$5\overline{)35}$	$5\overline{)15}$
$5\overline{)40}$	$5\overline{)0}$	$5\overline{)30}$
$5\overline{)25}$	$5\overline{)45}$	$5\overline{)10}$
$5\overline{)5}$	$5\overline{)40}$	$5\overline{)30}$
$5\overline{)15}$	$5\overline{)0}$	$5\overline{)20}$
$5\overline{)5}$	$5\overline{)35}$	

Score: __________ Time: __________ minutes __________ seconds

 0-7696-8503-X

Name ______________________________

Dividends Through Fifty-Four

Now, think about what happens when a number is divided by 6.

Example: $24 \div 6 = 4$

The dividend is 24. If you put 6 objects in each group, you have 4 equal groups.

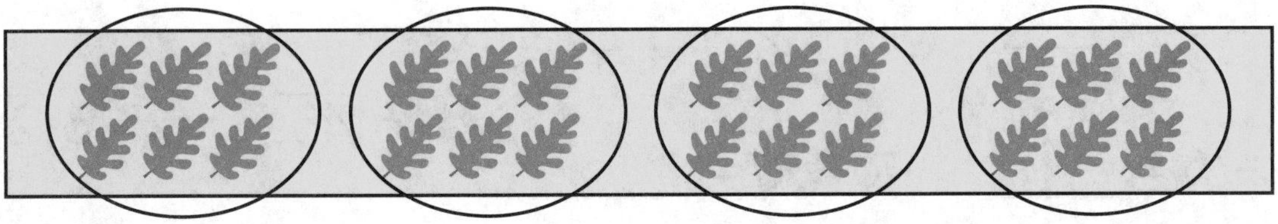

Remember: Division and multiplication are inverse operations.

Example: $6 \times 4 = 24$
$24 \div 6 = 4$

Apply what you have learned to the division facts of 6.

Examples: $0 \div 6 = 0$ $6 \div 1 = 6$ $6 \div 6 = 1$

■ Write a division fact related to each of these multiplication facts of 6.

$6 \times 1 = 6$	$6 \times 2 = 12$	$6 \times 3 = 18$
____ ÷ ____ = ____	____ ÷ ____ = ____	____ ÷ ____ = ____
$6 \times 4 = 24$	$6 \times 5 = 30$	$6 \times 6 = 36$
____ ÷ ____ = ____	____ ÷ ____ = ____	____ ÷ ____ = ____
$6 \times 7 = 42$	$6 \times 8 = 48$	$6 \times 9 = 54$
____ ÷ ____ = ____	____ ÷ ____ = ____	____ ÷ ____ = ____

Six as a Divisor

Name ______________________________

Practice

■ Divide.

30 ÷ 6 = ____	42 ÷ 6 = ____
24 ÷ 6 = ____	54 ÷ 6 = ____
36 ÷ 6 = ____	6 ÷ 6 = ____
0 ÷ 6 = ____	12 ÷ 6 = ____
48 ÷ 6 = ____	24 ÷ 6 = ____
42 ÷ 6 = ____	18 ÷ 6 = ____
54 ÷ 6 = ____	36 ÷ 6 = ____
6 ÷ 6 = ____	48 ÷ 6 = ____
18 ÷ 6 = ____	0 ÷ 6 = ____
12 ÷ 6 = ____	30 ÷ 6 = ____

$6\overline{)54}$	$6\overline{)18}$
$6\overline{)48}$	$6\overline{)24}$
$6\overline{)12}$	$6\overline{)0}$
$6\overline{)42}$	$6\overline{)30}$
$6\overline{)6}$	$6\overline{)36}$
$6\overline{)54}$	$6\overline{)12}$
$6\overline{)24}$	$6\overline{)48}$
$6\overline{)42}$	$6\overline{)36}$

FINISH

Circle any problems that you still find difficult to remember. Make your own flash cards to help you master these problems.

Score: ____________

Name ______________________________

Timed Test

■ Complete these facts as accurately and as quickly as you can.

$6 \div 6 =$ ____ $24 \div 6 =$ ____

$30 \div 6 =$ ____ $48 \div 6 =$ ____

$54 \div 6 =$ ____ $0 \div 6 =$ ____

$42 \div 6 =$ ____ $36 \div 6 =$ ____

$12 \div 6 =$ ____ $18 \div 6 =$ ____

$0 \div 6 =$ ____ $30 \div 6 =$ ____

$36 \div 6 =$ ____ $42 \div 6 =$ ____

$18 \div 6 =$ ____ $54 \div 6 =$ ____

$24 \div 6 =$ ____ $6 \div 6 =$ ____

$48 \div 6 =$ ____ $12 \div 6 =$ ____

$6\overline{)48}$ $6\overline{)42}$ $6\overline{)54}$

$6\overline{)30}$ $6\overline{)0}$ $6\overline{)18}$

$6\overline{)6}$ $6\overline{)48}$ $6\overline{)24}$

$6\overline{)12}$ $6\overline{)54}$ $6\overline{)30}$

$6\overline{)36}$ $6\overline{)6}$ $6\overline{)18}$

$6\overline{)12}$ $6\overline{)24}$ $6\overline{)36}$

$6\overline{)42}$ $6\overline{)0}$

Six as a Divisor

Score: __________ Time: __________ minutes __________ seconds

Name ______________________________

Dividends Through Sixty-Three

Now, think about what happens when a number is divided by 7.

Example: $63 \div 7 = 9$

The dividend is 63. If you put 7 objects in each group, you have 9 equal groups.

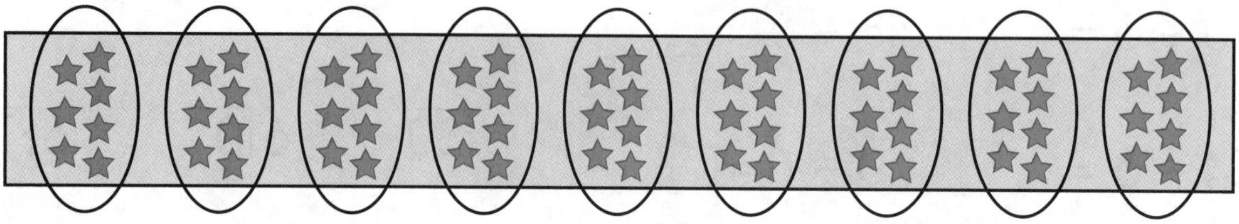

Remember: Division and multiplication are inverse operations.

Example: $7 \times 9 = 63$
$63 \div 7 = 9$

Apply what you have learned to the division facts of 7.

Examples: $0 \div 7 = 0$ $\quad 7 \div 1 = 7$ $\quad 7 \div 7 = 1$

■ Write a division fact related to each of these multiplication facts of 7.

7 x 1 = 7	7 x 2 = 14	7 x 3 = 21
___ ÷ ___ = ___	___ ÷ ___ = ___	___ ÷ ___ = ___
7 x 4 = 28	7 x 5 = 35	7 x 6 = 42
___ ÷ ___ = ___	___ ÷ ___ = ___	___ ÷ ___ = ___
7 x 7 = 49	7 x 8 = 56	7 x 9 = 63

Name ______________________

Practice

■ Divide.

$14 \div 7 =$ ____ $28 \div 7 =$ ____

$56 \div 7 =$ ____ $63 \div 7 =$ ____

$35 \div 7 =$ ____ $7 \div 7 =$ ____

$0 \div 7 =$ ____ $49 \div 7 =$ ____

$42 \div 7 =$ ____ $21 \div 7 =$ ____

$28 \div 7 =$ ____ $35 \div 7 =$ ____

$63 \div 7 =$ ____ $56 \div 7 =$ ____

$7 \div 7 =$ ____ $14 \div 7 =$ ____

$49 \div 7 =$ ____ $0 \div 7 =$ ____

$21 \div 7 =$ ____ $42 \div 7 =$ ____

$7\overline{)21}$ $7\overline{)49}$

$7\overline{)14}$ $7\overline{)0}$

$7\overline{)56}$ $7\overline{)28}$

$7\overline{)63}$ $7\overline{)35}$

$7\overline{)42}$ $7\overline{)7}$

$7\overline{)49}$ $7\overline{)63}$

$7\overline{)56}$ $7\overline{)21}$

$7\overline{)14}$ $7\overline{)28}$

FINISH

Circle any problems that you still find difficult to remember. Make your own flash cards to help you master these problems.

Score: ______________

Name ____________________

Timed Test

■ Complete these facts as accurately and as quickly as you can.

35 ÷ 7 = ____	28 ÷ 7 = ____
7 ÷ 7 = ____	49 ÷ 7 = ____
56 ÷ 7 = ____	21 ÷ 7 = ____
42 ÷ 7 = ____	14 ÷ 7 = ____
0 ÷ 7 = ____	7 ÷ 7 = ____
63 ÷ 7 = ____	35 ÷ 7 = ____
21 ÷ 7 = ____	42 ÷ 7 = ____
28 ÷ 7 = ____	63 ÷ 7 = ____
49 ÷ 7 = ____	0 ÷ 7 = ____
14 ÷ 7 = ____	56 ÷ 7 = ____

$7\overline{)7}$	$7\overline{)42}$	$7\overline{)0}$
$7\overline{)49}$	$7\overline{)63}$	$7\overline{)35}$
$7\overline{)0}$	$7\overline{)14}$	$7\overline{)56}$
$7\overline{)21}$	$7\overline{)7}$	$7\overline{)63}$
$7\overline{)28}$	$7\overline{)56}$	$7\overline{)42}$
$7\overline{)14}$	$7\overline{)49}$	$7\overline{)21}$
$7\overline{)28}$	$7\overline{)35}$	

Seven as a Divisor

Score: ________ Time: ________ minutes ________ seconds

Name ____________________________________

Dividends Through Seventy-Two

Now, think about what happens when a number is divided by 8.

Example: $48 \div 8 = 6$

The dividend is 48. If you put 8 objects in each group, you will have 6 equal groups.

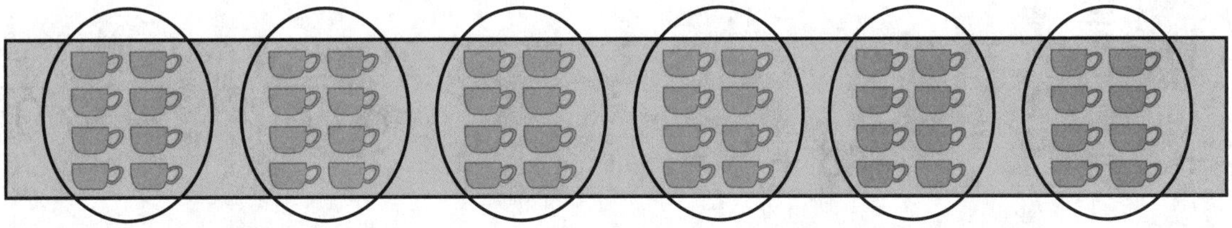

Remember: Division and multiplication are inverse operations.

Example: $8 \times 6 = 48$
$48 \div 8 = 6$

Apply what you have learned to the division facts of 8.

Examples: $0 \div 8 = 0$ $8 \div 1 = 8$ $8 \div 8 = 1$

■ Write a division fact related to each of these multiplication facts of 8.

$8 \times 1 = 8$	$8 \times 2 = 16$	$8 \times 3 = 24$
___ ÷ ___ = ___	___ ÷ ___ = ___	___ ÷ ___ = ___
$8 \times 4 = 32$	$8 \times 5 = 40$	$8 \times 6 = 48$
___ ÷ ___ = ___	___ ÷ ___ = ___	___ ÷ ___ = ___
$8 \times 7 = 56$	$8 \times 8 = 64$	$8 \times 9 = 72$
___ ÷ ___ = ___	___ ÷ ___ = ___	___ ÷ ___ = ___

 0-7696-8503-X

Name ________________________

Practice

■ Divide.

0 ÷ 8 = ____	40 ÷ 8 = ____	$8\overline{)48}$	$8\overline{)8}$
56 ÷ 8 = ____	72 ÷ 8 = ____	$8\overline{)56}$	$8\overline{)0}$
24 ÷ 8 = ____	48 ÷ 8 = ____	$8\overline{)64}$	$8\overline{)16}$
64 ÷ 8 = ____	32 ÷ 8 = ____	$8\overline{)72}$	$8\overline{)32}$
16 ÷ 8 = ____	8 ÷ 8 = ____	$8\overline{)40}$	$8\overline{)24}$
40 ÷ 8 = ____	0 ÷ 8 = ____	$8\overline{)56}$	$8\overline{)48}$
72 ÷ 8 = ____	56 ÷ 8 = ____	$8\overline{)16}$	$8\overline{)72}$
48 ÷ 8 = ____	24 ÷ 8 = ____	$8\overline{)32}$	$8\overline{)64}$
32 ÷ 8 = ____	64 ÷ 8 = ____		
8 ÷ 8 = ____	16 ÷ 8 = ____		

Circle any problems that you still find difficult to remember. Make your own flash cards to help you master these problems.

FINISH

Score: ____________

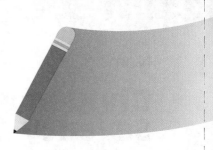

Name ______________________________

Timed Test

$32 \div 8 =$ ____ $56 \div 8 =$ ____

$72 \div 8 =$ ____ $16 \div 8 =$ ____

$8 \div 8 =$ ____ $48 \div 8 =$ ____

$0 \div 8 =$ ____ $40 \div 8 =$ ____

$64 \div 8 =$ ____ $24 \div 8 =$ ____

$40 \div 8 =$ ____ $8 \div 8 =$ ____

$56 \div 8 =$ ____ $0 \div 8 =$ ____

$24 \div 8 =$ ____ $64 \div 8 =$ ____

$16 \div 8 =$ ____ $32 \div 8 =$ ____

$8 \div 8 =$ ____ $48 \div 8 =$ ____

$8\overline{)8}$ $8\overline{)32}$ $8\overline{)64}$

$8\overline{)16}$ $8\overline{)0}$ $8\overline{)56}$

$8\overline{)40}$ $8\overline{)24}$ $8\overline{)72}$

$8\overline{)48}$ $8\overline{)16}$ $8\overline{)8}$

$8\overline{)24}$ $8\overline{)32}$ $8\overline{)0}$

$8\overline{)64}$ $8\overline{)56}$ $8\overline{)72}$

$8\overline{)40}$ $8\overline{)48}$

Score: __________ Time: __________ minutes __________ seconds

Name ______________________________

Dividends Through Eighty-One

Now, think about what happens when a number is divided by 9.

Example: 72 ÷ 9 = 8

The dividend is 72. If you put 9 objects in each group, you have 8 equal groups.

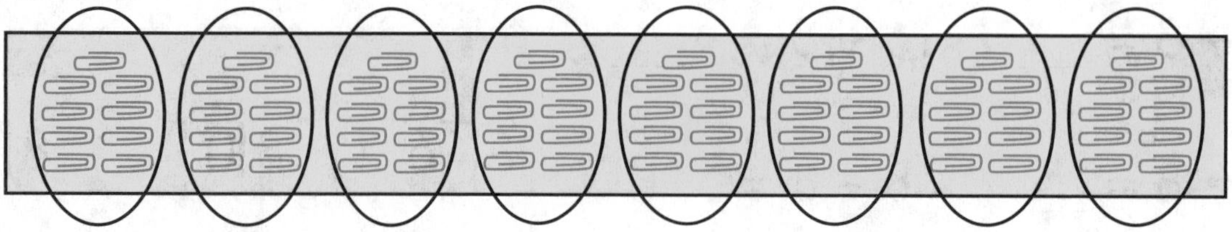

Remember: Division and multiplication are inverse operations.

Example: 9 x 8 = 72
72 ÷ 9 = 8

Apply what you have learned to the division facts of 9.

Examples: 0 ÷ 9 = 0 9 ÷ 1 = 9 9 ÷ 9 = 1

■ Write a division fact related to each multiplication fact of 9.

9 x 1 = 9	9 x 2 = 18	9 x 3 = 27
____ ÷ ____ = ____	____ ÷ ____ = ____	____ ÷ ____ = ____
9 x 4 = 36	9 x 5 = 45	9 x 6 = 54
____ ÷ ____ = ____	____ ÷ ____ = ____	____ ÷ ____ = ____
9 x 7 = 63	9 x 8 = 72	9 x 9 = 81
____ ÷ ____ = ____	____ ÷ ____ = ____	____ ÷ ____ = ____

Name ______________________

Practice

■ Divide.

27 ÷ 9 = ____	54 ÷ 9 = ____
72 ÷ 9 = ____	45 ÷ 9 = ____
81 ÷ 9 = ____	63 ÷ 9 = ____
36 ÷ 9 = ____	18 ÷ 9 = ____
54 ÷ 9 = ____	0 ÷ 9 = ____
9 ÷ 9 = ____	27 ÷ 9 = ____
45 ÷ 9 = ____	72 ÷ 9 = ____
63 ÷ 9 = ____	81 ÷ 9 = ____
18 ÷ 9 = ____	36 ÷ 9 = ____
0 ÷ 9 = ____	9 ÷ 9 = ____

$9\overline{)81}$	$9\overline{)27}$
$9\overline{)0}$	$9\overline{)63}$
$9\overline{)18}$	$9\overline{)72}$
$9\overline{)9}$	$9\overline{)45}$
$9\overline{)36}$	$9\overline{)54}$
$9\overline{)45}$	$9\overline{)9}$
$9\overline{)63}$	$9\overline{)81}$
$9\overline{)27}$	$9\overline{)0}$

4 ÷ 2 =

Circle any problems that you still find difficult to remember. Make your own flash cards to help you master these problems.

FINISH

Score: ____________

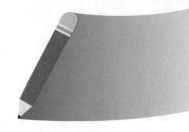

Name ____________________

Timed Test

■ Complete these facts as accurately and as quickly as you can.

Nine as a Divisor

45 ÷ 9 = ____ 9 ÷ 9 = ____

18 ÷ 9 = ____ 81 ÷ 9 = ____

0 ÷ 9 = ____ 36 ÷ 9 = ____

54 ÷ 9 = ____ 27 ÷ 9 = ____

9 ÷ 9 = ____ 63 ÷ 9 = ____

72 ÷ 9 = ____ 18 ÷ 9 = ____

0 ÷ 9 = ____ 45 ÷ 9 = ____

81 ÷ 9 = ____ 54 ÷ 9 = ____

63 ÷ 9 = ____ 72 ÷ 9 = ____

27 ÷ 9 = ____ 36 ÷ 9 = ____

$9\overline{)81}$ $9\overline{)36}$ $9\overline{)9}$

$9\overline{)18}$ $9\overline{)72}$ $9\overline{)45}$

$9\overline{)27}$ $9\overline{)81}$ $9\overline{)63}$

$9\overline{)9}$ $9\overline{)0}$ $9\overline{)18}$

$9\overline{)54}$ $9\overline{)72}$ $9\overline{)36}$

$9\overline{)45}$ $9\overline{)63}$ $9\overline{)27}$

$9\overline{)0}$ $9\overline{)18}$

Score: __________ Time: __________ minutes __________ seconds

Name ________________________________

Practice

■ Divide.

$64 \div 8 =$ ____	$25 \div 5 =$ ____	$10 \div 2 =$ ____	$81 \div 9 =$ ____
$4 \div 2 =$ ____	$9 \div 9 =$ ____	$8 \div 8 =$ ____	$36 \div 6 =$ ____
$5 \div 5 =$ ____	$0 \div 1 =$ ____	$6 \div 1 =$ ____	$18 \div 2 =$ ____
$4 \div 1 =$ ____	$24 \div 6 =$ ____	$18 \div 6 =$ ____	$24 \div 3 =$ ____
$0 \div 3 =$ ____	$20 \div 4 =$ ____	$30 \div 5 =$ ____	$16 \div 2 =$ ____
$54 \div 9 =$ ____	$42 \div 6 =$ ____	$0 \div 8 =$ ____	$6 \div 6 =$ ____
$21 \div 3 =$ ____	$9 \div 3 =$ ____	$4 \div 4 =$ ____	$63 \div 9 =$ ____
$28 \div 7 =$ ____	$12 \div 2 =$ ____	$32 \div 8 =$ ____	$36 \div 4 =$ ____
$9 \div 1 =$ ____	$3 \div 1 =$ ____	$42 \div 7 =$ ____	$7 \div 7 =$ ____
$45 \div 5 =$ ____	$12 \div 3 =$ ____	$28 \div 4 =$ ____	$12 \div 4 =$ ____

Continue this Practice on the next page.

Name ____________________________________

Practice

■ Divide.

$8\overline{)56}$	$1\overline{)9}$	$6\overline{)48}$	$6\overline{)0}$	$5\overline{)30}$	$4\overline{)28}$
$3\overline{)6}$	$1\overline{)7}$	$7\overline{)21}$	$8\overline{)0}$	$2\overline{)6}$	$7\overline{)42}$
$4\overline{)8}$	$6\overline{)54}$	$2\overline{)2}$	$3\overline{)18}$	$5\overline{)35}$	$5\overline{)0}$
$9\overline{)18}$	$4\overline{)20}$	$1\overline{)2}$	$8\overline{)32}$	$6\overline{)24}$	$2\overline{)12}$
$3\overline{)24}$	$5\overline{)15}$	$3\overline{)0}$	$9\overline{)63}$	$6\overline{)36}$	$3\overline{)27}$
$7\overline{)35}$	$4\overline{)12}$	$9\overline{)54}$	$1\overline{)0}$	$8\overline{)8}$	$8\overline{)48}$
$7\overline{)7}$	$2\overline{)8}$	$6\overline{)30}$	$9\overline{)27}$	$1\overline{)4}$	$9\overline{)45}$

All-Division Review

FINISH

Circle any problems that you still find difficult to remember. Make your own flash cards to help you master these problems.

Continue this Practice on the next page.

Name ______________________________

Timed Test

$30 \div 6 =$ ____	$42 \div 7 =$ ____	$24 \div 8 =$ ____	$1 \div 1 =$ ____
$6 \div 1 =$ ____	$18 \div 3 =$ ____	$7 \div 1 =$ ____	$48 \div 8 =$ ____
$3 \div 1 =$ ____	$4 \div 1 =$ ____	$4 \div 2 =$ ____	$15 \div 3 =$ ____
$20 \div 4 =$ ____	$16 \div 4 =$ ____	$45 \div 5 =$ ____	$16 \div 8 =$ ____
$0 \div 7 =$ ____	$25 \div 5 =$ ____	$18 \div 9 =$ ____	$8 \div 2 =$ ____
$49 \div 7 =$ ____	$0 \div 9 =$ ____	$20 \div 5 =$ ____	$5 \div 5 =$ ____
$24 \div 6 =$ ____	$32 \div 8 =$ ____	$6 \div 3 =$ ____	$0 \div 6 =$ ____
$16 \div 2 =$ ____	$18 \div 9 =$ ____	$54 \div 9 =$ ____	$40 \div 5 =$ ____
$40 \div 8 =$ ____	$9 \div 1 =$ ____	$72 \div 8 =$ ____	$14 \div 2 =$ ____
$9 \div 9 =$ ____	$56 \div 7 =$ ____	$35 \div 7 =$ ____	$36 \div 4 =$ ____

Score: __________ Time: __________ minutes __________ seconds

Name ______________________________

Timed Test

$1\overline{)0}$	$3\overline{)18}$	$7\overline{)35}$	$9\overline{)0}$	$8\overline{)24}$	$2\overline{)8}$
$8\overline{)32}$	$5\overline{)35}$	$6\overline{)36}$	$1\overline{)6}$	$4\overline{)36}$	$9\overline{)27}$
$2\overline{)16}$	$4\overline{)8}$	$7\overline{)21}$	$9\overline{)18}$	$5\overline{)30}$	$6\overline{)42}$
$2\overline{)12}$	$9\overline{)72}$	$6\overline{)0}$	$3\overline{)21}$	$1\overline{)4}$	$9\overline{)9}$
$8\overline{)16}$	$5\overline{)0}$	$6\overline{)24}$	$7\overline{)28}$	$9\overline{)1}$	$6\overline{)30}$
$8\overline{)8}$	$3\overline{)15}$	$2\overline{)14}$	$3\overline{)24}$	$5\overline{)25}$	$7\overline{)14}$
$1\overline{)5}$	$4\overline{)4}$	$4\overline{)32}$	$8\overline{)40}$	$2\overline{)2}$	$8\overline{)40}$

Score: __________ Time: __________ minutes __________ seconds

ANSWERS

6

Name ______________________

What Is Addition?

You add to find how many in all. The answer is called the **sum**.

3 birds plus 2 more birds equals 5 birds in all.

There are two ways to show the addition.

3 + 2 = 5

$$\begin{array}{r} 3 \\ +2 \\ \hline 5 \end{array}$$

You can draw a picture to find a sum.

Example: Find the sum. 2 + 4 = ____

Step 1: Draw 2 dots. ● ●

Step 2: Draw 4 more dots. ● ● ● ●

Step 3: Count all the dots.

Answer: 2 + 4 = 6

■ Draw a picture to find the sum.

3 + 1 = **4**   2 + 2 = **4**   4 + 2 = **6**

1 + 5 = **6**   2 + 3 = **5**   3 + 3 = **6**

7

Name ______________________

What Is Addition?

You can use counters to find a sum. You will need some pennies.

Example: Find the sum. 3 + 2 = ____

Step 1: Put 3 pennies in the box.

Step 2: Put 2 more pennies in the box.

Step 3: Count all the pennies.

Answer: 3 + 2 = 5

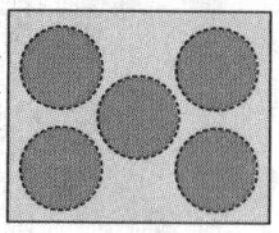

■ Use counters to find the sum.

4 + 3 = **7**   2 + 4 = **6**   3 + 4 = **7**

$$\begin{array}{r} 4 \\ +4 \\ \hline \mathbf{8} \end{array} \quad \begin{array}{r} 5 \\ +1 \\ \hline \mathbf{6} \end{array} \quad \begin{array}{r} 2 \\ +5 \\ \hline \mathbf{7} \end{array} \quad \begin{array}{r} 2 \\ +1 \\ \hline \mathbf{3} \end{array} \quad \begin{array}{r} 3 \\ +2 \\ \hline \mathbf{5} \end{array}$$

You can use a number line to find a sum.

Example: Find the sum. 5 + 3 = ____

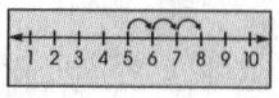

Step 1: Put your finger on 5.

Step 2: Move your finger 3 spaces to the right.

Step 3: Read the number your finger is on.

Answer: 5 + 3 = 8

■ Use the number line to find the sum.

4 + 1 = **5**   5 + 3 = **8**   3 + 5 = **8**

$$\begin{array}{r} 5 \\ +2 \\ \hline \mathbf{7} \end{array} \quad \begin{array}{r} 4 \\ +5 \\ \hline \mathbf{9} \end{array} \quad \begin{array}{r} 1 \\ +2 \\ \hline \mathbf{3} \end{array} \quad \begin{array}{r} 5 \\ +4 \\ \hline \mathbf{9} \end{array} \quad \begin{array}{r} 5 \\ +5 \\ \hline \mathbf{10} \end{array}$$

8

Name ______________________

Adding Zero

Zero is called the **identity element of addition**. This means that, when zero is added to a number, that number does not change.

Example: 3 + 0 = 3

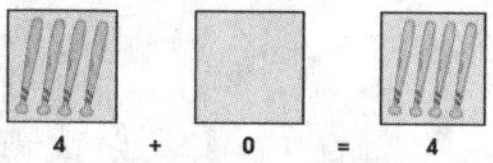

■ Add.

2 + 0 = **2**   3 + 0 = **3**

0 + 6 = **6**   0 + 4 = **4**

0 + 1 = **1**   4 + 0 = **4**

5 + 0 = **5**   0 + 3 = **3**

1 + 0 = **1**   0 + 2 = **2**

0 + 5 = **5**   6 + 0 = **6**

$$\begin{array}{r} 1 \\ +0 \\ \hline \mathbf{1} \end{array} \quad \begin{array}{r} 0 \\ +4 \\ \hline \mathbf{4} \end{array} \quad \begin{array}{r} 0 \\ +0 \\ \hline \mathbf{0} \end{array} \quad \begin{array}{r} 3 \\ +0 \\ \hline \mathbf{3} \end{array}$$

$$\begin{array}{r} 0 \\ +5 \\ \hline \mathbf{5} \end{array} \quad \begin{array}{r} 6 \\ +0 \\ \hline \mathbf{6} \end{array} \quad \begin{array}{r} 0 \\ +6 \\ \hline \mathbf{6} \end{array} \quad \begin{array}{r} 4 \\ +0 \\ \hline \mathbf{4} \end{array}$$

$$\begin{array}{r} 0 \\ +2 \\ \hline \mathbf{2} \end{array} \quad \begin{array}{r} 0 \\ +3 \\ \hline \mathbf{3} \end{array} \quad \begin{array}{r} 5 \\ +0 \\ \hline \mathbf{5} \end{array} \quad \begin{array}{r} 2 \\ +0 \\ \hline \mathbf{2} \end{array}$$

The numbers that are added together in an addition problem are called **addends**. The answer in an addition problem is called the **sum**.

5 + 0 = 5 (addend, addend, sum)

$$\begin{array}{rl} 5 & \text{addend} \\ +0 & \text{addend} \\ \hline 5 & \text{sum} \end{array}$$

9

Name ______________________

Counting On

If one of the addends in an addition fact is a lesser number like 1, 2, or 3, you can find the sum by "counting on" from the other addend.

Example: 3 + 2   Start at 3. Count on by moving 2 jumps on the number line. The sum is 5.

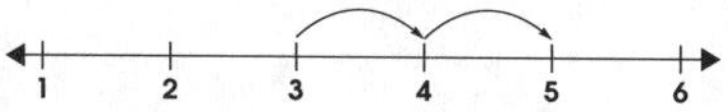

■ Complete each **T** by counting on by the number at the top. Use the number line to help you.

+1		+2		+3	
5	**6**	4	**6**	2	**5**
3	**4**	0	**2**	1	**4**
4	**5**	3	**5**	0	**3**
2	**3**	1	**3**		
0	**1**				

Counting numbers are all the whole numbers beginning with 1 and going as far as you want. 1, 2, 3, 4, . . .

Hint: Always add the smaller addend to the larger one, no matter which comes first.

10

Name ______________________

Changing the Order of the Addends

The **commutative property of addition** says that the sum is always the same no matter how the addends are arranged.

Example: 3 + 2 = 5 is the same as 2 + 3 = 5.

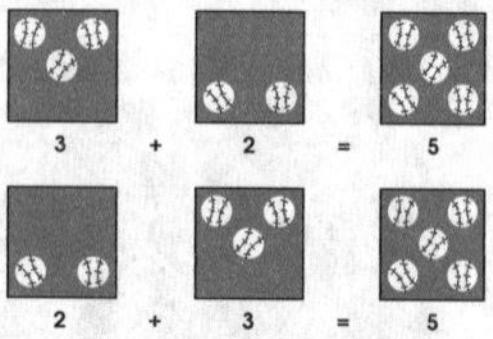

■ Use the commutative property to solve the problems below.

1 + 3 = **4**   4 + 2 = **6**   2 + 3 = **5**

3 + 1 = **4**   2 + 4 = **6**   3 + 2 = **5**

1 + 2 = **3**   1 + 4 = **5**   5 + 1 = **6**

2 + 1 = **3**   4 + 1 = **5**   1 + 5 = **6**

11

Name ______________________

Adding Doubles

Doubles are basic facts in which the addends are the same number.

Examples: 1 + 1 = 2

2 + 2 = 4

3 + 3 = 6

■ Add.

0 + 0 = **0**   2 + 2 = **4**

3 + 3 = **6**   1 + 1 = **2**

$$\begin{array}{r} 2 \\ +2 \\ \hline \mathbf{4} \end{array} \quad \begin{array}{r} 1 \\ +1 \\ \hline \mathbf{2} \end{array} \quad \begin{array}{r} 0 \\ +0 \\ \hline \mathbf{0} \end{array} \quad \begin{array}{r} 3 \\ +3 \\ \hline \mathbf{6} \end{array}$$

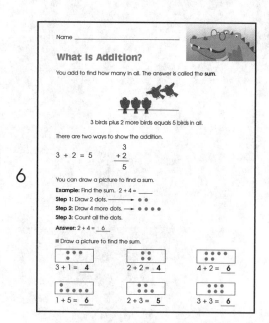

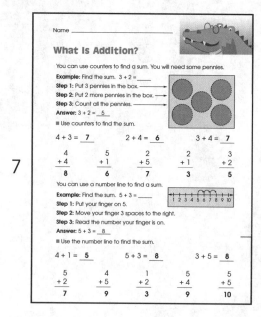

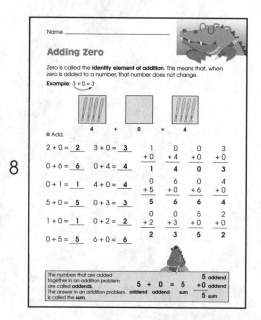

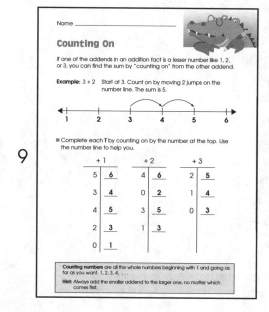

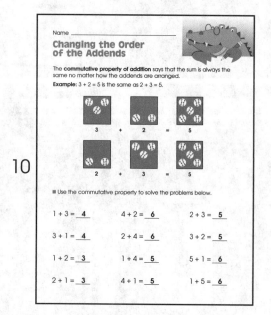

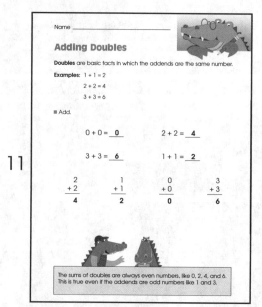

The sums of doubles are always even numbers, like 0, 2, 4, and 6. This is true even if the addends are odd numbers like 1 and 3.

12

Name ____________________

Practice

■ Add.

1	0	2	2	0	1	3	0	0
+ 4	+ 6	+ 1	+ 4	+ 5	+ 2	+ 3	+ 4	+ 1
5	**6**	**3**	**6**	**5**	**3**	**6**	**4**	**1**
0	2	0	3	1	0	1	5	3
+ 0	+ 2	+ 2	+ 2	+ 0	+ 3	+ 4	+ 0	+ 2
0	**4**	**2**	**5**	**1**	**3**	**5**	**5**	**5**
2	4	3	1	1	4	0	4	2
+ 3	+ 0	+ 3	+ 3	+ 4	+ 2	+ 3	+ 1	+ 0
5	**4**	**6**	**4**	**5**	**6**	**3**	**5**	**2**
3	1	1	2	6	1	2	3	5
+ 0	+ 5	+ 1	+ 2	+ 0	+ 3	+ 3	+ 1	+ 1
3	**6**	**2**	**4**	**6**	**4**	**5**	**4**	**6**

Score: ________

FINISH

13

Name ____________________

Practice

■ Add.

3	2	2	4
+ 3	+ 4	+ 1	+ 2
6	**6**	**3**	**6**
0	1	5	0
+ 1	+ 2	+ 0	+ 3
1	**3**	**5**	**3**
1	3	1	2
+ 0	+ 2	+ 3	+ 2
1	**5**	**4**	**4**
0	0	5	3
+ 2	+ 4	+ 1	+ 1
2	**4**	**6**	**4**
2	3	0	1
+ 1	+ 3	+ 5	+ 4
3	**6**	**5**	**5**

0 + 0 = **0**   1 + 1 = **2**

2 + 3 = **5**   2 + 0 = **2**

1 + 5 = **6**   5 + 1 = **6**

4 + 0 = **4**   0 + 6 = **6**

0 + 5 = **5**   3 + 1 = **4**

3 + 0 = **3**   1 + 4 = **5**

4 + 1 = **5**   6 + 0 = **6**

3 + 2 = **5**   2 + 2 = **4**

Score: ________

Circle any problems that you still find difficult to remember. Make your own flash cards to help you master these problems.

FINISH

14

Name ____________________

Timed Test

■ Improve your speed on these basic facts. Ask someone to time you. Record your time and score on each Timed Test page.

0 + 5 = **5**   1 + 1 = **2**   0 + 2 = **2**   2 + 1 = **3**

1 + 4 = **5**   5 + 0 = **5**   3 + 2 = **5**   6 + 0 = **6**

2 + 0 = **2**   2 + 3 = **5**   1 + 0 = **1**   1 + 5 = **6**

3 + 3 = **6**   4 + 2 = **6**   2 + 4 = **6**   5 + 1 = **6**

0 + 1 = **1**   0 + 3 = **3**   1 + 2 = **3**   2 + 2 = **4**

4 + 1 = **5**   1 + 3 = **4**   4 + 0 = **4**   3 + 1 = **4**

3 + 0 = **3**   0 + 6 = **6**   0 + 4 = **4**   0 + 0 = **0**

2 + 4 = **6**   3 + 3 = **6**   1 + 5 = **6**   3 + 2 = **5**

1 + 4 = **5**   5 + 0 = **5**   4 + 2 = **6**   2 + 2 = **4**

3 + 1 = **4**   1 + 1 = **2**   2 + 0 = **2**   1 + 2 = **3**

Score: ________   Time: ________ minutes ________ seconds

15

Name ____________________

Timed Test

1 + 4 = **5**   2 + 3 = **5**

5 + 1 = **6**   1 + 3 = **4**

0 + 6 = **6**   4 + 0 = **4**

2 + 4 = **6**   0 + 3 = **3**

2 + 0 = **2**   2 + 1 = **3**

6 + 0 = **6**   1 + 5 = **6**

0 + 4 = **4**   5 + 0 = **5**

3 + 3 = **6**   4 + 1 = **5**

2 + 1 = **3**   3 + 2 = **5**

1 + 1 = **2**   6 + 0 = **6**

0	3	3	1
+ 5	+ 1	+ 0	+ 2
5	**4**	**3**	**3**
4	0	3	3
+ 2	+ 0	+ 3	+ 2
6	**0**	**6**	**5**
1	4	2	0
+ 0	+ 1	+ 0	+ 1
1	**5**	**2**	**1**
0	1	2	5
+ 2	+ 1	+ 2	+ 1
2	**2**	**4**	**6**
1	1	0	2
+ 2	+ 0	+ 4	+ 4
3	**1**	**4**	**6**

Score: ________   Time: ________ minutes ________ seconds

16

Name ____________________

Timed Test

1 + 4 = **5**   2 + 2 = **4**

0 + 3 = **3**   3 + 0 = **3**

2 + 3 = **5**   0 + 6 = **6**

1 + 2 = **3**   4 + 1 = **5**

2 + 4 = **6**   1 + 3 = **4**

0 + 4 = **4**   0 + 3 = **3**

4 + 2 = **6**   0 + 1 = **1**

3 + 1 = **4**   3 + 2 = **5**

2 + 0 = **2**   1 + 2 = **3**

2 + 2 = **4**   4 + 1 = **5**

3	4	5	2
+ 3	+ 0	+ 0	+ 1
6	**4**	**5**	**3**
1	0	1	6
+ 1	+ 2	+ 0	+ 0
2	**2**	**1**	**6**
3	5	3	0
+ 2	+ 1	+ 1	+ 0
5	**6**	**4**	**0**
1	2	1	0
+ 5	+ 0	+ 2	+ 5
6	**2**	**3**	**5**
4	0	2	1
+ 2	+ 6	+ 2	+ 4
6	**6**	**4**	**5**

Score: ________   Time: ________ minutes ________ seconds

17

Name ____________________

Adding Zero

Remember: Zero is the identity element of addition. When zero is added to a number, that number does not change.

Example: 7 + 0 = 7

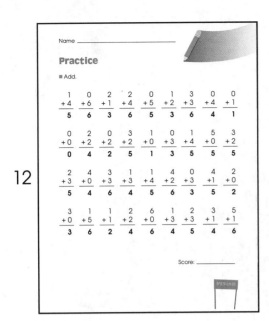

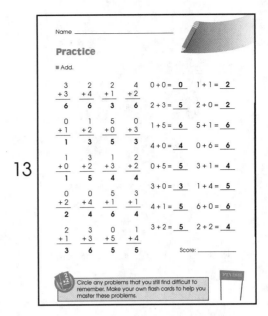

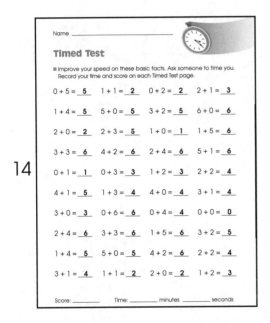

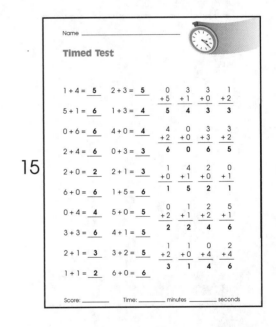

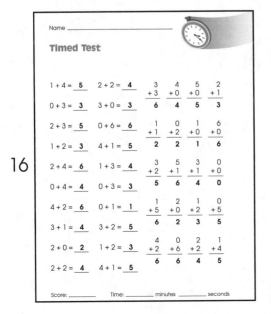

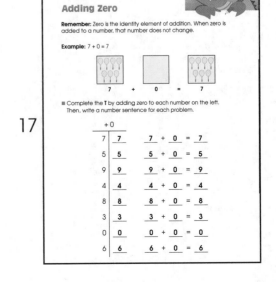

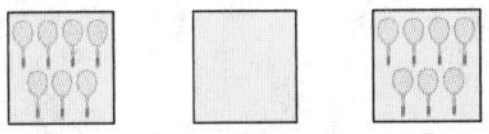

7 + 0 = 7

■ Complete the **T** by adding zero to each number on the left. Then, write a number sentence for each problem.

	+ 0	
7	**7**	**7** + **0** = **7**
5	**5**	**5** + **0** = **5**
9	**9**	**9** + **0** = **9**
4	**4**	**4** + **0** = **4**
8	**8**	**8** + **0** = **8**
3	**3**	**3** + **0** = **3**
0	**0**	**0** + **0** = **0**
6	**6**	**6** + **0** = **6**

18

Name ______________________

Changing the Order of the Addends

Remember: The commutative property of addition says that the sum is always the same no matter how the addends are arranged.

Example: 6 + 3 = 9 is the same as 3 + 6 = 9.

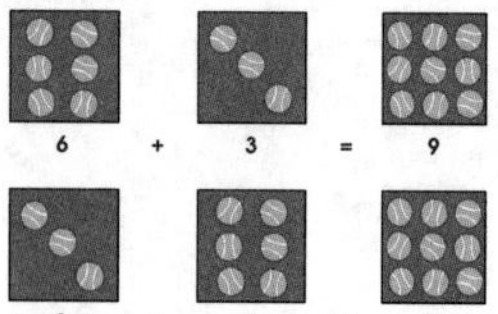

■ Write another addition fact using the numbers in each fact below.

7 + 1 = 8	6 + 4 = 10	9 + 0 = 9
1 + 7 = 8	4 + 6 = 10	0 + 9 = 9
6 + 1 = 7	6 + 2 = 8	9 + 1 = 10
1 + 6 = 7	2 + 6 = 8	1 + 9 = 10
7 + 2 = 9	8 + 1 = 9	8 + 2 = 10
2 + 7 = 9	1 + 8 = 9	2 + 8 = 10

19

Name ______________________

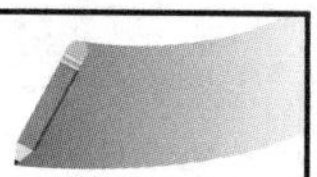

Practice

■ Add.

6	3	9	0	2	6	4	3	5
+ 3	+ 6	+ 0	+ 9	+ 6	+ 2	+ 4	+ 5	+ 3
9	9	9	9	8	8	8	8	8
9	1	4	5	8	0	8	2	1
+ 1	+ 9	+ 5	+ 4	+ 0	+ 8	+ 2	+ 8	+ 6
10	10	9	9	8	8	10	10	7
6	3	4	3	7	8	1	5	2
+ 1	+ 4	+ 3	+ 7	+ 3	+ 1	+ 8	+ 2	+ 5
7	7	7	10	10	9	9	7	7
5	7	2	6	4	0	7	7	1
+ 5	+ 2	+ 7	+ 4	+ 6	+ 7	+ 0	+ 1	+ 7
10	9	9	10	10	7	7	8	8

Score: ________

20

Name ______________________

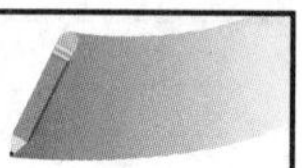

Practice

■ Add.

6	4	6	1
+ 4	+ 5	+ 2	+ 8
10	9	8	9
4	2	3	8
+ 4	+ 6	+ 7	+ 1
8	8	10	9
0	7	3	8
+ 7	+ 3	+ 6	+ 2
7	10	9	10
2	5	1	5
+ 8	+ 2	+ 7	+ 3
10	7	8	8
5	7	7	6
+ 4	+ 2	+ 3	+ 4
9	9	10	10

9 + 1 = 10	4 + 6 = 10
2 + 5 = 7	7 + 0 = 7
6 + 3 = 9	0 + 8 = 8
0 + 9 = 9	5 + 5 = 10
8 + 0 = 8	1 + 9 = 10
4 + 3 = 7	1 + 6 = 7
6 + 1 = 7	9 + 0 = 9
2 + 7 = 9	3 + 4 = 7

Score: ________

Circle any problems that you still find difficult to remember. Make your own flash cards to help you master these problems.

21

Name ______________________

Timed Test

■ Improve your speed on these basic facts. Ask someone to time you. Record your time and score on each Timed Test page.

0 + 8 = 8	5 + 3 = 8	5 + 4 = 9	2 + 6 = 8
2 + 5 = 7	2 + 8 = 10	0 + 7 = 7	7 + 0 = 7
7 + 3 = 10	8 + 0 = 8	5 + 2 = 7	3 + 7 = 10
1 + 6 = 7	3 + 6 = 9	3 + 5 = 8	8 + 1 = 9
7 + 1 = 8	6 + 4 = 10	4 + 6 = 10	0 + 9 = 9
3 + 4 = 7	1 + 8 = 9	2 + 7 = 9	6 + 2 = 8
6 + 1 = 7	4 + 5 = 9	1 + 7 = 8	4 + 3 = 7
6 + 3 = 9	8 + 2 = 10	4 + 4 = 8	5 + 5 = 10
1 + 9 = 10	7 + 2 = 9	9 + 1 = 10	9 + 0 = 9
3 + 7 = 10	2 + 8 = 10	5 + 4 = 9	4 + 6 = 10

Score: ________ Time: ________ minutes ________ seconds

22

Name ______________________

Timed Test

3 + 5 = 8	6 + 1 = 7
9 + 1 = 10	3 + 7 = 10
6 + 3 = 9	7 + 1 = 8
1 + 9 = 10	0 + 8 = 8
7 + 2 = 9	5 + 3 = 8
2 + 8 = 10	1 + 7 = 8
4 + 5 = 9	6 + 4 = 10
8 + 2 = 10	0 + 7 = 7
5 + 5 = 10	7 + 3 = 10
2 + 5 = 7	1 + 8 = 9

9	3	6	1
+ 0	+ 6	+ 2	+ 6
9	9	8	7
7	4	3	4
+ 3	+ 6	+ 4	+ 4
10	10	7	8
0	8	5	2
+ 9	+ 0	+ 2	+ 7
9	8	7	9
5	1	7	4
+ 4	+ 8	+ 0	+ 3
9	9	7	7
5	8	2	2
+ 5	+ 1	+ 6	+ 5
10	9	8	7

Score: ________ Time: ________ minutes ________ seconds

23

Name ______________________

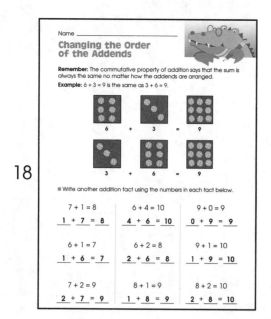

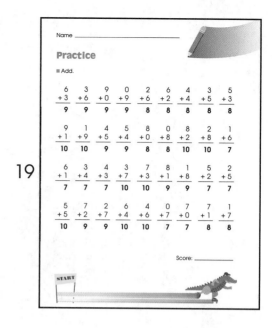

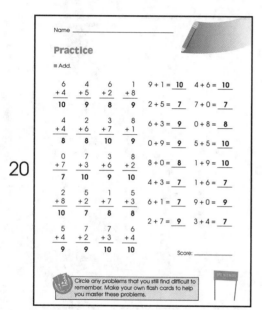

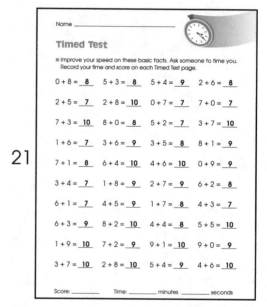

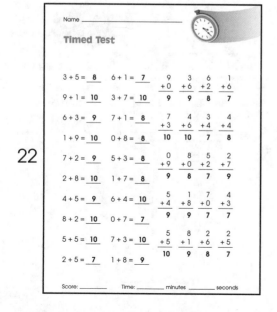

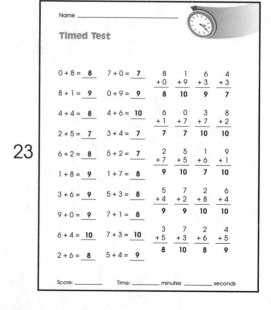

Timed Test

0 + 8 = 8	7 + 0 = 7
8 + 1 = 9	0 + 9 = 9
4 + 4 = 8	4 + 6 = 10
2 + 5 = 7	3 + 4 = 7
6 + 2 = 8	5 + 2 = 7
1 + 8 = 9	1 + 7 = 8
3 + 6 = 9	5 + 3 = 8
9 + 0 = 9	7 + 1 = 8
6 + 4 = 10	7 + 3 = 10
2 + 6 = 8	5 + 4 = 9

8	1	6	4
+ 0	+ 9	+ 3	+ 3
8	10	9	7
6	0	3	8
+ 1	+ 7	+ 7	+ 2
7	7	10	10
2	5	1	9
+ 7	+ 5	+ 6	+ 1
9	10	7	10
5	7	2	6
+ 4	+ 2	+ 8	+ 4
9	9	10	10
3	7	2	4
+ 5	+ 3	+ 6	+ 5
8	10	8	9

Score: ________ Time: ________ minutes ________ seconds

24

Name ____________

Thinking of Tens

Another way to remember certain sums is to think about tens.

Example: 8 + 6 = 14

Think: How much of 6 would be added to 8 to equal 10?
The answer is 8 + 2 = 10, with 4 left over. Therefore, 8 + 6 = 14.

■ Complete each of these number sentences.

9 + 4 is 9 + 1 (or 10), with 3 left over. Therefore, 9 + 4 = 13.

5 + 8 is 2 + 8 (or 10), with 3 left over. Therefore, 5 + 8 = 13.

9 + 7 is 9 + 1 (or 10), with 6 left over. Therefore, 9 + 7 = 16.

5 + 9 is 1 + 9 (or 10), with 4 left over. Therefore, 5 + 9 = 14.

4 + 7 is 3 + 7 (or 10), with 1 left over. Therefore, 4 + 7 = 11.

■ Think about tens as you complete these facts.

6 + 7 = 13 8 + 5 = 13 9 + 6 = 15 6 + 8 = 14

9 + 8 = 17 4 + 9 = 13 4 + 7 = 11 9 + 5 = 14

8 + 7 = 15 5 + 8 = 13 5 + 7 = 12 7 + 9 = 16

5 + 6 = 11 8 + 4 = 12 5 + 9 = 14 6 + 9 = 15

25

Name ____________

Adding Doubles

Remember: Two addends that are the same number are called doubles.

Example: 6 + 6 = 12

■ Add.

9 + 9 = 18 7 + 7 = 14 8 + 8 = 16 6 + 6 = 12

8	6	7	9
+ 8	+ 6	+ 7	+ 9
16	12	14	18

■ Add these doubles down and across.

3	3	6
3	3	6
6	6	12

4	4	8
4	4	8
8	8	16

Remember: The sums of doubles are always even numbers, like 10, 12, and 14. This is true even if the addends are odd numbers like 7 and 9.

26

Name ____________

Practice

■ Add.

8	7	4	6
+ 9	+ 6	+ 7	+ 5
17	13	11	11
8	8	9	6
+ 7	+ 5	+ 8	+ 7
15	13	17	13
3	5	9	8
+ 8	+ 8	+ 7	+ 3
11	13	16	11
6	7	9	5
+ 9	+ 8	+ 4	+ 6
15	15	13	11
7	9	4	9
+ 7	+ 6	+ 9	+ 3
14	15	13	12

7 + 4 = 11 9 + 2 = 11

8 + 8 = 16 6 + 8 = 14

6 + 6 = 12 5 + 9 = 14

3 + 9 = 12 4 + 8 = 12

8 + 4 = 12 7 + 9 = 16

7 + 5 = 12 9 + 5 = 14

9 + 9 = 18 5 + 7 = 12

8 + 6 = 14 2 + 9 = 11

Score: ____________

FINISH

27

Name ____________

Practice

■ Add.

9	6	5	8
+ 8	+ 7	+ 6	+ 3
17	13	11	11
3	7	6	9
+ 8	+ 8	+ 5	+ 6
11	15	11	15
7	9	3	8
+ 6	+ 9	+ 9	+ 5
13	18	12	13
8	5	9	6
+ 6	+ 8	+ 4	+ 9
14	13	13	15
8	9	8	9
+ 8	+ 2	+ 7	+ 3
16	11	15	12

9 + 7 = 16 5 + 7 = 12

4 + 8 = 12 8 + 9 = 17

9 + 5 = 14 7 + 5 = 12

6 + 8 = 14 8 + 7 = 15

7 + 9 = 16 4 + 9 = 13

4 + 7 = 11 8 + 4 = 12

7 + 7 = 14 7 + 4 = 11

6 + 6 = 12 5 + 9 = 14

Score: ____________

Circle any problems that you still find difficult to remember. Make your own flash cards to help you master these problems.

FINISH

28

Name ____________

Timed Test

■ Improve your speed on these basic facts. Ask someone to time you. Record your time and score on each Timed Test page.

9 + 6 = 15 9 + 8 = 17 8 + 6 = 14 5 + 7 = 12

5 + 8 = 13 5 + 9 = 14 4 + 7 = 11 9 + 2 = 11

2 + 9 = 11 7 + 6 = 13 9 + 4 = 13 7 + 8 = 15

9 + 5 = 14 3 + 9 = 12 6 + 8 = 14 8 + 8 = 16

7 + 4 = 11 8 + 3 = 11 8 + 5 = 13 6 + 5 = 11

9 + 3 = 12 6 + 7 = 13 3 + 8 = 11 4 + 6 = 10

5 + 6 = 11 8 + 7 = 15 9 + 7 = 16 7 + 9 = 16

8 + 9 = 17 4 + 8 = 12 7 + 5 = 12 4 + 9 = 13

8 + 4 = 12 6 + 9 = 15 9 + 9 = 18 6 + 6 = 12

7 + 8 = 15 8 + 6 = 14 7 + 7 = 14 3 + 9 = 12

Score: ________ Time: ________ minutes ________ seconds

29

Name ____________

Timed Test

3 + 8 = 11 8 + 8 = 16

8 + 4 = 12 6 + 5 = 11

9 + 7 = 16 7 + 6 = 13

5 + 6 = 11 8 + 9 = 17

7 + 9 = 16 5 + 7 = 12

9 + 6 = 15 8 + 6 = 14

4 + 8 = 12 6 + 7 = 13

9 + 3 = 12 9 + 9 = 18

6 + 9 = 15 5 + 9 = 14

8 + 7 = 15 2 + 9 = 11

4	9	2	9
+ 7	+ 4	+ 9	+ 5
11	13	11	14
7	8	6	8
+ 4	+ 7	+ 6	+ 3
11	15	12	11
7	9	4	7
+ 5	+ 2	+ 9	+ 8
12	11	13	15
9	5	3	8
+ 8	+ 8	+ 9	+ 5
17	13	12	13
6	7	7	8
+ 8	+ 7	+ 9	+ 4
14	14	16	12

Score: ________ Time: ________ minutes ________ seconds

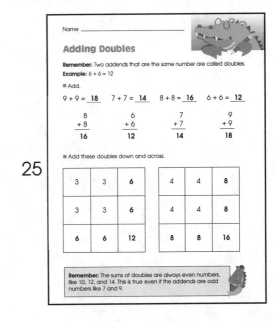

30

Name ______________________

Timed Test

5 + 7 = **12** 6 + 7 = **13**

8 + 9 = **17** 8 + 8 = **16**

4 + 8 = **12** 6 + 9 = **15**

9 + 9 = **18** 9 + 7 = **16**

7 + 5 = **12** 6 + 5 = **11**

8 + 6 = **14** 8 + 3 = **11**

7 + 7 = **14** 5 + 8 = **13**

3 + 8 = **11** 9 + 3 = **12**

9 + 5 = **14** 7 + 9 = **16**

8 + 7 = **15** 7 + 4 = **11**

7	9	5	4
+ 6	+ 2	+ 6	+ 7
13	**11**	**11**	**11**
9	7	8	2
+ 6	+ 4	+ 5	+ 9
15	**11**	**13**	**11**
9	6	6	8
+ 8	+ 6	+ 8	+ 7
17	**12**	**14**	**15**
3	8	4	9
+ 9	+ 4	+ 9	+ 4
12	**12**	**13**	**13**
5	7	6	8
+ 9	+ 8	+ 9	+ 3
14	**15**	**15**	**11**

Score: ________ Time: ________ minutes ________ seconds

32

Name ______________________

What Is Subtraction?

You subtract to find how many are left. The answer is called the **difference**.

5 birds take away 2 birds equals 3 birds.

There are two ways to show the subtraction.

5 - 2 = 3

5
- 2
3

You can draw a picture to find how many are left.

Example: Find the difference. 6 – 2 = ____

Step 1: Draw 6 dots. ⟶ ● ● ● ● ● ●

Step 2: Cross out 2 dots. ⟶ X X ● ● ● ●

Step 3: Count the remaining dots.

Answer: 6 – 2 = 4

■ Draw a picture to find the difference.

X ● ● ●	X X ● ●	X X ● ● ● ●
4 – 1 = **3**	4 – 2 = **2**	6 – 2 = **4**
X X X X X ●	X X X ● ●	X X X ● ● ●
6 – 5 = **1**	5 – 3 = **2**	6 – 3 = **3**

33

Name ______________________

What Is Subtraction?

You can use counters to find the difference. You will need some pennies.

Example: Find the difference. 5 – 2 = ____

Step 1: Put 5 pennies in the box. ⟶

Step 2: Take out 2 pennies. ⟶

Step 3: Count the pennies that are left. ⟶

Answer: 5 – 2 = 3

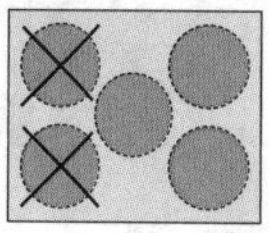

■ Use counters to find the difference.

6 – 3 = **3** 6 – 4 = **2** 7 – 4 = **3**

5	4	7	3	5
– 4	– 1	– 5	– 1	– 2
1	**3**	**2**	**2**	**3**

You can use a number line to find the difference.

Example: Find the answer. 8 – 3 = ____

Step 1: Put your finger on 8.

Step 2: Move your finger 3 spaces to the left.

Step 3: Read the number your finger is on.

Answer: 8 – 3 = 5

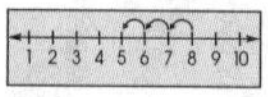

1 2 3 4 5 6 7 8 9 10

■ Use the number line to find the difference.

4 – 1 = **3** 5 – 3 = **2** 8 – 5 = **3**

4	7	3	6	6
– 2	– 5	– 2	– 4	– 5
2	**2**	**1**	**2**	**1**

34

Name ______________________

Subtracting Zero

Just as it is in addition, zero is the **identity element of subtraction**. This means that, when zero is subtracted from a number, the difference is that number.

Example: 3 – 0 = 3

3 – 0 = 3

■ Complete this **T** by subtracting zero from each number.

	– 0
1	**1**
3	**3**
2	**2**
0	**0**

■ Write the difference for each fact.

2 – 0 = **2** 0 – 0 = **0**

1 – 0 = **1** 3 – 0 = **3**

1	3	2	0
– 0	– 0	– 0	– 0
1	**3**	**2**	**0**

The answer in a subtraction problem is called the **difference**. The number from which the other is subtracted is called the **minuend**. The number being taken away is called the **subtrahend**.

35

Name ______________________

Subtracting Doubles

When the subtrahend is the same as the minuend, the difference is always zero.

Example: 2 – 2 = 0

2 – 2 = 0

Remember: If the difference is zero, the minuend and the subtrahend are the same number.

Example: If 6 – ? = 0, then 6 – 6 = 0.

■ Complete these facts by writing the missing numbers.

5 – 5 = **0** 8 – 8 = **0**

6 – **6** = 0 7 – **7** = 0

4 – 4 = 0 **9** – 9 = 0

1 – 1 = **0** **3** – 3 = 0

6	1	**9**	2
– 6	– **1**	– 9	– **2**
0	0	0	0
4	8	5	**3**
– 4	– 8	– **5**	– 3
0	**0**	0	0

36

Name ______________________

Counting Back

When the subtrahend is a lesser number like 1, 2, or 3, you can "count back" to find the difference.

Example: 3 – 1 = 2

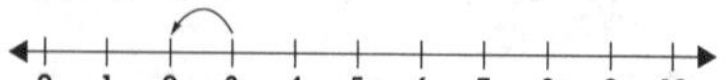

0 1 2 3 4 5 6 7 8 9 10

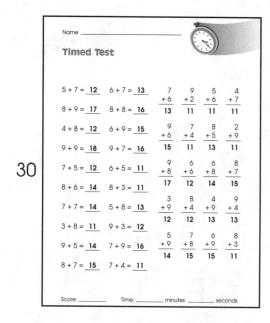

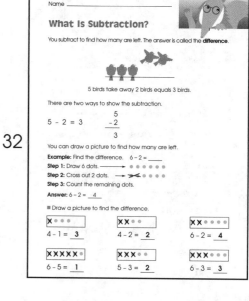

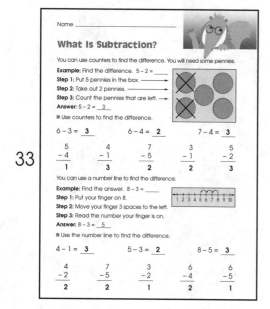

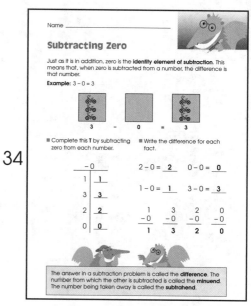

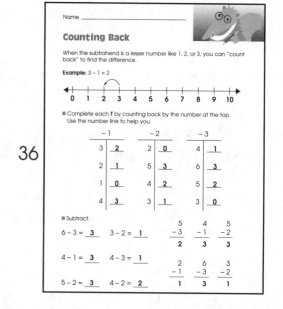

■ Complete each **T** by counting back by the number at the top. Use the number line to help you.

	– 1		– 2		– 3
3	**2**	2	**0**	4	**1**
2	**1**	5	**3**	6	**3**
1	**0**	4	**2**	5	**2**
4	**3**	3	**1**	3	**0**

■ Subtract.

6 – 3 = **3** 3 – 2 = **1**

4 – 1 = **3** 4 – 3 = **1**

5 – 2 = **3** 4 – 2 = **2**

5	4	5
– 3	– 1	– 2
2	**3**	**3**
2	6	3
– 1	– 3	– 2
1	**3**	**1**

37

Name ____________

Using Addition

You can use addition facts to help you learn subtraction facts. This is because addition and subtraction are inverse operations.

Example: You already know that 3 + 2 = 5.
Then, 5 − 2 = 3.
And, 5 − 3 = 2.

■ Write two different subtraction facts using the numbers in each addition sentence.

3 + 1 = 4	2 + 0 = 2	1 + 0 = 1
4 − **3** = **1**	**2** − **0** = **2**	**1** − **0** = **1**
4 − **1** = **3**	**2** − **2** = **0**	**1** − **1** = **0**
1 + 2 = 3	3 + 0 = 3	2 + 3 = 5
3 − **1** = **2**	**3** − **0** = **3**	**5** − **2** = **3**
3 − **2** = **1**	**3** − **3** = **0**	**5** − **3** = **2**

■ Write an addition fact using the numbers in each subtraction sentence.

3 − 2 = 1	4 − 1 = 3	5 − 3 = 2
2 + **1** = **3**	**1** + **3** = **4**	**3** + **2** = **5**
2 − 0 = 2	3 − 3 = 0	4 − 2 = 2
2 + **0** = **2**	**3** + **0** = **3**	**2** + **2** = **4**

38

Name ____________

Practice

■ Subtract.

0	8	9	7	8	5	3	1	4
−0	−7	−8	−6	−8	−4	−2	−1	−3
0	**1**	**1**	**1**	**0**	**1**	**1**	**0**	**1**
10	7	7	3	9	2	8	1	5
−9	−7	−5	−3	−6	−2	−5	−0	−2
1	**0**	**2**	**0**	**3**	**0**	**3**	**1**	**3**
9	5	4	11	12	9	11	8	2
−7	−3	−2	−8	−9	−9	−9	−6	−1
2	**2**	**2**	**3**	**3**	**0**	**2**	**2**	**1**
3	6	3	2	10	7	6	6	10
−0	−3	−1	−0	−8	−4	−5	−4	−7
3	**3**	**2**	**2**	**2**	**3**	**1**	**2**	**3**

Score: ____________

FINISH

39

Name ____________

Practice

■ Subtract.

8	11	4	6
−6	−9	−3	−6
2	**2**	**1**	**0**
10	5	2	3
−9	−3	−2	−2
1	**2**	**0**	**1**
7	9	11	6
−6	−9	−8	−4
1	**0**	**3**	**2**
8	0	5	7
−5	−0	−4	−5
3	**0**	**1**	**2**
3	8	6	5
−1	−8	−5	−2
2	**0**	**1**	**3**

9 − 8 = **1**	4 − 1 = **3**
1 − 0 = **1**	2 − 0 = **2**
4 − 2 = **2**	6 − 3 = **3**
5 − 5 = **0**	7 − 7 = **0**
8 − 7 = **1**	10 − 7 = **3**
2 − 1 = **1**	7 − 4 = **3**
3 − 0 = **3**	12 − 9 = **3**
1 − 1 = **0**	9 − 7 = **2**

Score: ____________

Circle any problems that you still find difficult to remember. Make your own flash cards to help you master these problems.

FINISH

40

Name ____________

Timed Test

3	6	11	2	11	4	3	6
−1	−6	−8	−0	−9	−3	−0	−5
2	**0**	**3**	**2**	**2**	**1**	**3**	**1**
6	2	5	6	10	1	5	9
−3	−2	−3	−4	−8	−0	−2	−8
3	**0**	**2**	**2**	**2**	**1**	**3**	**1**
9	0	4	9	12	5	4	10
−6	−0	−4	−9	−9	−5	−2	−9
3	**0**	**0**	**0**	**3**	**0**	**2**	**1**
7	3	8	8	4	7	7	2
−5	−2	−6	−7	−1	−7	−4	−1
2	**1**	**2**	**1**	**3**	**0**	**3**	**1**
5	8	3	9	8	10	1	7
−4	−5	−3	−7	−8	−7	−1	−6
1	**3**	**0**	**2**	**0**	**3**	**0**	**1**

Score: ________ Time: ________ minutes ________ seconds

41

Name ____________

Timed Test

8 − 7 = **1**	2 − 0 = **2**
1 − 0 = **1**	3 − 3 = **0**
7 − 4 = **3**	6 − 4 = **2**
5 − 4 = **1**	10 − 9 = **1**
1 − 1 = **0**	4 − 2 = **2**
7 − 5 = **2**	5 − 5 = **0**
3 − 0 = **3**	9 − 7 = **2**
11 − 9 = **2**	8 − 5 = **3**
3 − 2 = **1**	10 − 7 = **3**
12 − 9 = **3**	7 − 7 = **0**

11	7	4	6
−8	−6	−4	−3
3	**1**	**0**	**3**
6	4	8	5
−5	−1	−8	−2
1	**3**	**0**	**3**
2	8	0	9
−1	−6	−0	−6
1	**2**	**0**	**3**
3	9	10	2
−1	−9	−8	−2
2	**0**	**2**	**0**
5	4	9	6
−3	−3	−8	−6
2	**1**	**1**	**0**

Score: ________ Time: ________ minutes ________ seconds

42

Name ____________

Subtracting Zero

Knowing that zero is the identity element of subtraction helps you to know three of the facts in this new group. Just remember that zero subtracted from any number is that number.

Example: 5 − 0 = 5

■ Draw X's in these boxes to show this is true.

[XXXXX] − [ ] = [XXXXX]

5 − 0 = 5

■ Complete this T by subtracting zero from each number.

	−0
4	**4**
5	**5**
6	**6**

■ Now, write the answers for these facts.

6 − 0 = **6** 4 − 0 = **4**

5 − 0 = **5**

5	4	6
−0	−0	−0
5	**4**	**6**

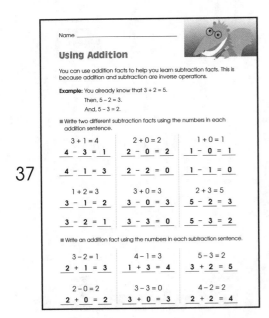

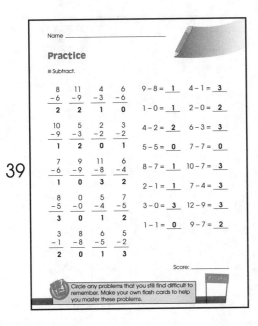

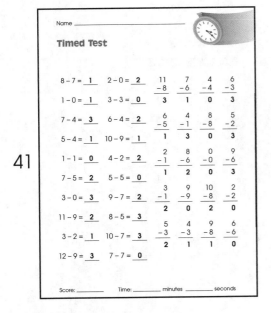

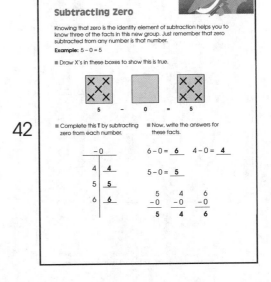

43

Name ______________________

Using Addition

You already have learned that addition and subtraction are opposite operations.

Example: If 1 + 4 = 5, then, 5 – 4 = 1. And, 5 – 1 = 4.

Notice that the sum in an addition fact becomes the minuend in a related subtraction fact.

Example: 1 + 4 = 5   5 – 4 = 1

■ Write two different subtraction facts using the numbers in each addition sentence.

6 + 2 = 8	5 + 3 = 8	5 + 1 = 6
8 – **2** = **6**	**8** – **5** = **3**	**6** – **5** = **1**
8 – **6** = **2**	**8** – **3** = **5**	**6** – **1** = **5**
5 + 2 = 7	3 + 6 = 9	5 + 4 = 9
7 – **2** = **5**	**9** – **3** = **6**	**9** – **5** = **4**
7 – **5** = **2**	**9** – **6** = **3**	**9** – **4** = **5**
3 + 4 = 7	4 + 2 = 6	6 + 1 = 7
7 – **3** = **4**	**6** – **4** = **2**	**7** – **6** = **1**
7 – **4** = **3**	**6** – **2** = **4**	**7** – **1** = **6**

44

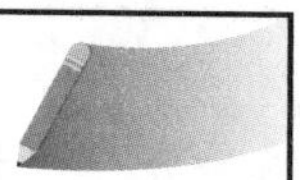

Name ______________________

Practice

■ Subtract.

5 – 0 = **5**	13 – 9 = **4**	7 – 3 = **4**	15 – 9 = **6**	12 – 7 = **5**	12 – 6 = **6**	6 – 2 = **4**	11 – 6 = **5**	9 – 3 = **6**
10 – 6 = **4**	7 – 2 = **5**	6 – 0 = **6**	13 – 7 = **6**	4 – 0 = **4**	9 – 4 = **5**	8 – 2 = **6**	13 – 8 = **5**	5 – 1 = **4**
12 – 8 = **4**	6 – 1 = **5**	10 – 5 = **5**	14 – 9 = **5**	11 – 7 = **4**	14 – 8 = **6**	10 – 4 = **6**	11 – 5 = **6**	8 – 4 = **4**
7 – 1 = **6**	9 – 5 = **4**	8 – 3 = **5**	9 – 4 = **5**	7 – 0 = **7**	15 – 9 = **6**	8 – 4 = **4**	13 – 9 = **4**	11 – 6 = **5**

Score: __________

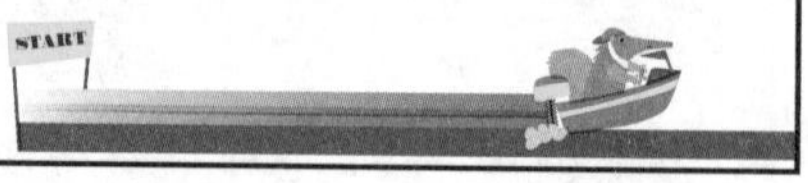

45

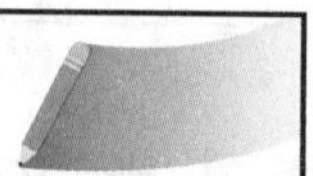

Name ______________________

Practice

■ Subtract.

12 – 7 = **5**	10 – 6 = **4**	7 – 2 = **5**	9 – 3 = **6**
6 – 2 = **4**	5 – 0 = **5**	7 – 3 = **4**	7 – 1 = **6**
11 – 6 = **5**	8 – 2 = **6**	11 – 7 = **4**	12 – 6 = **6**
8 – 3 = **5**	14 – 8 = **6**	4 – 0 = **4**	9 – 4 = **5**
13 – 7 = **6**	8 – 2 = **6**	9 – 5 = **4**	11 – 5 = **6**

5 – 1 = **4**   6 – 1 = **5**
13 – 8 = **5**   15 – 9 = **6**
8 – 4 = **4**   10 – 5 = **5**
6 – 0 = **6**   14 – 9 = **5**
10 – 4 = **6**   12 – 8 = **4**
13 – 9 = **4**   14 – 8 = **6**
11 – 5 = **6**   7 – 1 = **6**
9 – 4 = **5**   13 – 6 = **7**

Score: __________

46

Name ______________________

Timed Test

■ Complete these facts as accurately and as quickly as you can.

5 – 1 = **4**	6 – 1 = **5**	14 – 9 = **5**	9 – 5 = **4**	7 – 2 = **5**	13 – 9 = **4**	6 – 0 = **6**	15 – 9 = **6**
11 – 7 = **4**	9 – 3 = **6**	10 – 5 = **5**	8 – 2 = **6**	12 – 7 = **5**	10 – 6 = **4**	4 – 0 = **4**	13 – 7 = **6**
9 – 4 = **5**	7 – 3 = **4**	8 – 3 = **5**	12 – 8 = **4**	11 – 5 = **6**	5 – 0 = **5**	12 – 6 = **6**	6 – 2 = **4**
8 – 4 = **4**	7 – 1 = **6**	10 – 4 = **6**	11 – 6 = **5**	14 – 8 = **6**	13 – 8 = **5**	6 – 1 = **5**	9 – 3 = **6**
12 – 8 = **4**	14 – 9 = **5**	11 – 7 = **4**	8 – 2 = **6**	6 – 2 = **4**	5 – 0 = **5**	12 – 7 = **5**	10 – 5 = **5**

Score: ________ Time: ________ minutes ________ seconds

47

Name ______________________

Timed Test

9 – 5 = **4**   11 – 7 = **4**
11 – 5 = **6**   14 – 9 = **5**
6 – 2 = **4**   10 – 5 = **5**
13 – 8 = **5**   14 – 8 = **6**
8 – 3 = **5**   5 – 1 = **4**
6 – 0 = **6**   15 – 9 = **6**
12 – 8 = **4**   4 – 0 = **4**
8 – 2 = **6**   7 – 2 = **5**
5 – 0 = **5**   12 – 7 = **5**
9 – 3 = **6**   8 – 4 = **4**

15 – 9 = **6**	4 – 0 = **4**	7 – 2 = **5**	12 – 7 = **5**
8 – 4 = **4**	6 – 1 = **5**	13 – 9 = **4**	11 – 6 = **5**
7 – 3 = **4**	7 – 1 = **6**	9 – 4 = **5**	10 – 6 = **4**
13 – 7 = **6**	10 – 4 = **6**	12 – 6 = **6**	9 – 5 = **4**
6 – 2 = **4**	8 – 3 = **5**	10 – 5 = **5**	11 – 7 = **4**

Score: ________ Time: ________ minutes ________ seconds

48

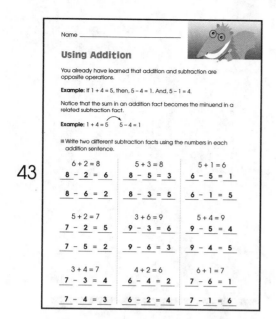

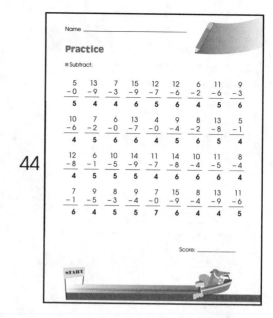

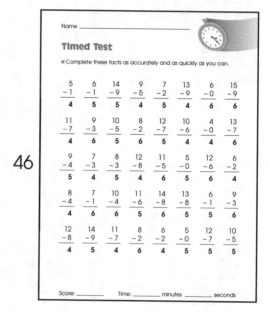

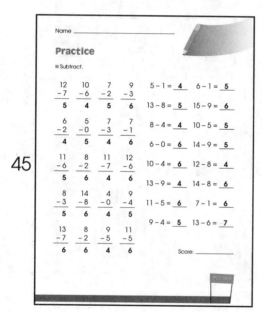

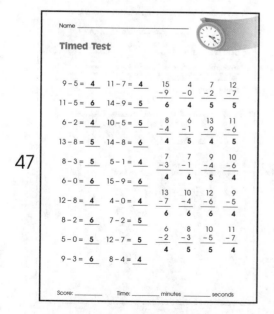

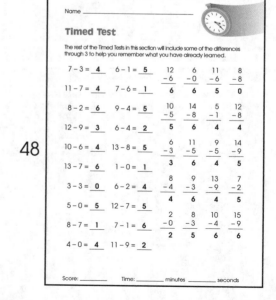

Name ______________________

Timed Test

The rest of the Timed Tests in this section will include some of the differences through 3 to help you remember what you have already learned.

7 – 3 = **4**   6 – 1 = **5**
11 – 7 = **4**   7 – 6 = **1**
8 – 2 = **6**   9 – 4 = **5**
12 – 9 = **3**   6 – 4 = **2**
10 – 6 = **4**   13 – 8 = **5**
13 – 7 = **6**   1 – 0 = **1**
3 – 3 = **0**   6 – 2 = **4**
5 – 0 = **5**   12 – 7 = **5**
8 – 7 = **1**   7 – 1 = **6**
4 – 0 = **4**   11 – 9 = **2**

12 – 6 = **6**	6 – 0 = **6**	11 – 6 = **5**	8 – 8 = **0**
10 – 5 = **5**	14 – 8 = **6**	5 – 1 = **4**	12 – 8 = **4**
6 – 3 = **3**	11 – 5 = **6**	9 – 5 = **4**	14 – 9 = **5**
8 – 4 = **4**	9 – 3 = **6**	13 – 9 = **4**	7 – 2 = **5**
2 – 0 = **2**	8 – 3 = **5**	10 – 4 = **6**	15 – 9 = **6**

Score: ________ Time: ________ minutes ________ seconds

49

Name ____________________

Counting Back

Remember: You can count back to find the difference when the subtrahend is a lesser number like 1, 2, or 3.

Example: 10 – 1 = 9

0 1 2 3 4 5 6 7 8 9 10 11 12

■ Complete these T's by subtracting the numbers at the top from those along the side. You may use the number line to help you count.

– 1		– 2		– 3	
10	9	11	9	10	7
9	8	9	7	12	9
8	7	10	8	11	8

■ Subtract.

9 – 2 = 7 11 – 3 = 8

10 – 3 = 7 8 – 1 = 7

11 – 2 = 9 12 – 3 = 9

8	10	11
– 1	– 2	– 3
7	8	8
10	12	9
– 1	– 3	– 1
9	9	8

50

Name ____________________

Using Addition

Use the higher addition facts and what you know about opposite operations to help you discover the higher subtraction facts.

Example: If 9 + 6 = 15, then, 15 – 9 = 6. And, 15 – 6 = 9.

■ Write two different subtraction problems for each addition sentence.

7 + 6 = 13	9 + 4 = 13	7 + 8 = 15
13 – 7 = 6	13 – 9 = 4	15 – 7 = 8
13 – 6 = 7	13 – 4 = 9	15 – 8 = 7
9 + 6 = 15	7 + 4 = 11	9 + 4 = 13
15 – 9 = 6	11 – 7 = 4	13 – 9 = 4
15 – 6 = 9	11 – 4 = 7	13 – 4 = 9
5 + 7 = 12	9 + 8 = 17	9 + 7 = 16
12 – 5 = 7	17 – 9 = 8	16 – 9 = 7
12 – 7 = 5	17 – 8 = 9	16 – 7 = 9

■ Write one subtraction fact related to each addition sentence.

7 + 7 = 14	8 + 8 = 16	9 + 9 = 18
14 – 7 = 7	16 – 8 = 8	18 – 9 = 9

51

Name ____________________

Practice

■ Subtract.

12	15	12	8
– 5	– 7	– 4	– 1
7	8	8	7
13	11	16	13
– 4	– 3	– 7	– 6
9	8	9	7
16	18	10	9
– 8	– 9	– 1	– 2
8	9	9	7
8	12	16	14
– 0	– 3	– 9	– 6
8	9	7	8
14	9	15	11
– 5	– 0	– 8	– 2
9	9	7	9

14 – 6 = 8 17 – 9 = 8

11 – 4 = 7 10 – 2 = 8

13 – 5 = 8 15 – 8 = 7

15 – 6 = 9 11 – 2 = 9

14 – 7 = 7 17 – 8 = 9

9 – 1 = 8 12 – 5 = 7

7 – 0 = 7 15 – 7 = 8

10 – 3 = 7 8 – 1 = 7

Score: __________

FINISH

52

Name ____________________

Practice

■ Subtract.

7	13	12	16
– 0	– 4	– 4	– 8
7	9	8	8
11	9	16	15
– 4	– 0	– 9	– 7
7	9	7	8
18	9	12	13
– 9	– 2	– 3	– 6
9	7	9	7
15	10	14	12
– 6	– 2	– 6	– 5
9	8	8	7
10	14	11	13
– 3	– 7	– 2	– 5
7	7	9	8

8 – 1 = 7 11 – 2 = 9

14 – 5 = 9 13 – 5 = 8

11 – 3 = 8 10 – 1 = 9

17 – 8 = 9 15 – 8 = 7

12 – 5 = 7 16 – 7 = 9

8 – 0 = 8 9 – 2 = 7

17 – 9 = 8 11 – 4 = 7

9 – 1 = 8 13 – 6 = 7

Score: __________

Circle any problems that you still find difficult to remember. Make your own flash cards to help you master these problems.

FINISH

53

Name ____________________

Timed Test

12	13	13	16	14	9	16	18
– 4	– 6	– 5	– 9	– 5	– 2	– 7	– 9
8	7	8	7	9	7	9	9
9	10	17	15	8	11	17	15
– 1	– 3	– 8	– 6	– 1	– 4	– 9	– 8
8	7	9	9	7	7	8	7
13	11	16	12	15	14	9	14
– 4	– 3	– 8	– 5	– 7	– 6	– 0	– 7
9	8	8	7	8	8	9	7
10	12	10	8	7	11	13	15
– 2	– 3	– 1	– 0	– 0	– 2	– 5	– 7
8	9	9	8	7	9	8	8
16	11	16	8	12	14	9	17
– 8	– 4	– 9	– 1	– 4	– 6	– 2	– 8
8	7	7	7	8	8	7	9

Score: ________ Time: ________ minutes ________ seconds

54

Name ____________________

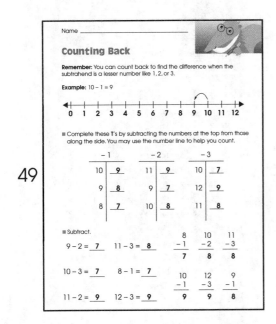

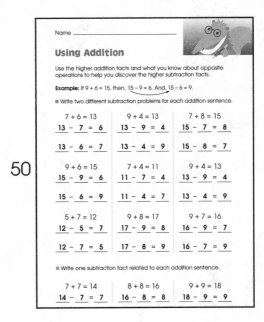

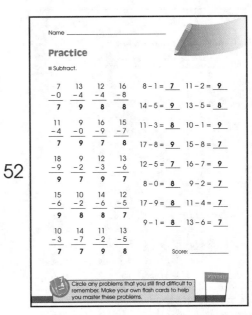

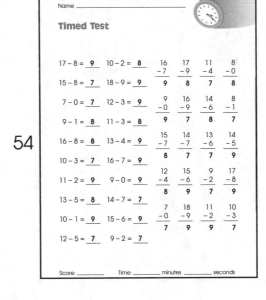

Timed Test

17 – 8 = 9 10 – 2 = 8

15 – 8 = 7 18 – 9 = 9

7 – 0 = 7 12 – 3 = 9

9 – 1 = 8 11 – 3 = 8

16 – 8 = 8 13 – 4 = 9

10 – 3 = 7 16 – 7 = 9

11 – 2 = 9 9 – 0 = 9

13 – 5 = 8 14 – 7 = 7

10 – 1 = 9 15 – 6 = 9

12 – 5 = 7 9 – 2 = 7

16	17	11	8
– 7	– 9	– 4	– 0
9	8	7	8
9	16	14	8
– 0	– 9	– 6	– 1
9	7	8	7
15	14	13	14
– 7	– 7	– 6	– 5
8	7	7	9
12	15	9	17
– 4	– 6	– 2	– 8
8	9	7	9
7	18	11	10
– 0	– 9	– 2	– 3
7	9	9	7

Score: ________ Time: ________ minutes ________ seconds

55

Name ______________________

Timed Test

12 − 5 = **7**	14 − 6 = **8**
16 − 7 = **9**	10 − 1 = **9**
9 − 2 = **7**	8 − 1 = **7**
11 − 2 = **9**	7 − 0 = **7**
13 − 5 = **8**	15 − 8 = **7**
9 − 1 = **8**	12 − 4 = **8**
14 − 5 = **9**	11 − 3 = **8**
13 − 6 = **7**	18 − 9 = **9**
9 − 0 = **9**	15 − 7 = **8**
10 − 2 = **8**	16 − 8 = **8**

17 − 8 = **9**	12 − 4 = **8**	15 − 6 = **9**	14 − 7 = **7**
13 − 4 = **9**	11 − 3 = **8**	18 − 9 = **9**	10 − 3 = **7**
15 − 7 = **8**	8 − 0 = **8**	12 − 3 = **9**	16 − 8 = **8**
16 − 9 = **7**	11 − 4 = **7**	17 − 9 = **8**	12 − 5 = **7**
14 − 5 = **9**	8 − 1 = **7**	10 − 2 = **8**	13 − 6 = **7**

Score: ________ Time: ________ minutes ________ seconds

56

Name ______________________

All-Addition Review

■ Here are 60 addition facts. Prove to yourself that you are an expert in addition. Concentrate on accuracy.

8 + 2 = **10**	1 + 8 = **9**	4 + 1 = **5**	7 + 8 = **15**
6 + 8 = **14**	5 + 9 = **14**	8 + 0 = **8**	3 + 9 = **12**
0 + 7 = **7**	7 + 4 = **11**	2 + 5 = **7**	4 + 9 = **13**
4 + 5 = **9**	9 + 6 = **15**	5 + 7 = **12**	7 + 1 = **8**
7 + 2 = **9**	9 + 5 = **14**	6 + 3 = **9**	4 + 4 = **8**
3 + 6 = **9**	1 + 7 = **8**	8 + 7 = **15**	3 + 5 = **8**
6 + 7 = **13**	5 + 2 = **7**	6 + 9 = **15**	5 + 0 = **5**
2 + 4 = **6**	9 + 8 = **17**	4 + 7 = **11**	1 + 2 = **3**
4 + 0 = **4**	5 + 8 = **13**	6 + 2 = **8**	4 + 8 = **12**
1 + 5 = **6**	5 + 6 = **11**	2 + 8 = **10**	2 + 7 = **9**
9 + 0 = **9**	2 + 6 = **8**	7 + 5 = **12**	5 + 3 = **8**
3 + 2 = **5**	2 + 3 = **5**	8 + 9 = **17**	7 + 6 = **13**
8 + 8 = **16**	7 + 7 = **14**	9 + 7 = **16**	8 + 1 = **9**
7 + 3 = **10**	3 + 4 = **7**	9 + 9 = **18**	4 + 2 = **6**
4 + 6 = **10**	1 + 6 = **7**	8 + 3 = **11**	9 + 1 = **10**

57

Name ______________________

All-Subtraction Review

■ Here are 60 subtraction facts. Prove to yourself that you are also an expert in subtraction. Concentrate on accuracy.

4 − 0 = **4**	16 − 9 = **7**	13 − 6 = **7**	7 − 3 = **4**
11 − 4 = **7**	17 − 9 = **8**	15 − 9 = **6**	2 − 1 = **1**
9 − 3 = **6**	2 − 2 = **0**	16 − 7 = **9**	13 − 4 = **9**
4 − 3 = **1**	14 − 5 = **9**	9 − 5 = **4**	6 − 2 = **4**
8 − 2 = **6**	10 − 7 = **3**	5 − 3 = **2**	9 − 6 = **3**
10 − 5 = **5**	5 − 5 = **0**	9 − 4 = **5**	11 − 3 = **8**
14 − 9 = **5**	9 − 2 = **7**	6 − 5 = **1**	12 − 7 = **5**
5 − 4 = **1**	13 − 5 = **8**	8 − 3 = **5**	9 − 7 = **2**
11 − 5 = **6**	12 − 6 = **6**	14 − 6 = **8**	12 − 3 = **9**
12 − 9 = **3**	15 − 6 = **9**	18 − 9 = **9**	12 − 8 = **4**
4 − 2 = **2**	12 − 4 = **8**	5 − 2 = **3**	11 − 2 = **9**
6 − 6 = **0**	16 − 8 = **8**	13 − 8 = **5**	5 − 1 = **4**
8 − 4 = **4**	14 − 7 = **7**	15 − 7 = **8**	14 − 8 = **6**
11 − 7 = **4**	13 − 9 = **4**	10 − 8 = **2**	12 − 5 = **7**
9 − 8 = **1**	11 − 6 = **5**	11 − 9 = **2**	13 − 7 = **6**

59

Name ______________________

What Is Multiplication?

You multiply to find how many there are in all in groups that are equal. The answer is called the **product**.

5 plums + 5 plums + 5 plums

Here are two ways to show the multiplication. You read the problem this way: **3 times 5 equals 15.**

3 x 5 = 15

$$\begin{array}{r} 3 \\ \times 5 \\ \hline 15 \end{array}$$

You can draw a picture to find a product.

Example: Find the answer. 4 x 2 = ____

Step 1: Draw 4 sets of 2 dots. ●● ●● ●● ●●

Step 2: Count all the dots.

Answer: 4 x 2 = 8

■ Draw a picture to find the product.

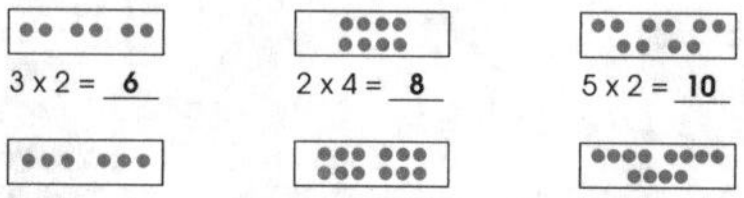

3 x 2 = **6**

2 x 4 = **8**

5 x 2 = **10**

2 x 3 = **6**

4 x 3 = **12**

3 x 4 = **12**

60

Name ______________________

What Is Multiplication?

You can use grid paper to find the product.

Example: Find the product. 4 x 5 = ____

Step 1: Draw a rectangle 5 units long and 4 units wide.

Step 2: Count the squares inside the rectangle.

Answer: 4 x 5 = 20

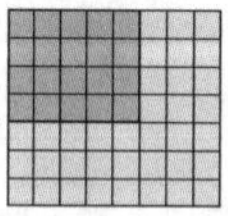

■ Use grid paper to find the product.

3 x 3 = **9** 2 x 5 = **10** 4 x 4 = **16**

3 x 5 = **15**	2 x 2 = **4**	6 x 2 = **12**	3 x 4 = **12**	6 x 3 = **18**

You can use a number line to find the product.

0 1 2 3 4 5 6 7 8 9 10 11 12 13 14 15 16 17

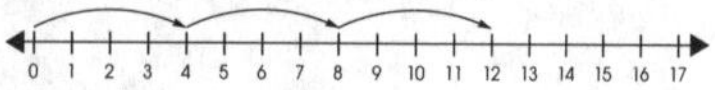

Example: Find the product. 3 x 4 = ____

Step 1: Put your finger on 0.

Step 2: Make 3 moves to the right of 4 spaces each.

Step 3: Read the number your finger is on.

Answer: 3 x 4 = 12

■ Use the number line to find the product.

3 x 3 = **9** 2 x 5 = **10** 4 x 4 = **16**

4 x 2 = **8**	3 x 4 = **12**	3 x 2 = **6**	2 x 6 = **12**	3 x 5 = **15**

61

Name ______________________

Products Through Nine

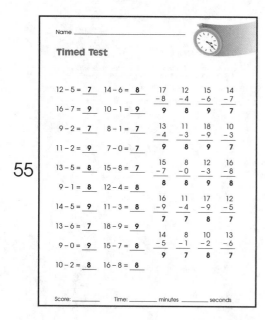

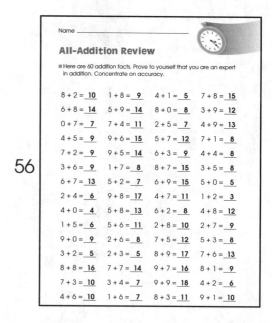

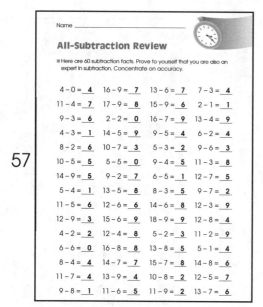

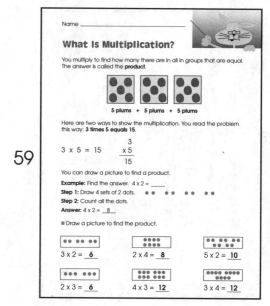

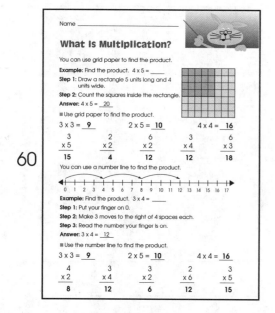

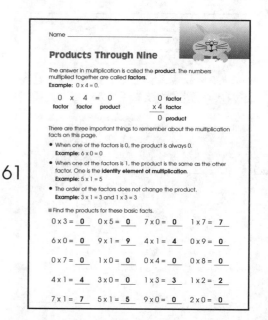

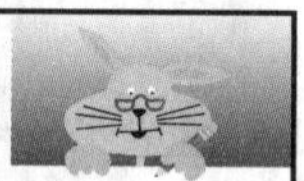

The answer in multiplication is called the **product**. The numbers multiplied together are called **factors**.

Example: 0 x 4 = 0.

0 x 4 = 0
factor factor product

$$\begin{array}{rl} 0 & \text{factor} \\ \times 4 & \text{factor} \\ \hline 0 & \text{product} \end{array}$$

There are three important things to remember about the multiplication facts on this page.

- When one of the factors is 0, the product is always 0.
  Example: 6 x 0 = 0
- When one of the factors is 1, the product is the same as the other factor. One is the **identity element of multiplication**.
  Example: 5 x 1 = 5
- The order of the factors does not change the product.
  Example: 3 x 1 = 3 and 1 x 3 = 3

■ Find the products for these basic facts.

0 x 3 = **0**	0 x 5 = **0**	7 x 0 = **0**	1 x 7 = **7**
6 x 0 = **0**	9 x 1 = **9**	4 x 1 = **4**	0 x 9 = **0**
0 x 7 = **0**	1 x 0 = **0**	0 x 4 = **0**	0 x 8 = **0**
4 x 1 = **4**	3 x 0 = **0**	1 x 3 = **3**	1 x 2 = **2**
7 x 1 = **7**	5 x 1 = **5**	9 x 0 = **0**	2 x 0 = **0**

62

Name ______________

Practice

■ Multiply.

0	1	2	4	9	5	0	1	0
x 0	x 2	x 0	x 1	x 0	x 1	x 3	x 9	x 5
0	**2**	**0**	**4**	**0**	**5**	**0**	**9**	**0**
1	5	1	0	9	7	1	0	0
x 1	x 0	x 8	x 7	x 1	x 1	x 7	x 9	x 8
1	**0**	**8**	**0**	**9**	**7**	**7**	**0**	**0**
4	8	1	1	3	1	3	0	0
x 0	x 0	x 4	x 0	x 1	x 3	x 0	x 1	x 4
0	**0**	**4**	**0**	**3**	**3**	**0**	**0**	**0**
2	6	8	1	0	6	7	0	1
x 1	x 0	x 1	x 5	x 6	x 1	x 0	x 2	x 6
2	**0**	**8**	**5**	**0**	**6**	**0**	**0**	**6**

Score: ______________

Circle any problems that you still find difficult to remember. Make your own flash cards to help you master these problems.

63

Name ______________

Timed Test

■ Improve your speed on these basic multiplication facts. Ask someone to time you. Record your time and score below and on page 150.

1 x 0 = **0** 2 x 1 = **2**
1 x 4 = **4** 0 x 4 = **0**
0 x 2 = **0** 7 x 1 = **7**
6 x 0 = **0** 9 x 0 = **0**
1 x 9 = **9** 0 x 5 = **0**
2 x 0 = **0** 7 x 0 = **0**
0 x 9 = **0** 1 x 7 = **7**
1 x 3 = **3** 4 x 0 = **0**
5 x 0 = **0** 1 x 5 = **5**
0 x 7 = **0** 9 x 1 = **9**

0	1	4	8
x 3	x 5	x 1	x 1
0	**5**	**4**	**8**
6	1	9	3
x 1	x 6	x 1	x 0
6	**6**	**9**	**0**
1	0	0	5
x 1	x 6	x 0	x 1
1	**0**	**0**	**5**
1	3	0	1
x 8	x 1	x 8	x 2
8	**3**	**0**	**2**
0	8	1	7
x 1	x 0	x 3	x 1
0	**0**	**3**	**7**

Score: ________ Time: ________ minutes ________ seconds

64

Name ______________

Products Through Eighteen

Remember: The answer in multiplication is called the **product**. The numbers that are multiplied together are called **factors**.

Multiplication is like addition in some ways. Like a sum, a product represents how many in all. What makes multiplication different is that one of the factors represents the number of things in a group and the other factor represents the number of groups.

Example: 2 x 4 = ?

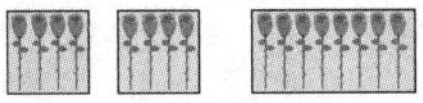

There are 2 groups of 4 roses each. Therefore, there are 8 roses in all.

2 x 4 = 8

Notice that the product is the same if you think of the problem as 4 groups of 2 roses each.

Notice that the product of 2 and another factor is always an even number, such as 0, 2, 4, 6, 8, 10, 12, 14, 16, or 18. These numbers are the first ten multiples of 2. They are the same as the products of 2 times any number from 0 through 9.

■ Complete these T's by multiplying the numbers by 2.

x 2		x 2		x 2		x 2		x 2	
4	**8**	5	**10**	9	**18**	0	**0**	2	**4**
1	**2**	3	**6**	7	**14**	6	**12**	8	**16**

65

Name ______________

Practice

■ Multiply.

2	4	2	6
x 3	x 2	x 0	x 2
6	**8**	**0**	**12**
2	2	2	7
x 1	x 6	x 4	x 2
2	**12**	**8**	**14**
2	0	9	1
x 7	x 2	x 2	x 2
14	**0**	**18**	**2**
5	2	2	2
x 2	x 9	x 8	x 3
10	**18**	**16**	**6**
1	2	3	2
x 2	x 6	x 2	x 9
2	**12**	**6**	**18**

2 x 5 = **10** 4 x 2 = **8**
9 x 2 = **18** 2 x 0 = **0**
3 x 2 = **6** 6 x 2 = **12**
0 x 2 = **0** 2 x 7 = **14**
2 x 1 = **2** 5 x 2 = **10**
2 x 9 = **18** 2 x 4 = **8**
8 x 2 = **16** 7 x 2 = **14**
2 x 3 = **6** 2 x 8 = **16**

Score: ______________

Circle any problems that you still find difficult to remember. Make your own flash cards to help you master these problems.

66

Name ______________

Timed Test

■ Complete these facts as accurately and as quickly as you can.

2 x 7 = **14** 3 x 2 = **6**
2 x 5 = **10** 9 x 2 = **18**
0 x 2 = **0** 2 x 0 = **0**
2 x 1 = **2** 5 x 2 = **10**
6 x 2 = **12** 2 x 3 = **6**
2 x 6 = **12** 2 x 8 = **16**
3 x 2 = **6** 9 x 2 = **18**
7 x 2 = **14** 4 x 2 = **8**
1 x 2 = **2** 2 x 2 = **4**
2 x 4 = **8** 2 x 9 = **18**

2	0	7	2
x 0	x 2	x 2	x 3
0	**0**	**14**	**6**
6	1	2	2
x 2	x 2	x 9	x 5
12	**2**	**18**	**10**
2	2	3	2
x 4	x 8	x 2	x 1
8	**16**	**6**	**2**
9	5	2	4
x 2	x 2	x 6	x 2
18	**10**	**12**	**8**
2	2	7	2
x 7	x 5	x 2	x 2
14	**10**	**14**	**4**

Score: ________ Time: ________ minutes ________ seconds

67

Name ______________

Products Through Twenty-Seven

When you multiply a number by 3, you triple that number. It is the same as adding that number three times.

Example: 3 x 4 = ?

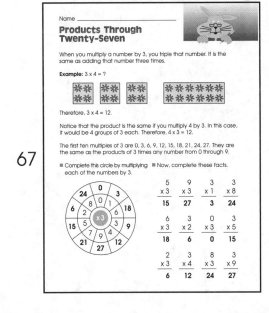

Therefore, 3 x 4 = 12.

Notice that the product is the same if you multiply 4 by 3. In this case, it would be 4 groups of 3 each. Therefore, 4 x 3 = 12.

The first ten multiples of 3 are 0, 3, 6, 9, 12, 15, 18, 21, 24, 27. They are the same as the products of 3 times any number from 0 through 9.

■ Complete this circle by multiplying each of the numbers by 3.

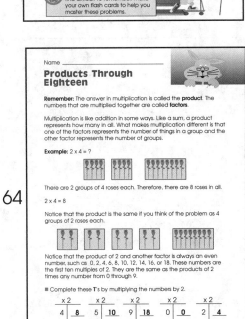

■ Now, complete these facts.

5	9	3	3
x 3	x 3	x 1	x 8
15	**27**	**3**	**24**
6	3	0	3
x 3	x 2	x 3	x 5
18	**6**	**0**	**15**
2	3	8	3
x 3	x 4	x 3	x 9
6	**12**	**24**	**27**

68

Name ______

Practice

■ Multiply.

3 x 3 **9**	3 x 0 **0**	5 x 3 **15**	3 x 2 **6**
9 x 3 **27**	3 x 6 **18**	2 x 3 **6**	3 x 7 **21**
3 x 4 **12**	8 x 3 **24**	1 x 3 **3**	3 x 9 **27**
6 x 3 **18**	4 x 3 **12**	3 x 5 **15**	7 x 3 **21**
0 x 3 **0**	2 x 3 **6**	3 x 1 **3**	3 x 8 **24**

3 x 0 = **0**	6 x 3 = **18**
0 x 3 = **0**	3 x 1 = **3**
3 x 8 = **24**	3 x 5 = **15**
3 x 7 = **21**	4 x 3 = **12**
8 x 3 = **24**	9 x 3 = **27**
3 x 4 = **12**	3 x 2 = **6**
1 x 3 = **3**	5 x 3 = **15**
7 x 3 = **21**	3 x 3 = **9**

Score: ______

Circle any problems that you still find difficult to remember. Make your own flash cards to help you master these problems.

69

Name ______

Timed Test

■ Complete these facts as accurately and as quickly as you can.

3 x 6 = **18**	3 x 3 = **9**
3 x 5 = **15**	3 x 1 = **3**
0 x 3 = **0**	3 x 4 = **12**
3 x 2 = **6**	1 x 3 = **3**
3 x 0 = **0**	3 x 9 = **27**
6 x 3 = **18**	2 x 3 = **6**
3 x 8 = **24**	3 x 3 = **9**
9 x 3 = **27**	8 x 3 = **24**
3 x 7 = **21**	4 x 3 = **12**
5 x 3 = **15**	3 x 1 = **3**

3 x 8 **24**	5 x 3 **15**	4 x 3 **12**	0 x 3 **0**
3 x 1 **3**	1 x 3 **3**	3 x 4 **12**	6 x 3 **18**
3 x 6 **18**	7 x 3 **21**	3 x 0 **0**	9 x 3 **27**
2 x 3 **6**	3 x 3 **9**	8 x 3 **24**	3 x 7 **21**
3 x 5 **15**	3 x 2 **6**	3 x 9 **27**	3 x 6 **18**

Score: ______ Time: ______ minutes ______ seconds

70

Name ______

Products Through Thirty-Six

The first ten multiples of 4 are 0, 4, 8, 12, 16, 20, 24, 28, 32, and 36. They are the same as the products of 4 times any number from 0 through 9.

Example: 4 x 5 = ?

Remember to think of one of the factors as the number of groups in all and the other as the number of objects in one group.

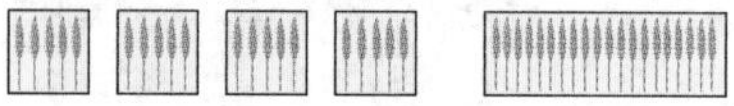

Therefore, 4 x 5 = 20.

■ Complete these T's by multiplying each of the numbers by 4.

	x 4
6	**24**
9	**36**
0	**0**
8	**32**
4	**16**

	x 4
2	**8**
7	**28**
1	**4**
3	**12**
5	**20**

■ Now, complete these facts.

4 x 9 = **36**	4 x 7 = **28**
3 x 4 = **12**	2 x 4 = **8**
4 x 2 = **8**	4 x 3 = **12**
8 x 4 = **32**	4 x 0 = **0**
1 x 4 = **4**	5 x 4 = **20**
6 x 4 = **24**	0 x 4 = **0**
4 x 1 = **4**	4 x 6 = **24**

71

Name ______

Practice

■ Multiply.

4 x 2 **8**	4 x 6 **24**	4 x 0 **0**	9 x 4 **36**
3 x 4 **12**	4 x 5 **20**	8 x 4 **32**	4 x 3 **12**
0 x 4 **0**	5 x 4 **20**	7 x 4 **28**	1 x 4 **4**
4 x 8 **32**	4 x 1 **4**	6 x 4 **24**	2 x 4 **8**
9 x 4 **36**	4 x 6 **24**	4 x 7 **28**	4 x 4 **16**

4 x 1 = **4**	0 x 4 = **0**
5 x 4 = **20**	4 x 3 = **12**
4 x 6 = **24**	7 x 4 = **28**
3 x 4 = **12**	1 x 4 = **4**
4 x 4 = **16**	4 x 5 = **20**
6 x 4 = **24**	4 x 8 = **32**
9 x 4 = **36**	8 x 4 = **32**
2 x 4 = **8**	4 x 0 = **0**

Score: ______

Circle any problems that you still find difficult to remember. Make your own flash cards to help you master these problems.

72

Name ______

Timed Test

■ Complete these facts as accurately and as quickly as you can.

4 x 4 = **16**	4 x 5 = **20**
2 x 4 = **8**	5 x 4 = **20**
4 x 8 = **32**	8 x 4 = **32**
0 x 4 = **0**	4 x 0 = **0**
4 x 3 = **12**	4 x 2 = **8**
3 x 4 = **12**	4 x 6 = **24**
6 x 4 = **24**	7 x 4 = **28**
1 x 4 = **4**	9 x 4 = **36**
4 x 7 = **28**	4 x 5 = **20**
4 x 9 = **36**	4 x 1 = **4**

4 x 5 **20**	8 x 4 **32**	9 x 4 **36**	4 x 3 **12**
4 x 4 **16**	7 x 4 **28**	0 x 4 **0**	4 x 1 **4**
4 x 6 **24**	4 x 0 **0**	4 x 9 **36**	5 x 4 **20**
4 x 2 **8**	4 x 8 **32**	1 x 4 **4**	6 x 4 **24**
9 x 4 **36**	3 x 4 **12**	4 x 7 **28**	2 x 4 **8**

Score: ______ Time: ______ minutes ______ seconds

73

Name ______

Products Through Forty-Five

The first ten multiples of 5 are 0, 5, 10, 15, 20, 25, 30, 35, 40, and 45. They are the same as the products of 5 times any number from 0 through 9.

Example: 5 x 3 = ?

Therefore, 5 x 3 = 15.

Remember, 3 x 5 is also 15.

Notice that when one of the factors is 5, the product always ends in a 5 or 0.

■ Complete this circle by multiplying each of the numbers by 5.

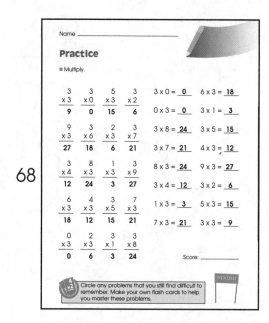

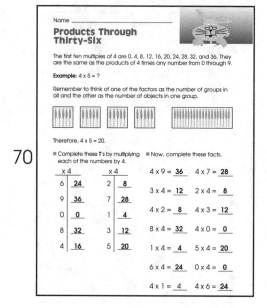

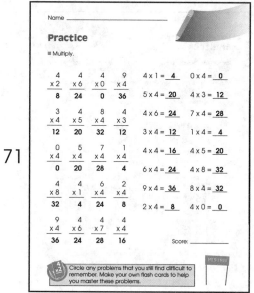

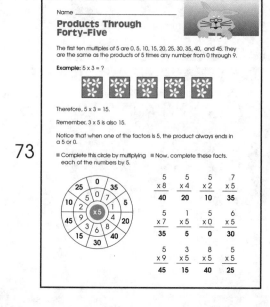

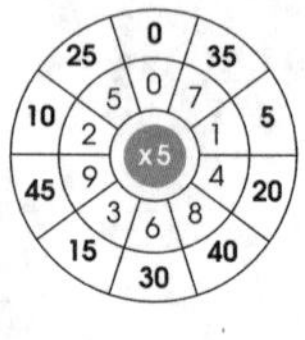

■ Now, complete these facts.

5 x 8 **40**	5 x 4 **20**	5 x 2 **10**	7 x 5 **35**
5 x 7 **35**	1 x 5 **5**	5 x 0 **0**	6 x 5 **30**
5 x 9 **45**	3 x 5 **15**	8 x 5 **40**	5 x 5 **25**

74

Name ____________

Practice

■ Multiply.

5 x 5 = 25	8 x 5 = 40	6 x 5 = 30	5 x 4 = 20
3 x 5 = 15	5 x 8 = 40	1 x 5 = 5	5 x 3 = 15
5 x 2 = 10	9 x 5 = 45	7 x 5 = 35	5 x 6 = 30
0 x 5 = 0	5 x 1 = 5	4 x 5 = 20	5 x 9 = 45
5 x 7 = 35	2 x 5 = 10	5 x 3 = 15	5 x 0 = 0

5 x 0 = 0	5 x 6 = 30
5 x 9 = 45	2 x 5 = 10
0 x 5 = 0	7 x 5 = 35
5 x 3 = 15	9 x 5 = 45
8 x 5 = 40	4 x 5 = 20
5 x 5 = 25	5 x 7 = 35
6 x 5 = 30	5 x 2 = 10
5 x 8 = 40	3 x 5 = 15

Score: ________

Circle any problems that you still find difficult to remember. Make your own flash cards to help you master these problems.

75

Name ____________

Timed Test

■ Complete these facts as accurately and as quickly as you can.

5 x 8 = 40	5 x 5 = 25
7 x 5 = 35	1 x 5 = 5
2 x 5 = 10	3 x 5 = 15
5 x 7 = 35	6 x 5 = 30
4 x 5 = 20	5 x 1 = 5
5 x 0 = 0	9 x 5 = 45
8 x 5 = 40	5 x 3 = 15
5 x 6 = 30	5 x 4 = 20
0 x 5 = 0	5 x 9 = 45
5 x 2 = 10	4 x 5 = 20

5 x 3 = 15	7 x 5 = 35	5 x 1 = 5	6 x 5 = 30
4 x 5 = 20	5 x 2 = 10	5 x 0 = 0	9 x 5 = 45
3 x 5 = 15	8 x 5 = 40	5 x 5 = 25	5 x 4 = 20
2 x 5 = 10	9 x 5 = 45	1 x 5 = 5	5 x 7 = 35
5 x 8 = 40	5 x 6 = 30	5 x 9 = 45	0 x 5 = 0

Score: ________ Time: ________ minutes ________ seconds

76

Name ____________

Products Through Fifty-Four

The first ten multiples of 6 are 0, 6, 12, 18, 24, 30, 36, 42, 48, and 54. They are the same as the products of 6 times any number from 0 through 9.

Example: 6 x 4 = ?

6 groups of 4 each

Therefore, 6 x 4 = 24.

Remember, 4 x 6 is also 24.

Notice that when you learn each set of facts, you are actually learning facts from other sets. For example, when you learned that 3 x 6 = 18, you also learned 6 x 3 = 18. This cuts down on the number of new facts you actually have to learn.

■ Complete these facts that you have already learned in which 6 is a factor.

6 x 4 = 24	6 x 0 = 0	6 x 5 = 30
6 x 2 = 12	6 x 3 = 18	6 x 1 = 6

■ Complete these T's by multiplying each of the numbers by 6.

x 6		x 6	
3	18	9	54
0	0	4	24
5	30	6	36
2	12	1	6
7	42	8	48

77

Name ____________

Practice

■ Multiply.

0 x 6 = 0	9 x 6 = 54	6 x 6 = 36	6 x 3 = 18
6 x 0 = 0	4 x 6 = 24	2 x 6 = 12	6 x 7 = 42
6 x 1 = 6	3 x 6 = 18	6 x 8 = 48	1 x 6 = 6
7 x 6 = 42	6 x 9 = 54	6 x 5 = 30	6 x 2 = 12
8 x 6 = 48	4 x 6 = 24	6 x 3 = 18	5 x 6 = 30

6 x 6 = 36	6 x 8 = 48
3 x 6 = 18	0 x 6 = 0
6 x 3 = 18	6 x 2 = 12
2 x 6 = 12	4 x 6 = 24
6 x 9 = 54	6 x 4 = 24
8 x 6 = 48	5 x 6 = 30
1 x 6 = 6	6 x 7 = 42
6 x 5 = 30	6 x 0 = 0

Score: ________

Circle any problems that you still find difficult to remember. Make your own flash cards to help you master these problems.

78

Name ____________

Timed Test

■ Complete these facts as accurately and as quickly as you can.

6 x 3 = 18	7 x 6 = 42
1 x 6 = 6	2 x 6 = 12
0 x 6 = 0	8 x 6 = 48
6 x 9 = 54	6 x 6 = 36
6 x 2 = 12	4 x 6 = 24
6 x 5 = 30	6 x 0 = 0
6 x 7 = 42	6 x 3 = 18
9 x 6 = 54	5 x 6 = 30
6 x 4 = 24	7 x 6 = 42
6 x 8 = 48	6 x 1 = 6

6 x 1 = 6	6 x 3 = 18	4 x 6 = 24	6 x 5 = 30
6 x 8 = 48	3 x 6 = 18	9 x 6 = 54	6 x 6 = 36
2 x 6 = 12	6 x 0 = 0	6 x 7 = 42	1 x 6 = 6
6 x 4 = 24	6 x 9 = 54	0 x 6 = 0	6 x 2 = 12
5 x 6 = 30	8 x 6 = 48	3 x 6 = 18	7 x 6 = 42

Score: ________ Time: ________ minutes ________ seconds

79

Name ____________

Products Through Sixty-Three

The first ten multiples of 7 are 0, 7, 14, 21, 28, 35, 42, 49, 56, and 63. They are the same as the products of 7 times any number from 0 through 9.

Example: 7 x 5 = ?

7 groups of 5 each

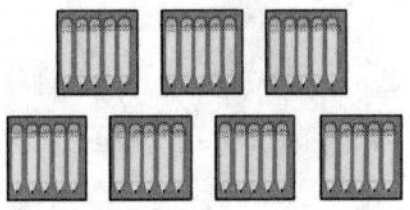

Therefore, 7 x 5 = 35.

Remember, 5 x 7 is also 35.

■ Complete these facts that you have already learned in which 7 is a factor.

3 x 7 = 21	1 x 7 = 7	5 x 7 = 35	2 x 7 = 14
0 x 7 = 0	4 x 7 = 28	6 x 7 = 42	

■ Complete this circle by multiplying each of the numbers by 7.

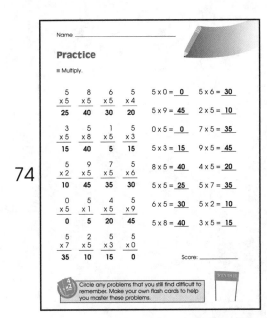

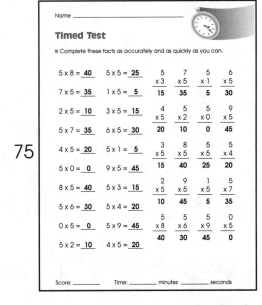

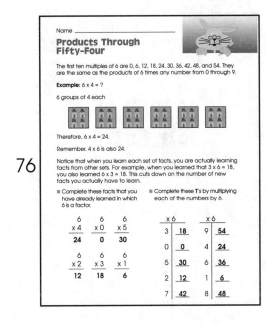

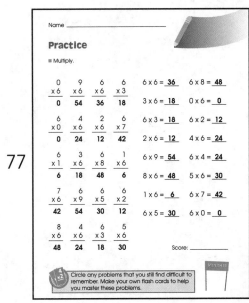

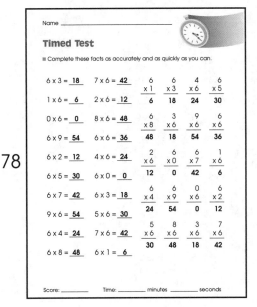

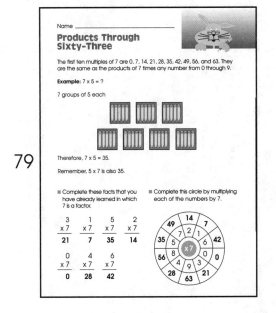

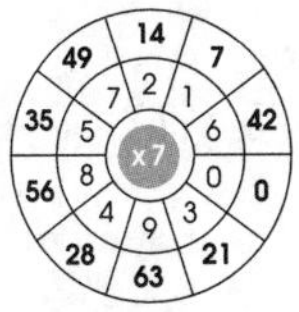

80

Name ____________________

Practice

■ Multiply.

7	5	7	9
x 7	x 7	x 4	x 7
49	**35**	**28**	**63**
7	3	7	4
x 0	x 7	x 8	x 7
0	**21**	**56**	**28**
7	6	1	7
x 3	x 7	x 7	x 9
21	**42**	**7**	**63**
7	8	7	0
x 5	x 7	x 2	x 7
35	**56**	**14**	**0**
2	7	7	7
x 7	x 6	x 8	x 1
14	**42**	**56**	**7**

7 x 4 = **28** 7 x 5 = **35**
2 x 7 = **14** 3 x 7 = **21**
7 x 1 = **7** 9 x 7 = **63**
7 x 7 = **49** 7 x 2 = **14**
7 x 8 = **56** 5 x 7 = **35**
1 x 7 = **7** 0 x 7 = **0**
7 x 3 = **21** 7 x 6 = **42**
8 x 7 = **56** 4 x 7 = **28**

Score: ____________

Circle any problems that you still find difficult to remember. Make your own flash cards to help you master these problems.

81

Name ____________________

Timed Test

■ Complete these facts as accurately and as quickly as you can.

7 x 6 = **42** 1 x 7 = **7**
8 x 7 = **56** 7 x 9 = **63**
2 x 7 = **14** 3 x 7 = **21**
5 x 7 = **35** 7 x 1 = **7**
0 x 7 = **0** 6 x 7 = **42**
7 x 2 = **14** 7 x 8 = **56**
7 x 0 = **0** 9 x 7 = **63**
4 x 7 = **28** 7 x 4 = **28**
7 x 7 = **49** 2 x 7 = **14**
7 x 5 = **35** 7 x 3 = **21**

0	7	7	7
x 7	x 3	x 8	x 6
0	**21**	**56**	**42**
7	6	7	7
x 2	x 7	x 5	x 4
14	**42**	**35**	**28**
7	5	1	4
x 9	x 7	x 7	x 7
63	**35**	**7**	**28**
7	9	2	3
x 1	x 7	x 7	x 7
7	**63**	**14**	**21**
8	7	7	7
x 7	x 5	x 7	x 0
56	**35**	**49**	**0**

Score: __________ Time: __________ minutes __________ seconds

82

Name ____________________

Timed Test

7 x 8 = **56** 7 x 4 = **28**
7 x 2 = **14** 7 x 1 = **7**
5 x 7 = **35** 7 x 9 = **63**
1 x 7 = **7** 7 x 2 = **14**
3 x 7 = **21** 7 x 3 = **21**
7 x 0 = **0** 7 x 5 = **35**
6 x 7 = **42** 0 x 7 = **0**
7 x 7 = **49** 4 x 7 = **28**
2 x 7 = **14** 9 x 7 = **63**
8 x 7 = **56** 7 x 6 = **42**

7	0	7	4
x 6	x 7	x 1	x 7
42	**0**	**7**	**28**
7	9	7	2
x 8	x 7	x 3	x 7
56	**63**	**21**	**14**
6	7	3	5
x 7	x 7	x 7	x 7
42	**49**	**21**	**35**
7	4	1	7
x 2	x 7	x 7	x 5
14	**28**	**7**	**35**
7	8	7	7
x 9	x 7	x 4	x 0
63	**56**	**28**	**0**

Score: __________ Time: __________ minutes __________ seconds

83

Name ____________________

Products Through Seventy-Two

The first ten multiples of 8 are 0, 8, 16, 24, 32, 40, 48, 56, 64, and 72. They are the same as the products of 8 times any number from 0 through 9.

Example: 8 x 6 = ?

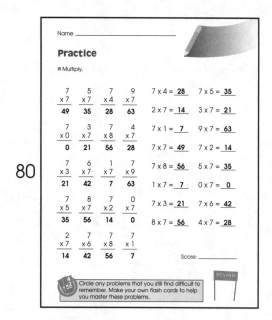

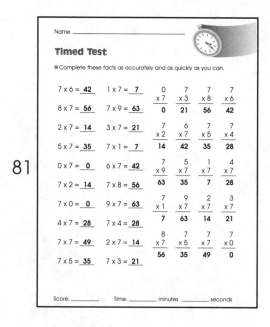

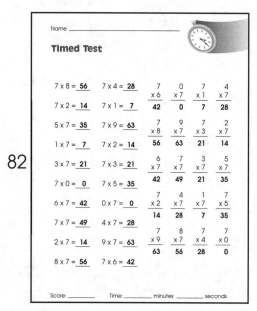

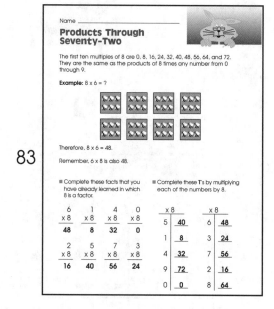

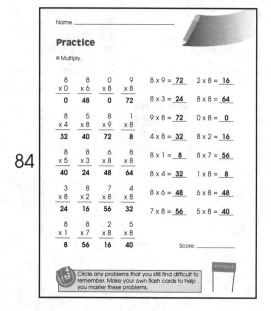

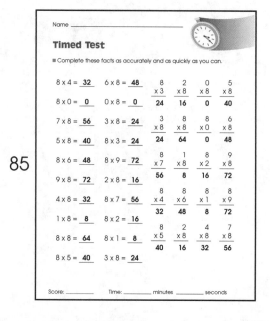

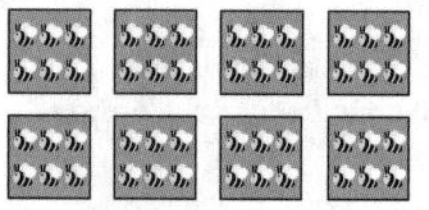

Therefore, 8 x 6 = 48.

Remember, 6 x 8 is also 48.

■ Complete these facts that you have already learned in which 8 is a factor.

6	1	4	0
x 8	x 8	x 8	x 8
48	**8**	**32**	**0**
2	5	7	3
x 8	x 8	x 8	x 8
16	**40**	**56**	**24**

■ Complete these T's by multiplying each of the numbers by 8.

	x 8
5	**40**
1	**8**
4	**32**
9	**72**
0	**0**

	x 8
6	**48**
3	**24**
7	**56**
2	**16**
8	**64**

84

Name ____________________

Practice

■ Multiply.

8	8	0	9
x 0	x 6	x 8	x 8
0	**48**	**0**	**72**
8	5	8	1
x 4	x 8	x 9	x 8
32	**40**	**72**	**8**
8	8	6	8
x 5	x 3	x 8	x 8
40	**24**	**48**	**64**
3	8	7	4
x 8	x 2	x 8	x 8
24	**16**	**56**	**32**
8	8	2	5
x 1	x 7	x 8	x 8
8	**56**	**16**	**40**

8 x 9 = **72** 2 x 8 = **16**
8 x 3 = **24** 8 x 8 = **64**
9 x 8 = **72** 0 x 8 = **0**
4 x 8 = **32** 8 x 2 = **16**
8 x 1 = **8** 8 x 7 = **56**
8 x 4 = **32** 1 x 8 = **8**
8 x 6 = **48** 6 x 8 = **48**
7 x 8 = **56** 5 x 8 = **40**

Score: ____________

Circle any problems that you still find difficult to remember. Make your own flash cards to help you master these problems.

85

Name ____________________

Timed Test

■ Complete these facts as accurately and as quickly as you can.

8 x 4 = **32** 6 x 8 = **48**
8 x 0 = **0** 0 x 8 = **0**
7 x 8 = **56** 3 x 8 = **24**
5 x 8 = **40** 8 x 3 = **24**
8 x 6 = **48** 8 x 9 = **72**
9 x 8 = **72** 2 x 8 = **16**
4 x 8 = **32** 8 x 7 = **56**
1 x 8 = **8** 8 x 2 = **16**
8 x 8 = **64** 8 x 1 = **8**
8 x 5 = **40** 3 x 8 = **24**

8	2	0	5
x 3	x 8	x 8	x 8
24	**16**	**0**	**40**
3	8	8	6
x 8	x 8	x 0	x 8
24	**64**	**0**	**48**
8	1	8	9
x 7	x 8	x 2	x 8
56	**8**	**16**	**72**
8	8	8	8
x 4	x 6	x 1	x 9
32	**48**	**8**	**72**
8	2	4	7
x 5	x 8	x 8	x 8
40	**16**	**32**	**56**

Score: __________ Time: __________ minutes __________ seconds

86

Name ______________________

Timed Test

8 x 9 = **72**	8 x 6 = **48**
6 x 8 = **48**	1 x 8 = **8**
8 x 2 = **16**	4 x 8 = **32**
0 x 8 = **0**	8 x 3 = **24**
7 x 8 = **56**	9 x 8 = **72**
8 x 5 = **40**	8 x 8 = **64**
5 x 8 = **40**	2 x 8 = **16**
8 x 7 = **56**	8 x 1 = **8**
8 x 0 = **0**	8 x 4 = **32**
9 x 8 = **72**	3 x 8 = **24**

8 x 4 = **32**	3 x 8 = **24**	8 x 0 = **0**	1 x 8 = **8**
9 x 8 = **72**	4 x 8 = **32**	8 x 3 = **24**	8 x 6 = **48**
2 x 8 = **16**	8 x 9 = **72**	5 x 8 = **40**	7 x 8 = **56**
8 x 5 = **40**	0 x 8 = **0**	8 x 4 = **32**	8 x 7 = **56**
8 x 1 = **8**	6 x 8 = **48**	2 x 8 = **16**	8 x 8 = **64**

Score: ________ Time: ________ minutes ________ seconds

87

Name ______________________

Products Through Eighty-One

The first ten multiples of 9 are 0, 9, 18, 27, 36, 45, 54, 63, 72, and 81. They are the same as the products of 9 times any number from 0 through 9.

Example: 9 x 4 = ?

9 groups of 4 each

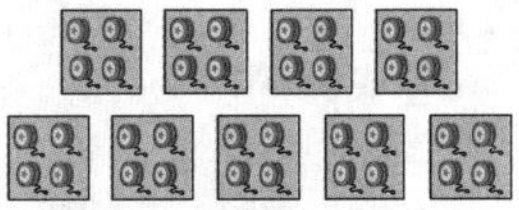

Therefore, 9 x 4 = 36. Remember, 4 x 9 is also 36.

■ Complete these facts that you have already learned in which 9 is a factor.

2 x 9 = **18**	0 x 9 = **0**	5 x 9 = **45**	6 x 9 = **54**	
4 x 9 = **36**	7 x 9 = **63**	1 x 9 = **9**	8 x 9 = **72**	3 x 9 = **27**

Here is the only new fact in this set in which 9 is a factor:

9 x 9 = **81**

■ Complete these T's by multiplying all the numbers by 9.

x9	
4	**36**
3	**27**
6	**54**
7	**63**
2	**18**

x9	
1	**9**
5	**45**
9	**81**
0	**0**
8	**72**

88

Name ______________________

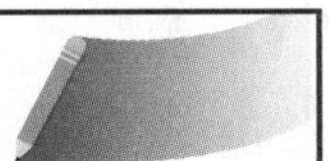

Practice

■ Complete these facts as accurately and as quickly as you can.

8 x 9 = **72**	9 x 5 = **45**	9 x 9 = **81**	1 x 9 = **9**
9 x 4 = **36**	9 x 8 = **72**	3 x 9 = **27**	0 x 9 = **0**
9 x 6 = **54**	9 x 7 = **63**	7 x 9 = **63**	2 x 9 = **18**
9 x 1 = **9**	9 x 3 = **27**	5 x 9 = **45**	9 x 0 = **0**
4 x 9 = **36**	9 x 2 = **18**	9 x 8 = **72**	6 x 9 = **54**

9 x 4 = **36**	9 x 9 = **81**
5 x 9 = **45**	1 x 9 = **9**
0 x 9 = **0**	7 x 9 = **63**
9 x 6 = **54**	3 x 9 = **27**
9 x 7 = **63**	9 x 2 = **18**
4 x 9 = **36**	9 x 8 = **72**
9 x 0 = **0**	2 x 9 = **18**
6 x 9 = **54**	9 x 3 = **27**

Score: ________

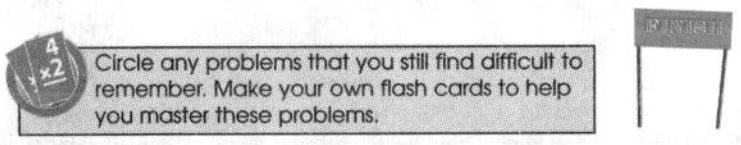

Circle any problems that you still find difficult to remember. Make your own flash cards to help you master these problems.

89

Name ______________________

Timed Test

■ Complete these facts as accurately and as quickly as you can.

0 x 9 = **0**	5 x 9 = **45**
7 x 9 = **63**	8 x 9 = **72**
9 x 0 = **0**	4 x 9 = **36**
6 x 9 = **54**	9 x 3 = **27**
1 x 9 = **0**	9 x 6 = **54**
9 x 5 = **45**	9 x 2 = **18**
9 x 9 = **81**	9 x 1 = **9**
9 x 8 = **72**	2 x 9 = **18**
8 x 9 = **72**	9 x 7 = **63**
9 x 4 = **36**	3 x 9 = **27**

9 x 1 = **9**	4 x 9 = **36**	0 x 9 = **0**	1 x 9 = **9**
8 x 9 = **72**	9 x 7 = **63**	3 x 9 = **27**	9 x 2 = **18**
7 x 9 = **63**	9 x 5 = **45**	4 x 9 = **36**	9 x 0 = **0**
5 x 9 = **45**	9 x 3 = **27**	2 x 9 = **18**	9 x 8 = **72**
6 x 9 = **54**	9 x 6 = **54**	9 x 9 = **81**	9 x 4 = **36**

Score: ________ Time: ________ minutes ________ seconds

90

Name ______________________

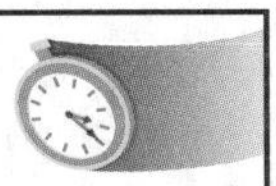

Timed Test

9 x 1 = **9**	4 x 9 = **36**
5 x 9 = **45**	0 x 9 = **0**
3 x 9 = **27**	9 x 7 = **63**
9 x 5 = **45**	7 x 9 = **63**
8 x 9 = **72**	9 x 9 = **81**
1 x 9 = **9**	9 x 3 = **27**
9 x 6 = **54**	9 x 2 = **18**
9 x 7 = **63**	9 x 8 = **72**
9 x 0 = **0**	2 x 9 = **18**
6 x 9 = **54**	9 x 4 = **36**

9 x 4 = **36**	9 x 9 = **81**	9 x 2 = **18**	7 x 9 = **63**
9 x 1 = **9**	9 x 6 = **54**	1 x 9 = **9**	6 x 9 = **54**
9 x 3 = **27**	5 x 9 = **45**	9 x 8 = **72**	9 x 7 = **63**
3 x 9 = **27**	9 x 5 = **45**	0 x 9 = **0**	4 x 9 = **36**
8 x 9 = **72**	9 x 0 = **0**	5 x 9 = **45**	2 x 9 = **18**

Score: ________ Time: ________ minutes ________ seconds

91

Name ______________________

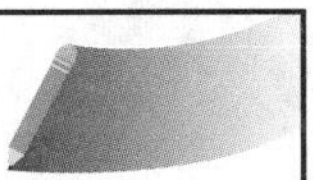

Practice

■ Multiply.

5 x 6 = **30**	2 x 5 = **10**	3 x 3 = **9**	4 x 4 = **16**	8 x 8 = **64**	1 x 0 = **0**	7 x 2 = **14**	6 x 7 = **42**
2 x 4 = **8**	9 x 6 = **54**	5 x 5 = **25**	9 x 4 = **36**	0 x 0 = **0**	6 x 3 = **18**	3 x 2 = **6**	7 x 9 = **63**
1 x 7 = **7**	8 x 0 = **0**	4 x 3 = **12**	6 x 8 = **48**	0 x 4 = **0**	4 x 9 = **36**	8 x 7 = **56**	1 x 8 = **8**
9 x 5 = **45**	8 x 1 = **8**	7 x 3 = **21**	2 x 2 = **4**	5 x 7 = **35**	4 x 5 = **20**	8 x 9 = **72**	1 x 6 = **6**
3 x 4 = **12**	3 x 9 = **27**	6 x 6 = **36**	5 x 4 = **20**	0 x 1 = **0**	7 x 8 = **56**	3 x 1 = **3**	9 x 7 = **63**

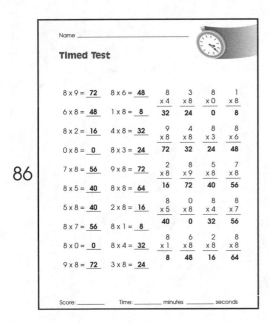

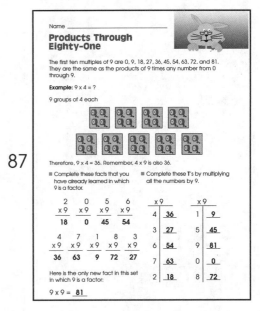

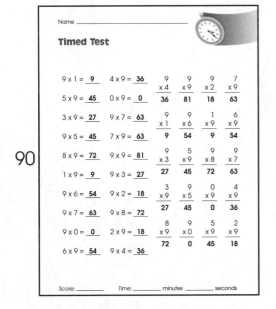

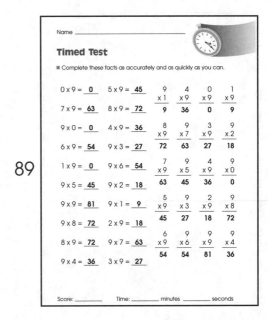

Continue this Review on the next page.

92

Name ____________________

Practice

9	3	2	4	0	5	1	6
x 1	x 8	x 3	x 6	x 6	x 8	x 5	x 5
9	**24**	**6**	**24**	**0**	**40**	**5**	**30**
3	7	0	5	8	3	4	0
x 0	x 4	x 9	x 2	x 5	x 5	x 1	x 2
0	**28**	**0**	**10**	**40**	**15**	**4**	**0**
2	6	2	7	1	9	5	7
x 0	x 1	x 7	x 0	x 2	x 8	x 0	x 7
0	**6**	**14**	**0**	**2**	**72**	**0**	**49**
8	9	7	1	0	6	4	2
x 2	x 0	x 5	x 4	x 7	x 4	x 7	x 9
16	**0**	**35**	**4**	**0**	**24**	**28**	**18**
5	9	5	0	9	3	8	1
x 9	x 2	x 3	x 3	x 9	x 7	x 4	x 3
45	**18**	**15**	**0**	**81**	**21**	**32**	**3**

Circle any problems that you still find difficult to remember. Make your own flash cards to help you master these problems.

Score: ____________

93

Name ____________________

Timed Test

■ Complete these facts as accurately and as quickly as you can.

5 x 4 = **20**	2 x 1 = **2**	0 x 1 = **0**	5 x 5 = **25**
1 x 0 = **0**	0 x 4 = **0**	7 x 3 = **21**	4 x 1 = **4**
9 x 6 = **54**	6 x 3 = **18**	8 x 0 = **0**	9 x 2 = **18**
4 x 4 = **16**	9 x 8 = **72**	9 x 1 = **9**	5 x 3 = **15**
9 x 3 = **27**	4 x 2 = **8**	9 x 7 = **63**	4 x 5 = **20**
3 x 4 = **12**	8 x 3 = **24**	2 x 8 = **16**	6 x 4 = **24**
0 x 9 = **0**	2 x 7 = **14**	8 x 1 = **8**	2 x 0 = **0**
3 x 3 = **9**	7 x 4 = **28**	3 x 5 = **15**	3 x 2 = **6**
9 x 9 = **81**	8 x 4 = **32**	1 x 1 = **1**	6 x 0 = **0**
1 x 3 = **3**	6 x 2 = **12**	7 x 9 = **63**	0 x 2 = **0**

Continue this Timed Test on the next page.

94

Name ____________________

Timed Test

6 x 9 = **54**	6 x 6 = **36**	2 x 4 = **8**	8 x 6 = **48**
4 x 0 = **0**	4 x 6 = **24**	7 x 1 = **7**	5 x 7 = **35**
5 x 6 = **30**	0 x 3 = **0**	1 x 9 = **9**	2 x 9 = **18**
4 x 9 = **36**	5 x 9 = **45**	8 x 9 = **72**	7 x 7 = **49**
1 x 4 = **4**	2 x 6 = **12**	9 x 5 = **45**	4 x 8 = **32**
3 x 1 = **3**	8 x 5 = **40**	8 x 7 = **56**	1 x 7 = **7**
2 x 2 = **4**	5 x 2 = **10**	1 x 5 = **5**	6 x 8 = **48**
7 x 6 = **42**	1 x 8 = **8**	7 x 8 = **56**	3 x 9 = **27**
0 x 7 = **0**	3 x 7 = **21**	3 x 0 = **0**	2 x 3 = **6**
3 x 6 = **18**	5 x 0 = **0**	0 x 8 = **0**	9 x 0 = **0**

Score: ________ Time: ________ minutes ________ seconds

95

Name ____________________

Timed Test

0 x 0 = **0**	5 x 7 = **35**	8 x 8 = **64**	0 x 5 = **0**
1 x 7 = **7**	0 x 9 = **0**	0 x 4 = **0**	5 x 8 = **40**
4 x 5 = **20**	6 x 1 = **6**	3 x 3 = **9**	2 x 6 = **12**
2 x 9 = **18**	8 x 0 = **0**	4 x 9 = **36**	8 x 5 = **40**
3 x 7 = **21**	2 x 5 = **10**	0 x 7 = **0**	1 x 8 = **8**
8 x 4 = **32**	7 x 6 = **42**	2 x 2 = **4**	7 x 9 = **63**
2 x 1 = **2**	9 x 2 = **18**	1 x 0 = **0**	9 x 8 = **72**
7 x 0 = **0**	1 x 3 = **0**	4 x 6 = **24**	5 x 4 = **20**
5 x 3 = **15**	6 x 5 = **30**	8 x 1 = **8**	6 x 9 = **54**
9 x 9 = **81**	4 x 1 = **1**	6 x 2 = **12**	0 x 1 = **0**

Continue this Timed Test on the next page.

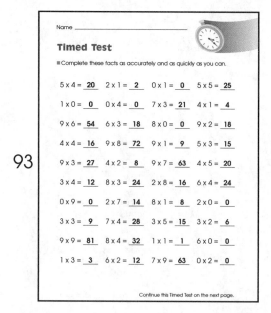

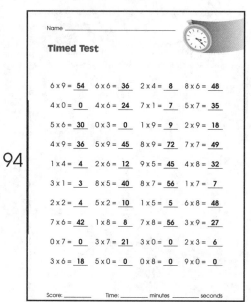

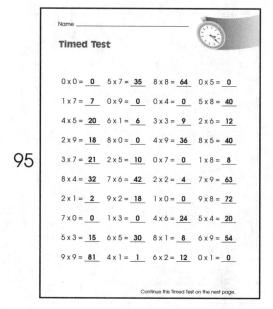

96

Name

Products Through One Hundred Twenty

Now you will learn about some higher facts.

The first thirteen multiples of 10 are 0, 10, 20, 30, 40, 50, 60, 70, 80, 90, 100, 110, and 120. They are the same as the products of 10 times any number from 0 through 12.

Here are some things to remember about the basic facts in which 10 is one of the factors:

- The product of 10 and another counting number always ends in 0. Here's a shortcut to find a product of 10 and another number: Simply annex (attach) a zero at the end of the other factor.

Examples: 10 x 6 = 60, 10 x 3 = 30, and 10 x 10 = 100

- Changing the order of the factors does not change the product. So, 10 x 7 is the same as 7 x 10.
- As you have learned with other facts, 10 x 0 is 0 and 10 x 1 is 10.

■ Complete these T's by multiplying each of the numbers by 10.

x 10	
6	60
2	20
12	120
4	40
7	70
9	90
1	10

x 10	
5	50
3	30
11	110
0	0
8	80
10	100

■ Now, complete these facts.

10 x 5 = 50 10 x 9 = 90
4 x 10 = 40 10 x 3 = 30
10 x 12 = 120 10 x 7 = 70
10 x 11 = 110 2 x 10 = 20
10 x 10 = 100 10 x 8 = 80
6 x 10 = 60 7 x 10 = 70
10 x 0 = 0 10 x 2 = 20
11 x 10 = 110 1 x 10 = 10

97

Name

Practice

■ Complete these facts as accurately and as quickly as you can.

10 x 8 = 80 10 x 5 = 50 10 x 3 = 30 10 x 12 = 120
11 x 10 = 110 10 x 8 = 80 12 x 10 = 120 10 x 4 = 40
10 x 9 = 90 10 x 2 = 20 10 x 4 = 40 10 x 0 = 100
10 x 7 = 70 10 x 6 = 60 10 x 2 = 20 10 x 9 = 90
10 x 5 = 50 10 x 1 = 10 10 x 12 = 120 10 x 7 = 70

10 x 6 = 60 7 x 10 = 70
0 x 10 = 0 10 x 12 = 120
10 x 2 = 20 10 x 4 = 40
6 x 10 = 60 1 x 10 = 10
3 x 10 = 30 12 x 10 = 120
10 x 7 = 70 10 x 10 = 100
10 x 11 = 110 11 x 10 = 110
10 x 0 = 0 10 x 1 = 10

Score: ____

Circle any problems that you still find difficult to remember. Make your own flash cards to help you master these problems.

98

Name

Timed Test

■ Complete these facts as accurately and as quickly as you can.

10 x 4 = 40 2 x 10 = 20
12 x 10 = 120 10 x 8 = 80
10 x 1 = 10 10 x 11 = 110
10 x 3 = 30 8 x 10 = 80
5 x 10 = 50 10 x 5 = 50
10 x 9 = 90 6 x 10 = 60
3 x 10 = 30 10 x 10 = 100
10 x 2 = 20 1 x 10 = 10
10 x 12 = 120 10 x 7 = 70
4 x 10 = 40 10 x 6 = 60

10 x 1 = 10 11 x 10 = 110 10 x 5 = 50 10 x 9 = 90
10 x 7 = 70 12 x 10 = 120 10 x 9 = 90 10 x 8 = 80
10 x 0 = 0 10 x 4 = 40 10 x 11 = 110 10 x 5 = 50
10 x 6 = 60 10 x 3 = 30 10 x 10 = 100 10 x 7 = 70
10 x 2 = 20 10 x 4 = 40 10 x 12 = 120 10 x 1 = 10

Score: ____ Time: ____ minutes ____ seconds

99

Name

Products Through One Hundred Thirty-Two

The first thirteen multiples of 11 are 0, 11, 22, 33, 44, 55, 66, 77, 88, 99, 110, 121, and 132. They are the same as the products of 11 times any number from 0 through 12.

Here are some things to remember about the basic facts in which 11 is one of the factors:

- All of the products from 11 x 2 through 11 x 9 are easy to remember because both digits in each product are the same as the second factor. Thus, 11 x 2 is 22, 11 x 5 is 55, and 11 x 9 is 99.
- That leaves only three other facts to learn. The first of these you already know: 11 x 10 is 110. The other two are new: 11 x 11 is 121 and 11 x 12 is 132.
- Changing the order of the factors does not change the product. So, 11 x 7 is the same as 7 x 11.
- As you have learned with other facts, 11 x 0 is 0 and 11 x 1 is 11.

■ Complete this circle by multiplying each of the numbers by 11.

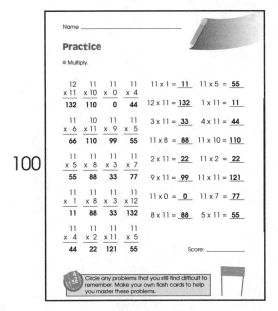

■ Now, complete these facts.

11 x 3 = 33 2 x 11 = 22
8 x 11 = 88 11 x 7 = 77
11 x 6 = 66 4 x 11 = 44
0 x 11 = 0 10 x 11 = 110
11 x 2 = 22 6 x 11 = 66
7 x 11 = 77 11 x 12 = 132
11 x 5 = 55 9 x 11 = 99

100

Name

Practice

■ Multiply.

12 x 11 = 132 11 x 10 = 110 11 x 0 = 0 11 x 4 = 44
11 x 6 = 66 10 x 11 = 110 11 x 9 = 99 11 x 5 = 55
11 x 5 = 55 11 x 8 = 88 11 x 3 = 33 11 x 7 = 77
11 x 1 = 11 11 x 8 = 88 11 x 3 = 33 11 x 12 = 132
11 x 4 = 44 11 x 2 = 22 11 x 11 = 121 11 x 5 = 55

11 x 1 = 11 11 x 5 = 55
12 x 11 = 132 1 x 11 = 11
3 x 11 = 33 4 x 11 = 44
11 x 8 = 88 11 x 10 = 110
2 x 11 = 22 11 x 2 = 22
9 x 11 = 99 11 x 11 = 121
11 x 0 = 0 11 x 7 = 77
8 x 11 = 88 5 x 11 = 55

Score: ____

Circle any problems that you still find difficult to remember. Make your own flash cards to help you master these problems.

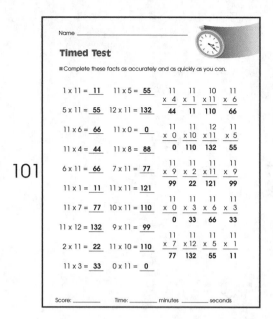

Timed Test

■ Complete these facts as accurately and as quickly as you can.

101

$1 \times 11 = \underline{11}$ $11 \times 5 = \underline{55}$

11	11	10	11
× 4	× 1	× 11	× 6
44	11	110	66

$5 \times 11 = \underline{55}$ $12 \times 11 = \underline{132}$

$11 \times 6 = \underline{66}$ $11 \times 0 = \underline{0}$

11	11	12	11
× 0	× 10	× 11	× 5
0	110	132	55

$11 \times 4 = \underline{44}$ $11 \times 8 = \underline{88}$

$6 \times 11 = \underline{66}$ $7 \times 11 = \underline{77}$

11	11	11	11
× 9	× 2	× 11	× 9
99	22	121	99

$11 \times 1 = \underline{11}$ $11 \times 11 = \underline{121}$

$11 \times 7 = \underline{77}$ $10 \times 11 = \underline{110}$

11	11	11	11
× 0	× 3	× 6	× 3
0	33	66	33

$11 \times 12 = \underline{132}$ $9 \times 11 = \underline{99}$

$2 \times 11 = \underline{22}$ $11 \times 10 = \underline{110}$

11	11	11	11
× 7	× 12	× 5	× 1
77	132	55	11

$11 \times 3 = \underline{33}$ $0 \times 11 = \underline{0}$

Score: _____   Time: _____ minutes _____ seconds

Products Through One Hundred Forty-Four

The first thirteen multiples of 12 are 0, 12, 24, 36, 48, 60, 72, 84, 96, 108, 120, 132, and 144. They are the same as the products of 12 times any number from 0 through 12.

Here are some things to remember about the basic facts in which 12 is one of the factors:

● Changing the order of the factors does not change the product. Therefore, you already know that 12 × 10 is 120 and 10 × 12 is 120.

● As you have learned with other facts, 12 × 0 is 0 and 12 × 1 is 12.

■ Complete these T's by multiplying each of the numbers by 12.   ■ Now, complete these facts.

102

× 12		× 12	
6	72	12	144
10	120	0	0
8	96	4	48
1	12	7	84
5	60	9	108
3	36	11	132
2	24		

$12 \times 2 = \underline{24}$ $12 \times 0 = \underline{0}$

$12 \times 5 = \underline{60}$ $12 \times 9 = \underline{108}$

$12 \times 4 = \underline{48}$ $12 \times 3 = \underline{36}$

$12 \times 12 = \underline{144}$ $12 \times 8 = \underline{96}$

$12 \times 6 = \underline{72}$ $12 \times 7 = \underline{84}$

$12 \times 1 = \underline{12}$ $12 \times 10 = \underline{120}$

$12 \times 11 = \underline{132}$

Practice

■ Multiply.

103

12	12	12	12
× 1	× 12	× 9	× 6
12	144	108	72

$12 \times 9 = \underline{108}$ $12 \times 4 = \underline{48}$

$4 \times 12 = \underline{48}$ $2 \times 12 = \underline{24}$

12	12	12	12
× 1	× 3	× 8	× 1
12	36	96	12

$12 \times 0 = \underline{0}$ $12 \times 10 = \underline{120}$

$10 \times 12 = \underline{120}$ $6 \times 12 = \underline{72}$

12	12	12	12
× 4	× 9	× 8	× 0
48	108	96	0

$3 \times 12 = \underline{36}$ $11 \times 12 = \underline{132}$

$9 \times 12 = \underline{108}$ $1 \times 12 = \underline{12}$

12	12	12	10
× 10	× 5	× 7	× 12
120	60	84	120

$12 \times 3 = \underline{36}$ $12 \times 12 = \underline{144}$

$5 \times 12 = \underline{60}$ $12 \times 6 = \underline{72}$

12	12	12	12
× 11	× 2	× 6	× 3
132	24	72	36

Score: _____

Circle any problems that you still find difficult to remember. Make your own flash cards to help you master these problems.

Timed Test

■ Complete these facts as accurately and as quickly as you can.

104

$1 \times 12 = \underline{12}$ $12 \times 2 = \underline{24}$

12	12	12	12
× 8	× 7	× 0	× 4
96	84	0	48

$6 \times 12 = \underline{72}$ $7 \times 12 = \underline{84}$

$12 \times 1 = \underline{12}$ $12 \times 9 = \underline{108}$

12	12	12	12
× 6	× 5	× 12	× 3
72	60	144	36

$12 \times 12 = \underline{144}$ $5 \times 12 = \underline{60}$

$12 \times 8 = \underline{96}$ $12 \times 4 = \underline{48}$

12	12	12	10
× 5	× 6	× 9	× 12
60	72	108	120

$12 \times 5 = \underline{60}$ $0 \times 12 = \underline{0}$

$9 \times 12 = \underline{108}$ $11 \times 12 = \underline{132}$

12	12	12	12
× 1	× 1	× 8	× 11
12	12	96	132

$12 \times 0 = \underline{0}$ $12 \times 3 = \underline{36}$

$12 \times 6 = \underline{72}$ $8 \times 12 = \underline{96}$

12	12	12	12
× 7	× 0	× 2	× 10
84	0	24	120

$3 \times 12 = \underline{36}$ $12 \times 7 = \underline{84}$

Score: _____   Time: _____ minutes _____ seconds

Timed Test

105

$11 \times 11 = \underline{121}$ $12 \times 8 = \underline{96}$ $1 \times 11 = \underline{11}$ $9 \times 10 = \underline{90}$

$3 \times 11 = \underline{33}$ $2 \times 11 = \underline{22}$ $2 \times 10 = \underline{20}$ $11 \times 5 = \underline{55}$

$10 \times 3 = \underline{30}$ $10 \times 7 = \underline{70}$ $7 \times 10 = \underline{70}$ $9 \times 11 = \underline{99}$

$8 \times 10 = \underline{80}$ $0 \times 12 = \underline{0}$ $11 \times 10 = \underline{110}$ $12 \times 0 = \underline{0}$

$12 \times 12 = \underline{144}$ $11 \times 12 = \underline{132}$ $6 \times 12 = \underline{72}$ $10 \times 10 = \underline{100}$

$5 \times 12 = \underline{60}$ $12 \times 4 = \underline{48}$ $10 \times 6 = \underline{60}$ $11 \times 8 = \underline{88}$

$11 \times 3 = \underline{33}$ $1 \times 10 = \underline{10}$ $0 \times 10 = \underline{0}$ $12 \times 3 = \underline{36}$

$11 \times 4 = \underline{44}$ $12 \times 9 = \underline{108}$ $12 \times 7 = \underline{84}$ $11 \times 5 = \underline{55}$

$5 \times 10 = \underline{50}$ $4 \times 12 = \underline{48}$ $9 \times 12 = \underline{108}$ $10 \times 4 = \underline{40}$

$10 \times 11 = \underline{110}$ $11 \times 2 = \underline{22}$ $10 \times 2 = \underline{20}$ $11 \times 6 = \underline{66}$

Score: _____   Time: _____ minutes _____ seconds

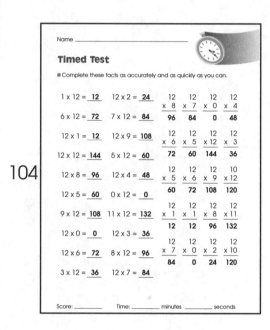

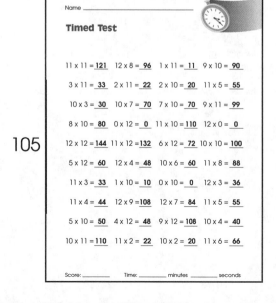

107

Name ____________________

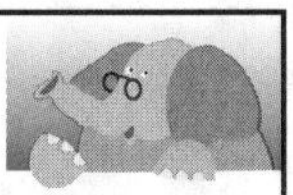

What Is Division?

You divide to answer questions such as how many groups of 3's are there in 12. The answer is called the **quotient**.

12 grapes divided into groups of 3 equals 4 equal groups.

Here are two ways to show the division.

$12 \div 3 = 4$ $\qquad$ $3\overline{)12}$ = 4

You read the problem this way: **12 divided by 3 equals 4.**

You can draw a picture to find a quotient.

Example: Find the quotient. $8 \div 2 =$ ____

Step 1: Draw 8 dots. Group them into 2's.

Step 2: Count all the groups.

Answer: $8 \div 2 =$ __4__

■ Draw a picture to find the quotient.

$6 \div 2 =$ **3**	$8 \div 4 =$ **2**	$10 \div 2 =$ **5**
$6 \div 3 =$ **2**	$12 \div 3 =$ **4**	$12 \div 4 =$ **3**

108

Name ____________________

What Is Division?

You can use a number line to find a quotient.

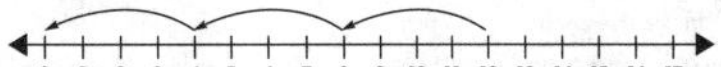

Example: Find the quotient. $12 \div 4 =$ ____

Step 1: Put your finger on 12.

Step 2: Make moves to the left of 4 spaces each, ending on zero.

Step 3: Count the number of moves you made.

Answer: $12 \div 4 =$ __3__

■ Use the number line to find the quotient.

$8 \div 2 =$ **4** $\qquad$ $15 \div 5 =$ **3** $\qquad$ $16 \div 4 =$ **4**

$2\overline{)8}$ **4**	$4\overline{)12}$ **3**	$2\overline{)6}$ **3**	$6\overline{)12}$ **2**	$5\overline{)15}$ **3**

Multiplication and division are **inverse operations.** $10 \div 2 = 5$ $\quad$ $5 \times 2 = 10$

You can use multiplication facts to find the quotient.

Example: Find the quotient. $20 \div 5 =$ ____

Think: Some number times 5 equals 20. ____ $\times 5 = 20$

Since $4 \times 5 = 20$, then $20 \div 5 =$ __4__

Answer: $20 \div 5 =$ __4__

■ Use a multiplication fact to find the quotient.

$9 \div 3 =$ **3** $\qquad$ $10 \div 5 =$ **2** $\qquad$ $16 \div 2 =$ **8**

$5\overline{)15}$ **3**	$2\overline{)4}$ **2**	$2\overline{)12}$ **6**	$6\overline{)18}$ **3**	$3\overline{)18}$ **6**

109

Name ____________________

Dividends Through Eighteen

Division is the operation in which a number is divided into equal parts. The **dividend** is the number being divided. The **divisor** is the number of equal parts, and the **quotient** is the number in each part.

Example: 15 (**dividend**) ÷ 3 (**divisor**) = 5 (**quotient**) $\qquad$ **divisor** $3\overline{)15}$ **dividend**, 5 **quotient**

When you divide a number by 1, the quotient will always be the same as the dividend.

Example: $6 \div 1 = 6$

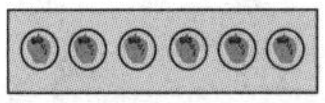

When you divide a number by 2, the quotient is half of the dividend.

Example: $6 \div 2 = 3$

■ Find the quotient for these facts.

$6 \div 1 =$ **6**	$18 \div 2 =$ **9**	$10 \div 2 =$ **5**	$0 \div 1 =$ **0**
$7 \div 1 =$ **7**	$6 \div 2 =$ **3**	$8 \div 1 =$ **8**	$5 \div 1 =$ **5**
$16 \div 2 =$ **8**	$14 \div 2 =$ **7**	$8 \div 2 =$ **4**	$1 \div 1 =$ **1**
$2 \div 1 =$ **2**	$9 \div 1 =$ **9**	$12 \div 2 =$ **6**	$4 \div 2 =$ **2**

110

Name ____________________

Practice

■ Divide.

$2 \div 1 =$ **2**	$8 \div 2 =$ **4**	$2\overline{)0}$ **0**	$1\overline{)4}$ **4**
$6 \div 2 =$ **3**	$4 \div 1 =$ **4**	$2\overline{)8}$ **4**	$2\overline{)12}$ **6**
$7 \div 1 =$ **7**	$14 \div 2 =$ **7**	$2\overline{)18}$ **9**	$1\overline{)0}$ **0**
$10 \div 2 =$ **5**	$2 \div 2 =$ **1**	$1\overline{)5}$ **5**	$1\overline{)9}$ **9**
$9 \div 1 =$ **9**	$0 \div 1 =$ **0**	$2\overline{)14}$ **7**	$2\overline{)6}$ **3**
$8 \div 1 =$ **8**	$18 \div 2 =$ **9**	$1\overline{)3}$ **3**	$2\overline{)16}$ **8**
$3 \div 1 =$ **3**	$12 \div 2 =$ **6**	$1\overline{)6}$ **6**	$2\overline{)2}$ **1**
$0 \div 2 =$ **0**	$4 \div 2 =$ **2**	$1\overline{)8}$ **8**	$1\overline{)1}$ **1**
$16 \div 2 =$ **8**	$5 \div 1 =$ **5**		
$6 \div 1 =$ **6**	$1 \div 1 =$ **1**		

Circle any problems that you still find difficult to remember. Make your own flash cards to help you master these problems.

FINISH

Score: __________

111

Name ____________________

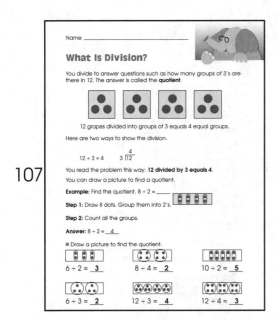

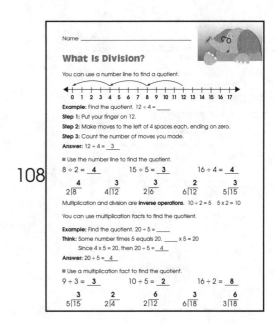

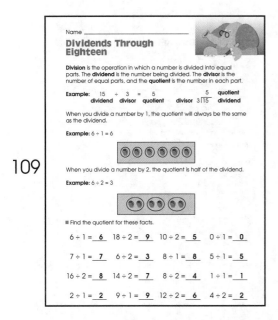

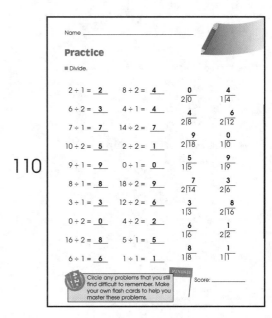

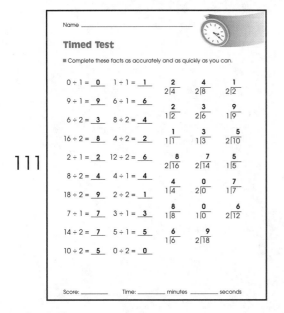

Timed Test

■ Complete these facts as accurately and as quickly as you can.

$0 \div 1 =$ **0**	$1 \div 1 =$ **1**	$2\overline{)4}$ **2**	$2\overline{)8}$ **4**	$2\overline{)2}$ **1**
$9 \div 1 =$ **9**	$6 \div 1 =$ **6**	$1\overline{)2}$ **2**	$2\overline{)6}$ **3**	$1\overline{)9}$ **9**
$6 \div 2 =$ **3**	$8 \div 2 =$ **4**	$1\overline{)1}$ **1**	$1\overline{)3}$ **3**	$2\overline{)10}$ **5**
$16 \div 2 =$ **8**	$4 \div 2 =$ **2**	$2\overline{)16}$ **8**	$2\overline{)14}$ **7**	$1\overline{)5}$ **5**
$2 \div 1 =$ **2**	$12 \div 2 =$ **6**	$1\overline{)4}$ **4**	$2\overline{)0}$ **0**	$1\overline{)7}$ **7**
$8 \div 2 =$ **4**	$4 \div 1 =$ **4**	$1\overline{)8}$ **8**	$1\overline{)0}$ **0**	$2\overline{)12}$ **6**
$18 \div 2 =$ **9**	$2 \div 2 =$ **1**	$1\overline{)6}$ **6**	$2\overline{)18}$ **9**	
$7 \div 1 =$ **7**	$3 \div 1 =$ **3**			
$14 \div 2 =$ **7**	$5 \div 1 =$ **5**			
$10 \div 2 =$ **5**	$0 \div 2 =$ **0**			

Score: ________ Time: ________ minutes ________ seconds

112

Name ____________

Dividends Through Twenty-Seven

Now, think about what happens when a number is divided by 3.

Example: 18 ÷ 3 = 6

The dividend is 18. If you put 3 objects in each group, you have 6 equal groups.

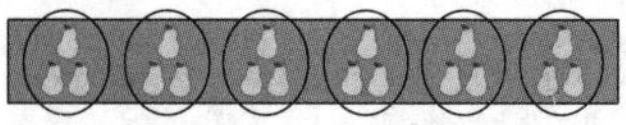

Division and multiplication are **inverse operations**.

Example: 6 x 3 = 18
18 ÷ 3 = 6

When you divide, you cannot have 0 as a divisor. It doesn't make sense to divide a number into zero groups. However, you could have a 0 as a dividend. But, no matter how many groups you divide 0 into, the quotient will always be 0.

Examples: 0 ÷ 2 = 0   0 ÷ 5 = 0

Apply what you have learned to the division facts of 3.

Examples: 0 ÷ 3 = 0   3 ÷ 1 = 3   3 ÷ 3 = 1

■ Complete this circle by dividing each of the numbers by 3.

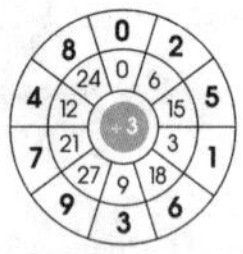

113

Name ____________

Practice

■ Divide.

24 ÷ 3 = **8**   12 ÷ 3 = **4** $3\overline{)21}$ **7** $3\overline{)12}$ **4**

3 ÷ 3 = **1**   9 ÷ 3 = **3** $3\overline{)3}$ **1** $3\overline{)18}$ **6**

18 ÷ 3 = **6**   0 ÷ 3 = **0** $3\overline{)27}$ **9** $3\overline{)0}$ **0**

6 ÷ 3 = **2**   27 ÷ 3 = **9** $3\overline{)6}$ **2** $3\overline{)24}$ **8**

15 ÷ 3 = **5**   24 ÷ 3 = **8** $3\overline{)15}$ **5** $3\overline{)9}$ **3**

21 ÷ 3 = **7**   18 ÷ 3 = **6** $3\overline{)27}$ **9** $3\overline{)15}$ **5**

9 ÷ 3 = **3**   6 ÷ 3 = **2** $3\overline{)18}$ **6** $3\overline{)21}$ **7**

0 ÷ 3 = **0**   3 ÷ 3 = **1** $3\overline{)24}$ **8** $3\overline{)12}$ **4**

12 ÷ 3 = **4**   15 ÷ 3 = **5**

27 ÷ 3 = **9**   21 ÷ 3 = **7**

Circle any problems that you still find difficult to remember. Make your own flash cards to help you master these problems.

FINISH   Score: ____________

114

Name ____________

Timed Test

■ Complete these facts as accurately and as quickly as you can.

15 ÷ 3 = **5**   24 ÷ 3 = **8** $3\overline{)27}$ **9** $3\overline{)21}$ **7** $3\overline{)12}$ **4**

21 ÷ 3 = **7**   9 ÷ 3 = **3** $3\overline{)0}$ **0** $3\overline{)15}$ **5** $3\overline{)6}$ **2**

3 ÷ 3 = **1**   12 ÷ 3 = **4** $3\overline{)18}$ **6** $3\overline{)9}$ **3** $3\overline{)3}$ **1**

24 ÷ 3 = **8**   27 ÷ 3 = **9** $3\overline{)12}$ **4** $3\overline{)21}$ **7** $3\overline{)6}$ **2**

18 ÷ 3 = **6**   0 ÷ 3 = **0** $3\overline{)24}$ **8** $3\overline{)9}$ **3** $3\overline{)18}$ **6**

6 ÷ 3 = **2**   15 ÷ 3 = **5** $3\overline{)3}$ **1** $3\overline{)27}$ **9** $3\overline{)15}$ **5**

12 ÷ 3 = **4**   18 ÷ 3 = **6** $3\overline{)21}$ **7** $3\overline{)0}$ **0**

0 ÷ 3 = **0**   3 ÷ 3 = **1**

9 ÷ 3 = **3**   6 ÷ 3 = **2**

27 ÷ 3 = **9**   21 ÷ 3 = **7**

Score: ________   Time: ________ minutes ________ seconds

115

Name ____________

Dividends Through Thirty-Six

Now, think about what happens when a number is divided by 4.

Example: 12 ÷ 4 = 3

The dividend is 12. If you put 4 objects in each group, you have 3 equal groups.

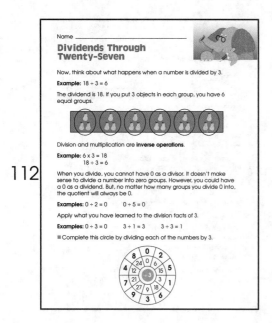

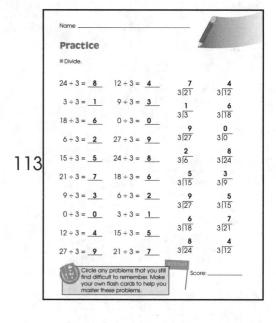

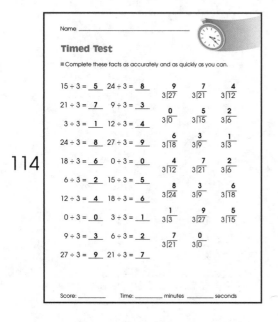

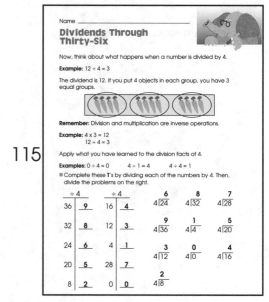

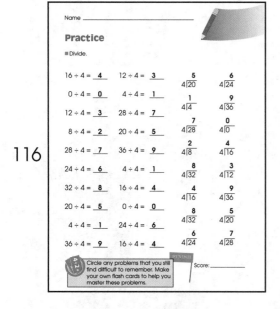

Remember: Division and multiplication are inverse operations.

Example: 4 x 3 = 12
12 ÷ 4 = 3

Apply what you have learned to the division facts of 4.

Examples: 0 ÷ 4 = 0   4 ÷ 1 = 4   4 ÷ 4 = 1

■ Complete these **T**'s by dividing each of the numbers by 4. Then, divide the problems on the right.

÷ 4	
36	**9**
32	**8**
24	**6**
20	**5**
8	**2**

÷ 4	
16	**4**
12	**3**
4	**1**
28	**7**
0	**0**

$4\overline{)24}$ **6** $4\overline{)32}$ **8** $4\overline{)28}$ **7**

$4\overline{)36}$ **9** $4\overline{)4}$ **1** $4\overline{)20}$ **5**

$4\overline{)12}$ **3** $4\overline{)0}$ **0** $4\overline{)16}$ **4**

$4\overline{)8}$ **2**

116

Name ____________

Practice

■ Divide.

16 ÷ 4 = **4**   12 ÷ 4 = **3** $4\overline{)20}$ **5** $4\overline{)24}$ **6**

0 ÷ 4 = **0**   4 ÷ 4 = **1** $4\overline{)4}$ **1** $4\overline{)36}$ **9**

12 ÷ 4 = **3**   28 ÷ 4 = **7** $4\overline{)28}$ **7** $4\overline{)0}$ **0**

8 ÷ 4 = **2**   20 ÷ 4 = **5** $4\overline{)8}$ **2** $4\overline{)16}$ **4**

28 ÷ 4 = **7**   36 ÷ 4 = **9** $4\overline{)32}$ **8** $4\overline{)12}$ **3**

24 ÷ 4 = **6**   4 ÷ 4 = **1** $4\overline{)16}$ **4** $4\overline{)36}$ **9**

32 ÷ 4 = **8**   16 ÷ 4 = **4** $4\overline{)32}$ **8** $4\overline{)20}$ **5**

20 ÷ 4 = **5**   0 ÷ 4 = **0** $4\overline{)24}$ **6** $4\overline{)28}$ **7**

4 ÷ 4 = **1**   24 ÷ 4 = **6**

36 ÷ 4 = **9**   16 ÷ 4 = **4**

Circle any problems that you still find difficult to remember. Make your own flash cards to help you master these problems.

FINISH   Score: ____________

117

Name ______________________

Timed Test

■ Complete these facts as accurately and as quickly as you can.

28 ÷ 4 = 7	4 ÷ 4 = 1	$\overset{9}{4\overline{)36}}$	$\overset{0}{4\overline{)0}}$	$\overset{3}{4\overline{)12}}$
16 ÷ 4 = 4	0 ÷ 4 = 0	$\overset{1}{4\overline{)4}}$	$\overset{2}{4\overline{)8}}$	$\overset{8}{4\overline{)32}}$
24 ÷ 4 = 6	36 ÷ 4 = 9	$\overset{4}{4\overline{)16}}$	$\overset{9}{4\overline{)36}}$	$\overset{7}{4\overline{)28}}$
20 ÷ 4 = 5	32 ÷ 4 = 8	$\overset{5}{4\overline{)20}}$	$\overset{3}{4\overline{)12}}$	$\overset{2}{4\overline{)8}}$
4 ÷ 4 = 1	12 ÷ 4 = 3	$\overset{6}{4\overline{)24}}$	$\overset{0}{4\overline{)0}}$	$\overset{1}{4\overline{)4}}$
8 ÷ 4 = 2	28 ÷ 4 = 7	$\overset{2}{4\overline{)8}}$	$\overset{4}{4\overline{)16}}$	$\overset{5}{4\overline{)20}}$
32 ÷ 4 = 8	0 ÷ 4 = 0	$\overset{8}{4\overline{)32}}$	$\overset{7}{4\overline{)28}}$	
12 ÷ 4 = 3	20 ÷ 4 = 5			
36 ÷ 4 = 9	8 ÷ 4 = 2			
16 ÷ 4 = 4	24 ÷ 4 = 6			

Score: ______ Time: ______ minutes ______ seconds

118

Name ______________________

Dividends Through Forty-Five

Now, think about what happens when a number is divided by 5.

Example: 15 ÷ 5 = 3

The dividend is 15. If you put 5 objects in each group, you have 3 equal groups.

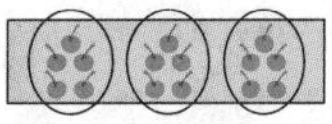

Remember: Division and multiplication are inverse operations.

Example: 5 x 3 = 15
15 ÷ 5 = 3

Apply what you have learned to the division facts of 5.

Examples: 0 ÷ 5 = 0 5 ÷ 1 = 5 5 ÷ 5 = 1

■ Complete this circle by dividing each of the numbers by 5. Then, divide the problems on the right.

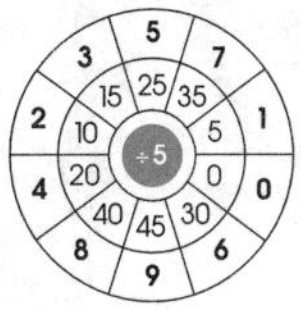

$\overset{3}{5\overline{)15}}$	$\overset{5}{5\overline{)25}}$	$\overset{0}{5\overline{)0}}$
$\overset{4}{5\overline{)20}}$	$\overset{8}{5\overline{)40}}$	$\overset{2}{5\overline{)10}}$
$\overset{7}{5\overline{)35}}$	$\overset{1}{5\overline{)5}}$	$\overset{6}{5\overline{)30}}$
$\overset{9}{5\overline{)45}}$		

119

Name ______________________

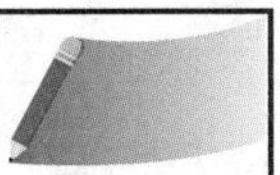

Practice

■ Divide.

10 ÷ 5 = 2	5 ÷ 5 = 1	$\overset{3}{5\overline{)15}}$	$\overset{6}{5\overline{)30}}$
35 ÷ 5 = 7	45 ÷ 5 = 9	$\overset{1}{5\overline{)5}}$	$\overset{2}{5\overline{)10}}$
15 ÷ 5 = 3	20 ÷ 5 = 4	$\overset{9}{5\overline{)45}}$	$\overset{5}{5\overline{)25}}$
30 ÷ 5 = 6	40 ÷ 5 = 8	$\overset{7}{5\overline{)35}}$	$\overset{0}{5\overline{)0}}$
5 ÷ 5 = 1	0 ÷ 5 = 0	$\overset{8}{5\overline{)40}}$	$\overset{4}{5\overline{)20}}$
25 ÷ 5 = 5	15 ÷ 5 = 3	$\overset{3}{5\overline{)15}}$	$\overset{2}{5\overline{)10}}$
45 ÷ 5 = 9	35 ÷ 5 = 7	$\overset{4}{5\overline{)20}}$	$\overset{6}{5\overline{)30}}$
20 ÷ 5 = 4	10 ÷ 5 = 2	$\overset{9}{5\overline{)45}}$	$\overset{8}{5\overline{)40}}$
40 ÷ 5 = 8	30 ÷ 5 = 6		
0 ÷ 5 = 0	25 ÷ 5 = 5		

Circle any problems that you still find difficult to remember. Make your own flash cards to help you master these problems.

Score: ______

120

Name ______________________

Timed Test

■ Complete these facts as accurately and as quickly as you can.

5 ÷ 5 = 1	20 ÷ 5 = 4	$\overset{2}{5\overline{)10}}$	$\overset{8}{5\overline{)40}}$	$\overset{9}{5\overline{)45}}$
45 ÷ 5 = 9	35 ÷ 5 = 7	$\overset{4}{5\overline{)20}}$	$\overset{7}{5\overline{)35}}$	$\overset{3}{5\overline{)15}}$
30 ÷ 5 = 6	15 ÷ 5 = 3	$\overset{8}{5\overline{)40}}$	$\overset{0}{5\overline{)0}}$	$\overset{6}{5\overline{)30}}$
40 ÷ 5 = 8	10 ÷ 5 = 2	$\overset{5}{5\overline{)25}}$	$\overset{9}{5\overline{)45}}$	$\overset{2}{5\overline{)10}}$
0 ÷ 5 = 0	5 ÷ 5 = 1	$\overset{1}{5\overline{)5}}$	$\overset{8}{5\overline{)40}}$	$\overset{6}{5\overline{)30}}$
15 ÷ 5 = 3	45 ÷ 5 = 9	$\overset{3}{5\overline{)15}}$	$\overset{0}{5\overline{)0}}$	$\overset{4}{5\overline{)20}}$
25 ÷ 5 = 5	40 ÷ 5 = 8	$\overset{1}{5\overline{)5}}$	$\overset{7}{5\overline{)35}}$	
20 ÷ 5 = 4	30 ÷ 5 = 6			
10 ÷ 5 = 2	0 ÷ 5 = 0			
35 ÷ 5 = 7	25 ÷ 5 = 5			

Score: ______ Time: ______ minutes ______ seconds

121

Name ______________________

Dividends Through Fifty-Four

Now, think about what happens when a number is divided by 6.

Example: 24 ÷ 6 = 4

The dividend is 24. If you put 6 objects in each group, you have 4 equal groups.

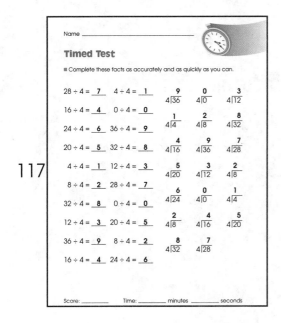

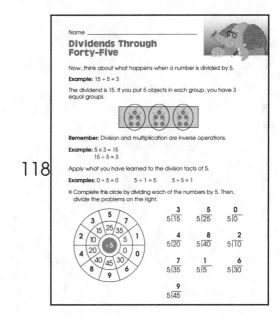

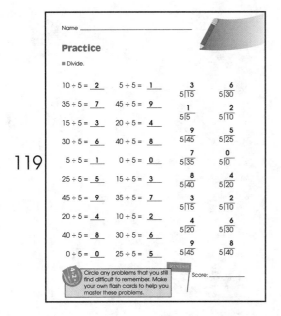

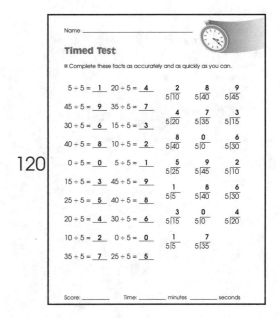

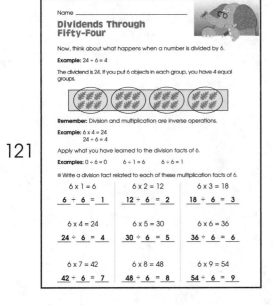

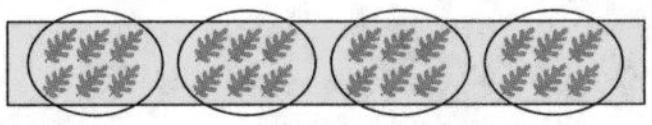

Remember: Division and multiplication are inverse operations.

Example: 6 x 4 = 24
24 ÷ 6 = 4

Apply what you have learned to the division facts of 6.

Examples: 0 ÷ 6 = 0 6 ÷ 1 = 6 6 ÷ 6 = 1

■ Write a division fact related to each of these multiplication facts of 6.

6 x 1 = 6	6 x 2 = 12	6 x 3 = 18
6 ÷ 6 = 1	12 ÷ 6 = 2	18 ÷ 6 = 3
6 x 4 = 24	6 x 5 = 30	6 x 6 = 36
24 ÷ 6 = 4	30 ÷ 6 = 5	36 ÷ 6 = 6
6 x 7 = 42	6 x 8 = 48	6 x 9 = 54
42 ÷ 6 = 7	48 ÷ 6 = 8	54 ÷ 6 = 9

122

Name ____________

Practice

■ Divide. Record your score—the number correct—on each Practice page and again on page 268.

0 ÷ 6 = **0**	30 ÷ 6 = **5**	6)24 = **4**	6)36 = **6**
18 ÷ 6 = **3**	24 ÷ 6 = **4**	6)0 = **0**	6)42 = **7**
36 ÷ 6 = **6**	48 ÷ 6 = **8**	6)18 = **3**	6)30 = **5**
6 ÷ 6 = **1**	54 ÷ 6 = **9**	6)54 = **9**	6)6 = **1**
30 ÷ 6 = **5**	42 ÷ 6 = **7**	6)48 = **8**	6)12 = **2**
12 ÷ 6 = **2**	0 ÷ 6 = **0**	6)36 = **6**	6)42 = **7**
24 ÷ 6 = **4**	18 ÷ 6 = **3**	6)12 = **2**	6)18 = **3**
48 ÷ 6 = **8**	36 ÷ 6 = **6**	6)48 = **8**	6)24 = **4**
54 ÷ 6 = **9**	6 ÷ 6 = **1**		
42 ÷ 6 = **7**	12 ÷ 6 = **2**		

START

Score: ____________

123

Name ____________

Timed Test

■ Complete these facts as accurately and as quickly as you can.

6 ÷ 6 = **1**	24 ÷ 6 = **4**	6)48 = **8**	6)42 = **7**	6)54 = **9**
30 ÷ 6 = **5**	48 ÷ 6 = **8**	6)30 = **5**	6)0 = **0**	6)18 = **3**
54 ÷ 6 = **9**	0 ÷ 6 = **0**	6)6 = **1**	6)48 = **8**	6)24 = **4**
42 ÷ 6 = **7**	36 ÷ 6 = **6**	6)12 = **2**	6)54 = **9**	6)30 = **5**
12 ÷ 6 = **2**	18 ÷ 6 = **3**	6)36 = **6**	6)6 = **1**	6)18 = **3**
0 ÷ 6 = **0**	30 ÷ 6 = **5**	6)12 = **2**	6)24 = **4**	6)36 = **6**
36 ÷ 6 = **6**	42 ÷ 6 = **7**	6)42 = **7**	6)0 = **0**	
18 ÷ 6 = **3**	54 ÷ 6 = **9**			
24 ÷ 6 = **4**	6 ÷ 6 = **1**			
48 ÷ 6 = **8**	12 ÷ 6 = **2**			

Score: ________ Time: ________ minutes ________ seconds

124

Name ____________

Dividends Through Sixty-Three

Now, think about what happens when a number is divided by 7.

Example: 63 ÷ 7 = 9

The dividend is 63. If you put 7 objects in each group, you have 9 equal groups.

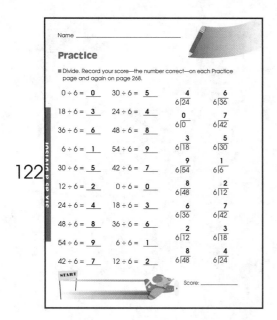

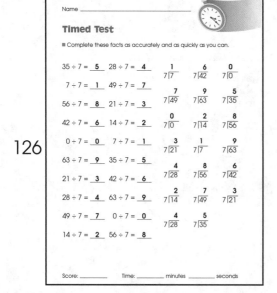

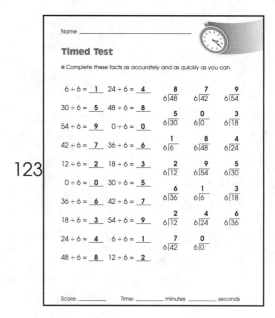

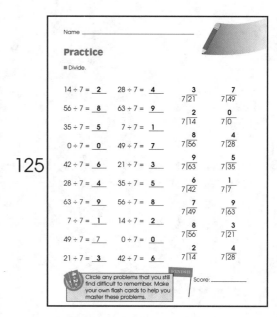

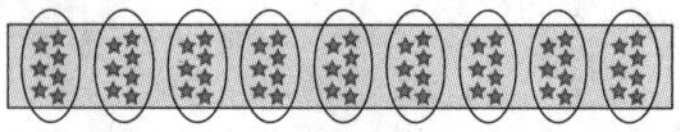

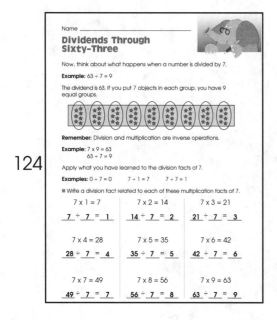

Remember: Division and multiplication are inverse operations.

Example: 7 x 9 = 63
63 ÷ 7 = 9

Apply what you have learned to the division facts of 7.

Examples: 0 ÷ 7 = 0 7 ÷ 1 = 7 7 ÷ 7 = 1

■ Write a division fact related to each of these multiplication facts of 7.

7 x 1 = 7	7 x 2 = 14	7 x 3 = 21
7 ÷ **7** = **1**	**14** ÷ **7** = **2**	**21** ÷ **7** = **3**
7 x 4 = 28	7 x 5 = 35	7 x 6 = 42
28 ÷ **7** = **4**	**35** ÷ **7** = **5**	**42** ÷ **7** = **6**
7 x 7 = 49	7 x 8 = 56	7 x 9 = 63
49 ÷ **7** = **7**	**56** ÷ **7** = **8**	**63** ÷ **7** = **9**

125

Name ____________

Practice

■ Divide.

14 ÷ 7 = **2**	28 ÷ 7 = **4**	7)21 = **3**	7)49 = **7**
56 ÷ 7 = **8**	63 ÷ 7 = **9**	7)14 = **2**	7)0 = **0**
35 ÷ 7 = **5**	7 ÷ 7 = **1**	7)56 = **8**	7)28 = **4**
0 ÷ 7 = **0**	49 ÷ 7 = **7**	7)63 = **9**	7)35 = **5**
42 ÷ 7 = **6**	21 ÷ 7 = **3**	7)42 = **6**	7)7 = **1**
28 ÷ 7 = **4**	35 ÷ 7 = **5**	7)49 = **7**	7)63 = **9**
63 ÷ 7 = **9**	56 ÷ 7 = **8**	7)56 = **8**	7)21 = **3**
7 ÷ 7 = **1**	14 ÷ 7 = **2**	7)14 = **2**	7)28 = **4**
49 ÷ 7 = **7**	0 ÷ 7 = **0**		
21 ÷ 7 = **3**	42 ÷ 7 = **6**		

Circle any problems that you still find difficult to remember. Make your own flash cards to help you master these problems.

FINISH

Score: ____________

126

Name ____________

Timed Test

■ Complete these facts as accurately and as quickly as you can.

35 ÷ 7 = **5**	28 ÷ 7 = **4**	7)7 = **1**	7)42 = **6**	7)0 = **0**
7 ÷ 7 = **1**	49 ÷ 7 = **7**	7)49 = **7**	7)63 = **9**	7)35 = **5**
56 ÷ 7 = **8**	21 ÷ 7 = **3**	7)0 = **0**	7)14 = **2**	7)56 = **8**
42 ÷ 7 = **6**	14 ÷ 7 = **2**	7)21 = **3**	7)7 = **1**	7)63 = **9**
0 ÷ 7 = **0**	7 ÷ 7 = **1**	7)28 = **4**	7)56 = **8**	7)42 = **6**
63 ÷ 7 = **9**	35 ÷ 7 = **5**	7)14 = **2**	7)49 = **7**	7)21 = **3**
21 ÷ 7 = **3**	42 ÷ 7 = **6**	7)28 = **4**	7)35 = **5**	
28 ÷ 7 = **4**	63 ÷ 7 = **9**			
49 ÷ 7 = **7**	0 ÷ 7 = **0**			
14 ÷ 7 = **2**	56 ÷ 7 = **8**			

Score: ________ Time: ________ minutes ________ seconds

127

Name ____________________

Dividends Through Seventy-Two

Now, think about what happens when a number is divided by 8.

Example: 48 ÷ 8 = 6

The dividend is 48. If you put 8 objects in each group, you will have 6 equal groups.

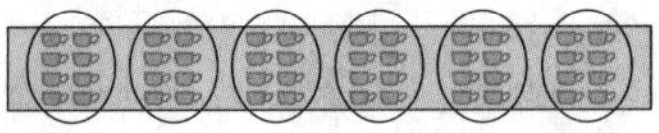

Remember: Division and multiplication are inverse operations.

Example: 8 x 6 = 48
48 ÷ 8 = 6

Apply what you have learned to the division facts of 8.

Examples: 0 ÷ 8 = 0 8 ÷ 1 = 8 8 ÷ 8 = 1

■ Write a division fact related to each of these multiplication facts of 8.

8 x 1 = 8	8 x 2 = 16	8 x 3 = 24
8 ÷ 8 = 1	16 ÷ 8 = 2	24 ÷ 8 = 3
8 x 4 = 32	8 x 5 = 40	8 x 6 = 48
32 ÷ 8 = 4	40 ÷ 8 = 5	48 ÷ 8 = 6
8 x 7 = 56	8 x 8 = 64	8 x 9 = 72
56 ÷ 8 = 7	64 ÷ 8 = 8	72 ÷ 8 = 9

128

Name ____________________

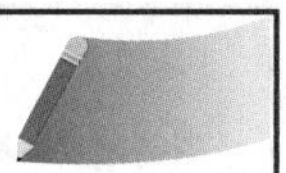

Practice

■ Divide.

0 ÷ 8 = 0	40 ÷ 8 = 5	$8\overline{)48}$ = 6	$8\overline{)8}$ = 1
56 ÷ 8 = 7	72 ÷ 8 = 9	$8\overline{)56}$ = 7	$8\overline{)0}$ = 0
24 ÷ 8 = 3	48 ÷ 8 = 6	$8\overline{)64}$ = 8	$8\overline{)16}$ = 2
64 ÷ 8 = 8	32 ÷ 8 = 4	$8\overline{)72}$ = 9	$8\overline{)32}$ = 4
16 ÷ 8 = 2	8 ÷ 8 = 1	$8\overline{)40}$ = 5	$8\overline{)24}$ = 3
40 ÷ 8 = 5	0 ÷ 8 = 0	$8\overline{)56}$ = 7	$8\overline{)48}$ = 6
72 ÷ 8 = 9	56 ÷ 8 = 7	$8\overline{)16}$ = 2	$8\overline{)72}$ = 9
48 ÷ 8 = 6	24 ÷ 8 = 3	$8\overline{)32}$ = 4	$8\overline{)64}$ = 8
32 ÷ 8 = 4	64 ÷ 8 = 8		
8 ÷ 8 = 1	16 ÷ 8 = 2		

Circle any problems that you still find difficult to remember. Make your own flash cards to help you master these problems.

Score: __________

129

Name ____________________

Timed Test

32 ÷ 8 = 4	56 ÷ 8 = 7	$8\overline{)8}$ = 1	$8\overline{)32}$ = 4	$8\overline{)64}$ = 8
72 ÷ 8 = 9	16 ÷ 8 = 2	$8\overline{)16}$ = 2	$8\overline{)0}$ = 0	$8\overline{)56}$ = 7
8 ÷ 8 = 1	48 ÷ 8 = 6	$8\overline{)40}$ = 5	$8\overline{)24}$ = 3	$8\overline{)72}$ = 9
0 ÷ 8 = 0	40 ÷ 8 = 5	$8\overline{)48}$ = 6	$8\overline{)16}$ = 2	$8\overline{)8}$ = 1
64 ÷ 8 = 8	24 ÷ 8 = 3	$8\overline{)24}$ = 3	$8\overline{)32}$ = 4	$8\overline{)0}$ = 0
40 ÷ 8 = 5	8 ÷ 8 = 1	$8\overline{)64}$ = 8	$8\overline{)56}$ = 7	$8\overline{)72}$ = 9
56 ÷ 8 = 7	0 ÷ 8 = 0	$8\overline{)40}$ = 5	$8\overline{)48}$ = 6	
24 ÷ 8 = 3	64 ÷ 8 = 8			
16 ÷ 8 = 2	32 ÷ 8 = 4			
8 ÷ 8 = 1	48 ÷ 8 = 6			

Score: ________ Time: ________ minutes ________ seconds

130

Name ____________________

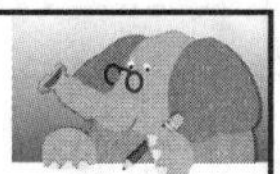

Dividends Through Eighty-One

Now, think about what happens when a number is divided by 9.

Example: 72 ÷ 9 = 8

The dividend is 72. If you put 9 objects in each group, you have 8 equal groups.

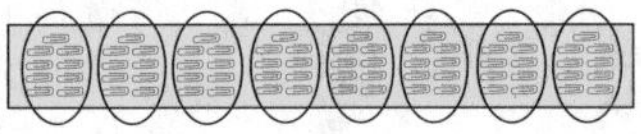

Remember: Division and multiplication are inverse operations.

Example: 9 x 8 = 72
72 ÷ 9 = 8

Apply what you have learned to the division facts of 9.

Examples: 0 ÷ 9 = 0 9 ÷ 1 = 9 9 ÷ 9 = 1

■ Write a division fact related to each multiplication fact of 9.

9 x 1 = 9	9 x 2 = 18	9 x 3 = 27
9 ÷ 9 = 1	18 ÷ 9 = 2	27 ÷ 9 = 3
9 x 4 = 36	9 x 5 = 45	9 x 6 = 54
36 ÷ 9 = 4	45 ÷ 9 = 5	54 ÷ 9 = 6
9 x 7 = 63	9 x 8 = 72	9 x 9 = 81
63 ÷ 9 = 7	72 ÷ 9 = 8	81 ÷ 9 = 9

131

Name ____________________

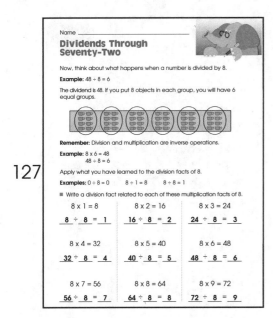

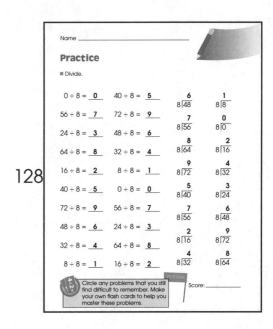

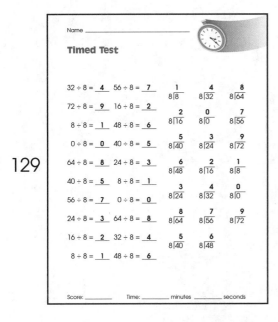

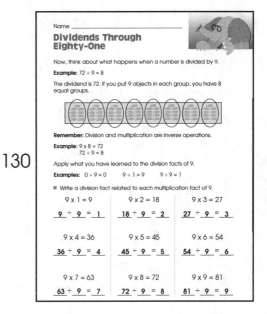

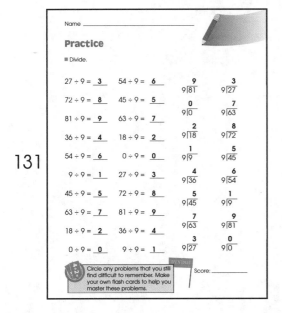

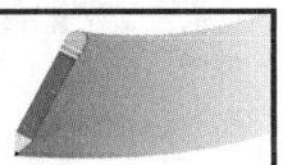

Practice

■ Divide.

27 ÷ 9 = 3	54 ÷ 9 = 6	$9\overline{)81}$ = 9	$9\overline{)27}$ = 3
72 ÷ 9 = 8	45 ÷ 9 = 5	$9\overline{)0}$ = 0	$9\overline{)63}$ = 7
81 ÷ 9 = 9	63 ÷ 9 = 7	$9\overline{)18}$ = 2	$9\overline{)72}$ = 8
36 ÷ 9 = 4	18 ÷ 9 = 2	$9\overline{)9}$ = 1	$9\overline{)45}$ = 5
54 ÷ 9 = 6	0 ÷ 9 = 0	$9\overline{)36}$ = 4	$9\overline{)54}$ = 6
9 ÷ 9 = 1	27 ÷ 9 = 3	$9\overline{)45}$ = 5	$9\overline{)9}$ = 1
45 ÷ 9 = 5	72 ÷ 9 = 8	$9\overline{)63}$ = 7	$9\overline{)81}$ = 9
63 ÷ 9 = 7	81 ÷ 9 = 9	$9\overline{)27}$ = 3	$9\overline{)0}$ = 0
18 ÷ 9 = 2	36 ÷ 9 = 4		
0 ÷ 9 = 0	9 ÷ 9 = 1		

Circle any problems that you still find difficult to remember. Make your own flash cards to help you master these problems.

Score: __________

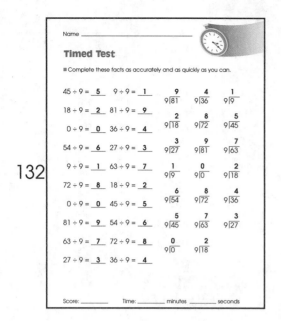

132

Name ______________________

Timed Test

■ Complete these facts as accurately and as quickly as you can.

45 ÷ 9 = 5	9 ÷ 9 = 1
18 ÷ 9 = 2	81 ÷ 9 = 9
0 ÷ 9 = 0	36 ÷ 9 = 4
54 ÷ 9 = 6	27 ÷ 9 = 3
9 ÷ 9 = 1	63 ÷ 9 = 7
72 ÷ 9 = 8	18 ÷ 9 = 2
0 ÷ 9 = 0	45 ÷ 9 = 5
81 ÷ 9 = 9	54 ÷ 9 = 6
63 ÷ 9 = 7	72 ÷ 9 = 8
27 ÷ 9 = 3	36 ÷ 9 = 4

9)81 = 9	9)36 = 4	9)9 = 1
9)18 = 2	9)72 = 8	9)45 = 5
9)27 = 3	9)81 = 9	9)63 = 7
9)9 = 1	9)0 = 0	9)18 = 2
9)54 = 6	9)72 = 8	9)36 = 4
9)45 = 5	9)63 = 7	9)27 = 3
9)0 = 0	9)18 = 2	

Score: ________ Time: ________ minutes ________ seconds

133

Name ______________________

Practice

■ Divide.

64 ÷ 8 = 8	25 ÷ 5 = 5	10 ÷ 2 = 5	81 ÷ 9 = 9
4 ÷ 2 = 2	9 ÷ 9 = 1	8 ÷ 8 = 1	36 ÷ 6 = 6
5 ÷ 5 = 1	0 ÷ 1 = 0	6 ÷ 1 = 6	18 ÷ 2 = 9
4 ÷ 1 = 4	24 ÷ 6 = 4	18 ÷ 6 = 3	24 ÷ 3 = 8
0 ÷ 3 = 0	20 ÷ 4 = 5	30 ÷ 5 = 6	16 ÷ 2 = 8
54 ÷ 9 = 6	42 ÷ 6 = 7	0 ÷ 8 = 0	6 ÷ 6 = 1
21 ÷ 3 = 7	9 ÷ 3 = 3	4 ÷ 4 = 1	63 ÷ 9 = 7
28 ÷ 7 = 4	12 ÷ 2 = 6	32 ÷ 8 = 4	36 ÷ 4 = 9
9 ÷ 1 = 9	3 ÷ 1 = 3	42 ÷ 7 = 6	7 ÷ 7 = 1
45 ÷ 5 = 9	12 ÷ 3 = 4	28 ÷ 4 = 7	12 ÷ 4 = 3

START

Continue this Practice on the next page.

134

Name ______________________

Practice

■ Divide.

8)56 = 7	1)9 = 9	6)48 = 8	6)0 = 0	5)30 = 6	4)28 = 7
3)6 = 2	1)7 = 7	7)21 = 3	8)0 = 0	2)6 = 3	7)42 = 6
4)8 = 2	6)54 = 9	2)2 = 1	3)18 = 6	5)35 = 7	5)0 = 0
9)18 = 2	4)20 = 5	1)2 = 2	8)32 = 4	6)24 = 4	2)12 = 6
3)24 = 8	5)15 = 3	3)0 = 0	9)63 = 7	6)36 = 6	3)27 = 9
7)35 = 5	4)12 = 3	9)54 = 6	1)0 = 0	8)8 = 1	8)48 = 6
7)7 = 1	2)8 = 4	6)30 = 5	9)27 = 3	1)4 = 4	9)45 = 5

FINISH

Circle any problems that you still find difficult to remember. Make your own flash cards to help you master these problems.

Continue this Practice on the next page.

135

Name ______________________

Timed Test

30 ÷ 6 = 5	42 ÷ 7 = 6	24 ÷ 8 = 3	1 ÷ 1 = 1
6 ÷ 1 = 6	18 ÷ 3 = 6	7 ÷ 1 = 7	48 ÷ 8 = 6
3 ÷ 1 = 3	4 ÷ 1 = 4	4 ÷ 2 = 2	15 ÷ 3 = 5
20 ÷ 4 = 5	16 ÷ 4 = 4	45 ÷ 5 = 9	16 ÷ 8 = 2
0 ÷ 7 = 0	25 ÷ 5 = 5	18 ÷ 9 = 2	8 ÷ 2 = 4
49 ÷ 7 = 7	0 ÷ 9 = 0	20 ÷ 5 = 4	5 ÷ 5 = 1
24 ÷ 6 = 4	32 ÷ 8 = 4	6 ÷ 3 = 2	0 ÷ 6 = 0
16 ÷ 2 = 8	18 ÷ 9 = 2	54 ÷ 9 = 6	40 ÷ 5 = 8
40 ÷ 8 = 5	9 ÷ 1 = 9	72 ÷ 8 = 9	14 ÷ 2 = 7
9 ÷ 9 = 1	56 ÷ 7 = 8	35 ÷ 7 = 5	36 ÷ 4 = 9

Score: ________ Time: ________ minutes ________ seconds

136

Name ______________________

Timed Test

1)0 = 0	3)18 = 6	7)35 = 5	9)0 = 0	8)24 = 3	2)8 = 4
8)32 = 4	5)35 = 7	6)36 = 6	1)6 = 6	4)36 = 9	9)27 = 3
2)16 = 8	4)8 = 2	7)21 = 3	9)18 = 2	5)30 = 6	6)42 = 7
2)12 = 6	9)72 = 8	6)0 = 0	3)21 = 7	1)4 = 4	9)9 = 1
8)16 = 2	5)0 = 0	6)24 = 4	7)28 = 4	1)9 = 9	6)30 = 5
8)8 = 1	3)15 = 5	2)14 = 7	3)24 = 8	5)25 = 5	7)14 = 2
1)5 = 5	4)4 = 1	4)32 = 8	8)40 = 5	2)2 = 1	8)40 = 5

Score: ________ Time: ________ minutes ________ seconds

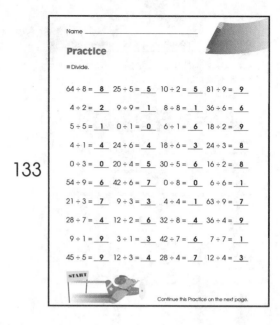

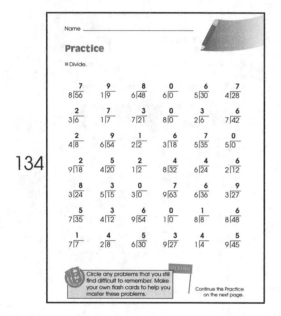

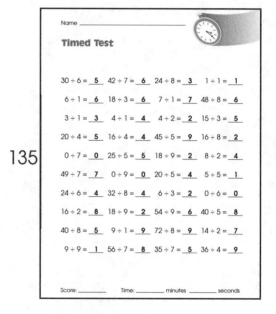

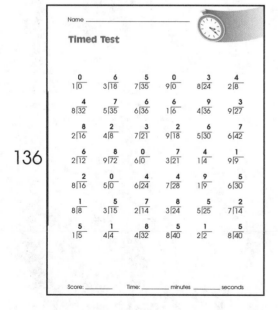